lonely

Sinhala

Phrasebook & Dictionary

Acknowledgments
Language Writer Swarna Pragnaratne
Cover Image Researcher Gwen Cotter

Published by Lonely Planet Global Limited
CRN 554153

5th Edition – May 2024
ISBN 978 1 78657 084 0
Text © Lonely Planet 2024
Cover Image Sri Lankan Women Picking Tea Leaves Concept
Rawpixel.com/Shutterstock ©
Illustrations Jules Chapple

Printed in Malaysia 10 9 8 7 6 5 4 3 2 1

Contact lonelyplanet.com/contact

All rights reserved. No part of this publication may be reproduced, stored in a retrieval system or transmitted in any form by any means, electronic, mechanical, photocopying, recording or otherwise, except brief extracts for the purpose of review, without the written permission of the publisher. Lonely Planet and the Lonely Planet logo are trade marks of Lonely Planet and are registered in the U.S. Patent and Trademark Office and in other countries. Lonely Planet does not allow its name or logo to be appropriated by commercial establishments, such as retailers, restaurants or hotels. Please let us know of any misuses: www.lonelyplanet.com/legal/intellectual-property

Although the authors and Lonely Planet try to make the information as accurate as possible, we accept no responsibility for any loss, injury or inconvenience sustained by anyone using this book.

Paper in this book is certified against the Forest Stewardship Council™ standards. FSC™ promotes environmentally responsible, socially beneficial and economically viable management of the world's forests.

acknowledgments

about the author

Swarna Pragnaratne started her career as a teacher of Sinhala, English and Pali in Sri Lanka, where she was born and still visits regularly. She branched into interpreting and translating, and after immigrating to Australia continued to work in this field. Swarna has over 30 years' experience and finds great satisfaction in this work. She was appointed as an examiner to the first-ever panel for Sinhala examinations conducted by the National Accreditation Authority for Translation and Interpreting, and continues her work on this panel. Swarna is currently an Interpreter and Translator for NAATI in Melbourne.

from the author

This book has been a stepping stone to a vision in my life, and I was keen to enable visitors to Sri Lanka to get by with ease in communication and socialising. My thanks go out to Ramani Liyanaratchi who was ever willing to 'jog my memory' about Sinhalese grammar; to my friend Charmaine Pereira for the loan of a very informative book dating back to 1821; and to Dr Piyasoma Medis from Sydney for checking over the phrasebook. To the Publishing Manager, the editors and the rest of the supportive team at Lonely Planet, I offer my sincere appreciation for your patience and friendliness, which made it enjoyable. Last but not least, I am deeply grateful to my sister Suranyani Dodamwala for all her encouragement throughout the entire exercise.

CONTENTS

Sri Lanka

About Sinhalese

Sinhala is one of the two official languages of Sri Lanka, a nation of more than twenty million people. It is the first language of more than 75% of the population. Around 20%, mostly in the north, speak the second of Sri Lanka's official languages – Tamil – and a number of other languages, creoles and dialects are spoken in various parts of the country. English is spoken by approximately 10% of the population.

An Indo-Aryan language, Sinhala developed in isolation from other members of its language family – as a result, and because of influences from Tamil, it was even classified as a Dravidian language. Other members of the Indo-Aryan family include Bengali, Hindi and Punjabi. Its closest relative is Divehi, spoken in the Maldive Islands. Modern Sinhala is a language that has been greatly affected by travel and trade over the centuries, and loan words can be found from a number of languages, including Dutch, Portuguese, English and Malay.

According to Sinhalese tradition, the 6th century introduction of the language to the island is attributed to a sequence of events commencing with a journey by Prince Vijaya from the kingdom of Sinhapura (Bengal). Banished to sea by the king, Vijaya and his followers landed on an island, defeated its evil 'demon inhabitants', then settled down to create a dynasty. Thus Sri Lanka was born.

There is certainly some fact behind this traditional explanation, and the date given in the story accounts neatly for the development of unique characteristics that distinguish Sinhala from other Indo-Aryan languages. The portrayal of demons might be more

ABOUT SINHALESE

fanciful though. Recent archaeological findings suggest that the 'demons' had, in fact, established agricultural practices, including irrigation, used iron and made pottery – not normally the work of demons!

Two forms of Sinhala are in use today, a literary written form and a spoken form. The written language retains a number of features that link it back to the ancient Indian languages Pali and Sanscrit, and is most commonly associated with Buddhism and education. Spoken Sinhala, however, is the focus of this book for obvious reasons, and while some scholars suggest that differences between the two forms are so great that they might almost be considered distinct languages, it is the spoken form that everyone understands.

Although the grammar of Sinhala may at first seem daunting to English speakers, its relative flexibility allows speakers to have a go at making sentences and still be understood. The sounds are quite similar to those found in English and, as is the case with every country you visit, your efforts to speak the language will be rewarded, sometimes with laughter (of the appreciative kind) and certainly with approval.

ABBREVIATIONS USED IN THIS BOOK

adj	adjective	n	noun
f	feminine	neut	neuter
inf	informal	pl	plural
lit	literal	sg	singular
m	masculine	v	verb

PRONUNCIATION

Pronunciation of Sinhala is not difficult – many of the sounds are similar to English and, unlike other languages in the region, there are no tones.

You'll find, however, that many of the transliterations contain consonant clusters that may be unfamiliar. Don't be put off by their appearance – the sounds themselves aren't too complicated. One example is sth, as in sthoo-thiy (**ස්තුතියි**), 'thank you'. To pronounce this correctly, try saying the 'ss' in 'hiss' followed by 'toothy'. Another example is dhy, as in vi-dhyaah-vah (**විද්‍යා**), 'science'. The dhyaah, here, is pronounced similarly to 'd', followed by the 'yar' in 'yarn' – but remember it's only one syllable.

Throughout the book, we've split the transliterations into syllables to aid pronunciation. This is particularly important where a consonant is doubled in a word, as you need to pronounce them both for the correct meaning to be understood. For example, to avoid confusion between mah-lah **මල** ('flower') and mal-lah **මල්ල** ('bag'), each 'l' needs to be pronounced clearly in the latter.

PRONUNCIATION TIPS

aspirated consonants	pronounced with a puff of air after the sound; this is the way the letters 'p', 't' and 'k' are pronounced in English at the beginning of a word
unaspirated consonants	pronounced without a puff of air – compare 'pot' (aspirated) with 'spot' (unaspirated)
diphthongs	the sound produced by the combination of two vowels, for example, the 'ai' in 'aisle'

VOWELS

There are 12 vowels in Sinhala, which can be divided into two groups: short and long, with six in each.

	Short Vowels	
Script	Transliteration	Pronunciation
අ	ah	as the 'u' in 'cup'
ඇ	a	as the 'a' in 'pat'
එ	e	as the 'e' in 'pet'
ඉ	i	as the 'i' in 'pit'
ඔ	o	as the 'o' in 'pot'
උ	u	as the 'u' in 'put'
	Long Vowels	
ආ	aah	as the 'a' in 'part'
ඈ	aa	as the 'a' in 'ant'
ඒ	eh	as the 'a' in 'bathe'
ඊ	ee	as the 'ee' in 'see'
ඕ	oh	as the 'o' in 'port'
ඌ	oo	as the 'oo' in 'pool'

In script, vowels only appear as separate characters at the beginning of a word, for example, in ee-lahn-gah (ඊළඟ), 'next', the ඊ (ee) is clearly visible. When vowels appear elsewhere in a word, they're indicated by a symbol added to the consonant they follow. Within a word, ee is represented by කී, for example, in aah-di-kaah-lee-nah (ආදිකාලින) 'ancient', it appears in combination with ල (lah) to form ලී (lee) (see Applying Vowels to Consonants on page 14).

	Vowel Combinations (Diphthongs)	
Script	Transliteration	Pronunciation
ආයි	ai	as the 'ai' in 'aisle'
ඖ	au	as the 'ou' in 'ounce'
ඒයි	ei	as the 'ei' in 'weight'
ඔයි	oi	as the 'oi' in 'oil'

CONSONANTS

Consonants in Sinhala are represented as syllabic units – they all have an inherent ah sound in their basic form. These syllabic units form the foundation for writing all of the possible sounds in Sinhala. To represent sounds other than ah sounds, the basic form is used in conjunction with additional characters or symbols (see page 15).

Unaspirated Consonants		
Script	Transliteration	Pronunciation
ක	kah	as the 'cu' in 'cup'
ග	gah	as the 'gu' in 'gun'
ජ	jah	as the 'ju' in 'jump'
ට	tah	as the 'tu' in 'tug'
ඩ	dah	as the 'du' in 'duck'
ණ[1]	nah	as the 'nu' in 'nun'
ත	thah	as the 'thu' in 'thump'
ද	dhah	as the 'the' in 'mother'
න[1]	nah	as the 'nu' in 'nun'
ප	pah	as the 'pu' in 'punt'
බ	bah	as the 'bu' in 'bun'
ම	mah	as the 'mu' in 'mum'
ය	yah	as the 'yu' in 'yuck'
ර	rah	as the 'ru' in 'rum'
ල[2]	lah	as the 'lu' in 'luck'
ව	wah	as the 'wo' in 'won'
	vah*	as the 'va' in 'vantage'
හ	hah	as the 'hu' in 'hut'
ස	sah	as the 'su' in 'sun'
ළ[2]	lah	as the 'lu' in 'luck'
ශ[3]	shah	as the 'shu' in 'shut'
ෂ[3]	shah	as the 'shu' in 'shut'
ච	chah	as the 'chu' in 'chuck'
ඥ	gnah	as the 'ny' in 'Kenya', plus the 'u' in 'cup'

* generally, vah is used in verbs and wah in all other words

Letters marked with numbers (nah, **ණ**; nah, **න**; lah, **ළ**; lah, **ල**; shah, **ෂ**; shah, **ශ**) are pronounced very similarly but are used in words totally different from each other in meaning. In spoken language, this is not a problem – your meaning would be clear through context – but in written language you'd need to be cautious to avoid confusing your message:

¹	**ණ**	nah	**තණ**	thah-nah	grass
	න	nah	**තන**	thah-nah	breast
²	**ළ**	lah	**මළ**	mah-lah	flower
	ල	lah	**මල**	mah-lah	dead

With shah (**ෂ**) and shah (**ශ**), you wouldn't create the wrong word by using the wrong letter, as they're not used in the same combination of letters – you would just create a word that doesn't exist. For example, if you used **ෂ** instead of **ශ** in the word **ජූෂ** yu-shah ('juice'), the word would have no meaning. Likewise, if you used **ශ** instead of **ෂ** in the word **මාංශ** maahn-shah ('flesh'), it would have no meaning.

Applying Vowels to Consonants

As mentioned earlier in this chapter, vowel sounds within a word are indicated by attaching a number of different characters or symbols to a consonant; these symbols can appear above, below, before or after the consonant. A symbol is also added to a consonant when it's pronounced on its own, without any vowel.

In the following table, we've used kah (**ක**) as an example.

SYLLABIC SINHALA

Unlike English, vowels and consonants in Sinhala aren't written separately, but together as syllabic units. That is to say, each character represents a syllable, not just a single letter.

Script	Symbol(s) Added	Translit-eration	Pronunciation
ක	◌̆	k	as the 'k' in 'skin'
කා	◌ා	kaah	as 'k' plus the 'a' in 'part'
කි	◌ි	ki	as 'k' plus the 'i' in 'pit'
කී	◌ී	kee	as 'k' plus the 'ee' in 'see'
කු	◌ු	ku	as 'k' plus the 'u' in 'put'
කූ	◌ූ	koo	as 'k' plus the 'oo' in 'pool'
කෙ	◌ෙ	ke	as 'k' plus the 'e' in 'pet'
කේ	◌ේ	keh	as 'k' plus the 'ai' in 'bait'
කො	◌ො	ko	as 'k' plus the 'o' in 'pot'
කෝ	◌ෝ	koh	as 'k' plus the 'o' in 'port'

PRONUNCIATION

Aspirated Consonants

There are seven aspirated consonants in Sinhala. All have un-aspirated counterparts and are pronounced the same but with a puff of air (see page 11).

	Aspirated		Unaspirated
බ	khah	ක	kah
ඝ	ghah	ග	gah
ධ	_tah*	ට	tah
ථ	_thah*	ත	thah
ධ	_dhah*	ද	dhah
ඵ	phah	ප	pah
භ	bhah	බ	bah

* underlining has been used in the transliterations to distinguish between the unaspirated and aspirated sounds

THE SINHALESE ALPHABET

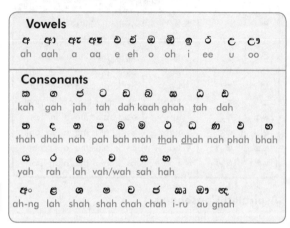

Vowels

අ	ආ	ඇ	ඈ	එ	ඒ	ඔ	ඕ	ඉ	ඊ	උ	ඌ
ah	aah	a	aa	e	eh	o	oh	i	ee	u	oo

Consonants

ක	ග	ජ	ට	ඩ	බ	ස	ධ	ඬ
kah	gah	jah	tah	dah	kaah	ghah	<u>tah</u>	dah

ත	ද	න	ප	බ	ම	ථ	ධ	ණ	එ	හ
thah	dhah	nah	pah	bah	mah	<u>thah</u>	<u>dhah</u>	nah	phah	bhah

ය	ර	ල	ව	ස	හ
yah	rah	lah	vah/wah	sah	hah

අං	ළ	ශ	ෂ	ච	ජ	සෘ	ඖ	ඥ
ah-ng	lah	shah	shah	chah	chah	i-ru	au	gnah

PRONUNCIATION

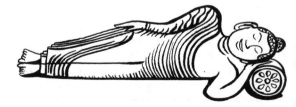

Spoken Sinhala and written Sinhala vary quite considerably. In many respects, the spoken language is far simpler – for example, you don't need to worry about gender agreement between nouns and verbs.

You'll also come across a number of words that have been borrowed from English (eg, bahs, 'bus'), which will make things easier for you.

This chapter gives the basics of Sinhalese grammar, which will enable you to construct your own sentences and communicate with ease.

WORD ORDER

Unlike English, where the word order is subject-verb-object, the word order in Sinhala is generally subject-object-verb:

I bought a book.
   mah-mah po-thahk gahth-thaah   **මම පොතක් ගත්තා.**
   (lit: I book bought)

ARTICLES

Sinhala doesn't use the definite article ('the'), so po-thah (**පොත**) can mean 'book' or 'the book' – context will usually make it clear which is meant.

Nouns borrowed from English, however, are always followed by e-kah (**එක**), meaning 'one':

(the) bus	bahs e-kah	**බස් එක**
(the) piano	pi-yaah-noh e-kah	**යානෝ එක**
(the) station	steh-shahn e-kah	**ස්ටේෂන් එක**

There's no corresponding word for the indefinite article ('a/an'). To make a noun indefinite, just add k (**ක්**) to the end of the final syllable:

book	po-thah	පොත
a book	po-thahk	පොතක්
egg	bith-thah-rah-yah	බිත්තරය
an egg	bith-thah-rah-yahk	බිත්තරයක්

However, this rule only applies to nouns ending in the short vowel sounds (ah, a, e, i, o, and u) – these are always inanimate (non-living) nouns.

For nouns ending in the long vowel sounds aah and ee – always animate (living) nouns – the final vowel sound changes to ek. Note that singular nouns never end in the other long vowel sounds (aa, oo, eh and oh) or in consonants unless they're loan words.

child	lah-mah-yaah	ළමයා
a child	lah-mah-yek	ළමයෙක්
passenger	mah-gi-yaah	මගියා
a passenger	mah-gi-yek	මගියෙක්

For English loan words, the final e-kah (**එක**) becomes e-kahk (**එකක්**) to indicate the indefinite article:

a bus	bahs e-kahk	බස් එකක්
a piano	pi-yaah-noh e-kahk	යානෝ එකක්
a station	steh-shahn e-kahk	ස්ටේෂන් එකක්

GRAMMATICAL TERMS

A number of basic grammatical terms are used in this chapter. Here's a general summary of them:

adjective	adds information about a noun *red* wine
adverb	adds information about a verb or adjective He runs *quickly.* *very* big
conjunction	joins together sentences or parts of a sentence Wash the car *and* walk the dog.
noun	a person (John), thing (book), place (beach) or concept (happiness)
object	refers to the noun or pronoun that is affected by the verb Paul washes the *dog.*
preposition	introduces information about location, place or direction *at* the market *towards* the city
pronoun	usually takes the place of a noun *he* sings instead of Paul sings
subject	refers to the noun or pronoun that is performing an action *The man* washes the dog.
verb	an action or doing word He *runs* fast.

GRAMMAR

NOUNS
Gender

Nouns are masculine, feminine or neuter in gender. It's important to know the gender of a noun as the verb endings must agree in written language (see Verbs, page 27). In spoken language, however, there's no agreement.

Gender is easy to remember in Sinhala. Generally, it reflects human gender: boy, man, husband etc are masculine; girl, woman, wife etc are feminine; and all inanimate nouns are neuter:

man	mi-ni-haah (m)	මිනිහා
woman	ga-ha-ni-yah (f)	ගැහැනිය
knife	pi-hi-yah (neut)	පිහිය

Nouns that could refer to a male or a female (child, bus driver etc) are neuter. You can specify the gender of such nouns by placing ga-ha-nu, 'female', or pi-ri-mi, 'male', before the noun:

child	lah-mah-yaah	ළමයා
boy	pi-ri-mi lah-mah-yaah	පිරිමි ළමයා
girl	ga-ha-nu lah-mah-yaah	ගැහැනු ළමයා
driver	ri-yah-du-raah	රියදුරා
male driver	pi-ri-mi ri-yah-du-raah	පිරිමි රියදුරා
female driver	ga-ha-nu ri-yah-du-raah	ගැහැනු රියදුරා

Plurals

Plurals of nouns vary but always involve changing the final syllable of the singular – usually it's shortened, sometimes even dropped:

tree	gah-sah	ගස
trees	gahs	ගස්
pillar	kah-nu-wah	කණුව
pillars	kah-nu	කණු

To pluralise English loan words, e-kah is always dropped:

| car | kaahr e-kah | කාර් එක |
| cars | kaahr | කාර් |

There's no single rule for pluralising nouns, however, and even words with the same or similar endings don't necessarily follow the same pattern. Don't be put off though – you'll still be understood if you use the singular form (which is given in the dictionary) and no one will mind the odd mistake.

CASE

In English, we're able to recognise the 'role' a noun plays in a sentence – who is performing an action, to whom, with what and so on – by its position in the sentence and/or by the use of prepositions.

Many other languages, however, for example, German, Russian and Sinhala, use what are know as 'cases' to make these distinctions. Different endings act as labels to indicate the role of a noun and its relationship to other words in a sentence.

In Sinhala, there are nine cases, known as vi-bahk-thi (විභක්ති):

Nominative	prah-thah-maah	ප්‍රථමා
Accusative	kahr-mah	කර්ම
Genitive	sahm-bahn-dhah	සම්බන්ධ
Dative	sahm-prah-dhaah-nah	සම්ප්‍රදාන
Instrumental	kath-roo	කතෘ
Ablative	ah-vah-dhi	අවධි
Agentive	kah-rah-nah	කරණ
Locative	aah-dhaah-rah	ආධාර
Vocative	aah-lah-pah-nah	ආලපන

While endings vary, you can use the following ones or even use no endings and still be understood. Where case endings have no English equivalent, they are given in the literal translations in their transliterated form. This has been applied throughout the book.

Nominative
The nominative case refers to the subject of the sentence, and is also the form you'll find in a dictionary. It indicates 'who' or 'what' is performing the action.

The child went home.
   lah-mah-yaah ge-dhe-rah   ළමයා ගෙදර ගියා.
   gi-yeh-yah
   (lit: child home went)

Accusative
The accusative case refers to the direct object of a sentence. It indicates 'what' or 'whom' the verb affects.

The dog is chasing the child.
   bahl-laah lah-mah-yaah-vah   බල්ලා ළමයාව
   pahn-nah-nah-vaah   පන්නනවා.
   (lit: dog child-vah chasing)

Genitive
The genitive case refers to possession. It indicates 'whose', 'of what' or 'of whom'.

The child's hand is injured.
   lah-mah-yaah-geh ah-thah   ළමයාගේ අත
   thu-vaah-lai   තුවාලයි.
   (lit: child's hand injured)

Dative
The dative case refers to the indirect object. It indicates the person or object 'to whom' or 'to which' something is given, done, lent and so on.

I gave the child some food.
   mah-mah lah-mah-yaah-tah   මම ළමයාට කෑම
   kaa-mah dun-naah   දුන්නා.
   (lit: I child-to food gave)

GRAMMAR

Instrumental

The instrumental case has several functions. It's used to answer a number of questions, including 'with what' and 'by what means'.

The child hit the dog with the stick.
   lah-mah-yaah bahl-laah-tah   ළමයා බල්ලාට
   koh-tu-ven ga-hu-vaah   කෝටුවෙන් ගැහුවා.
   (lit: child to-dog with-stick hit)

Ablative

The ablative case is used to denote 'from where' or 'from whom'.

The thief stole money from the child.
   so-raah lah-mah-yaah-gen   සොරා ළමයාගෙන්
   mu-dhal so-rah-kahm   මුදල් සොරකම්
   kah-leh-yah   කළේය.
   (lit: thief from-child money stole)

Agentive

The agentive case is used to denote 'by whom'.

The vase was broken by the child.
   lah-mah-yaah vi-sin   ළමයා විසින්
   mahl bah-dhu-nah kah-dah-nah   මල් බඳුන කඩන
   lah-dhee   ලදි.
   (lit: child by flower vase broken)

Locative

The locative case indicates where an action takes place. It's always used with prepositions indicating location, such as 'in', 'on', 'by', 'at' and 'about'.

The child's in the house.
   lah-mah-yaah ge-yah a-thu-leh   ළමයා ගෙය ඇතුළේ.
   (lit: child house in)

GRAMMAR

Vocative

The vocative case is used when addressing people directly.

<u>Child</u>, come here!
  <u>lah-mah-yaah</u> me-he en-nah!   **ළමයා මෙහෙ එන්න !**
  (lit: <u>child</u> here come!)

ADJECTIVES

The adjective always precedes the noun it describes:

tall man	u-sah mi-ni-haah	**උස මිනිහා**
	(lit: tall man)	
big house	lo-ku ge-yah	**ලොකු ගෙය**
	(lit: big house)	

Comparatives

To create comparatives, simply place either i-thaah (**ඉතා**) or vah-daah (**වඩා**) before the adjective. The two alternatives are interchangeable:

tall	u-sah	**උස**
taller	i-thaah u-sah	**ඉතා උස**
big	lo-ku	**ලොකු**
bigger	vah-daah lo-ku	**වඩා ලොකු**

Superlatives

To create superlatives in Sinhala, add i-thaah-mahth (**ඉතාමත්**) or vah-daah-mahth (**වඩාමත්**) before the adjective. Another way of looking at this is to add mahth to the end of the comparative indicator (i-thaah or vah-daah):

tallest	i-thaah-mahth	**ඉතාමත්**
	u-sah	**උස**
biggest	vah-daah-mahth	**වඩාමත්**
	lo-ku	**ලොකු**

GRAMMAR

PRONOUNS

All subject and object pronouns are the same, except for he/him:

Subject Pronouns	Object Pronouns	Transliteration	Script
Singular			
I	me	mah-mah	මම
you	you	o-bah	ඔබ
he	–	o-hu	ඔහු
–	him	a-yaah	එයා
she	her	a-yah	ඇය
it	it	eh-kah/e-yah	ඒක/එය
Plural			
we	us	ah-pi	අපි
you	you	o-bah(-laa)	ඔබ(ලා)
they	them	o-vun	ඔවුන්

Note that eh-kah, 'it', is more common in spoken language than e-yah which tends to be reserved for written language.

The subject pronoun always precedes the verb. If the sentence contains an object pronoun as well, it is placed between the subject pronoun and the verb:

I gave it to my mother.

mah-mah e-yah mah-geh
ahm-maah-tah dhun-naah
(lit: I it my mother-to gave)

මම එය මගේ
අම්මට දුන්නා.

GRAMMAR

VERBS

In both spoken and written Sinhala, the present tense is the same as the future tense – context differentiates between the two. In the past tense, both the stem and the endings change.

Spoken Language

In spoken language, the present/future tense is the form of the verb that usually appears in the dictionary . The verb doesn't change according to gender or number (singular or plural) and always ends in -nah-vaah (**නවා**).

To form the past tense, nah is dropped and the vowel in the first syllable of the verb changes. Again the verb remains the same, irrespective of gender or number. There are various patterns which affect the vowel change and it's something that must be learned, however, you'll find you'll still be understood even if you don't get it quite right.

As an example, 'eat', kah-nah-vaah (**කනවා**) has the following forms in the present/future and past tenses, which are added to the pronouns:

Spoken Language: Present/Future & Past Tenses			
I	mah-mah	මම	Present/future:
you (sg)	o-bah	ඔබ	kah-nah-vaah
he/she	o-hu/a-yah	ඔහු/ඇය	**කනවා**
it	eh-kah/e-yah	ඒක/එය	
we	a-pi	අපි	Past:
you (pl)	o-bah-laah	ඔබලා	kaa-vaah
they	o-vun	ඔවුන්	**කෑවා**

GRAMMAR

Written Language

In written language, the verb changes in the third person singular (he, she, it) according to the gender of the subject. Neuter takes the same verb endings as masculine:

| fall | va-te-nah-vaah | **වැටෙන** |

The boy falls. (m)
pi-ri-mi lah-mah-yaah
va-tu-neh-yah
(lit: male child falls)
පිරිමි ළමයා වැටුණේය .

The tree falls. (neut)
gah-sah
va-tu-neh-yah
(lit: tree falls)
ගස වැටුණේය .

The girl falls. (f)
ga-hu-nu lah-mah-yaah
va-tu-naah-yah
(lit: female child falls)
ගැහැනු ළමයා වැටුණාය .

Present/Future Tense

The verb endings for the present and future tenses in written language are as follows:

Written Language: Present/Future Tense		
I	mah-mah ...-n-ne-mi	මම ... න්නෙමි
you (sg)	o-bah ...-n-neh-yah	ඔබ ... න්නේය
he	o-hu ...-n-neh-yah	ඔහු ... න්නේය
she	a-yah ...-n-naah-yah	ඇය ... න්නාය
it	eh-kah/e-yah	ඒක/එය
	...-n-neh-yah	... න්නේය
we	a-pi ...-n-ne-mu	අපි ... න්නෙමු
you (pl)	o-bah-laah ...-n-noh-yah	ඔබ ... න්නෝය
they	o-vun ...-n-noh-yah	ඔබලා ... න්නෝය

So, in written language, the verb kah-nah-vaah (කනවා), 'eat', would be conjugated as follows in the present/future tense:

I eat; will eat	mah-mah kahn-ne-mi	මම කන්නෙමි
you eat; will eat	o-bah kahn-neh-yah	ඔබ කන්නේය
he eats; will eat	o-hu kahn-neh-yah	ඔහු කන්නේය
she eats; will eat	a-yah kahn-naah-yah	ඇය කන්නීය
we eat; will eat	a-pi kahn-ne-mu	අපි කන්නෙමු
you eat; will eat	o-bah-laah	ඔබලා
	kahn-noh-yah	කන්නොය
they eat; will eat	o-vun kahn-noh-yah	ඔවිහු කන්නොය

Past Tense
In the past tense, the stem is the same as in spoken language and the verb ending either starts with v or with n, depending on the last syllable of the verb stem. There's no hard-and-fast rule and whichever you choose, you'll find you'll still be understood.

Written Language: Past Tense		
I	mah-mah ...-ve-mi/ ne-mi	මම ...වෙමි/ නෙමි
you (sg)	o-bah ...-veh-yah/ neh-yah	ඔබ ...වේය/ නේය
he/she	o-hu/a-yah/eh-kah/e-yah ...-veh-yah/neh-yah	ඔහු/ඇය/එක/එය ...වේය/නේය
it	eh-kah/e-yah	එක/එය
we	a-pi ...-ve-mu/ne-mu	අපි ...වෙමු/නෙමු
you (pl)	o-bah-laah ...-voh-yah/ noh-yah	ඔබලා ...වොය/නොය
they	o-vun ...-voh-yah/ noh-yah	ඔවිහු ...වොය/නොය

GRAMMAR

In written language, the verb kah-nah-vaah (කනවා) would be conjugated as follows in the past tense:

I ate	mah-mah kaa-ve-mi	මම කෑවෙම්
you ate	o-bah kaa-veh-yah	ඔබ කෑවේය
he ate	o-hu kaa-veh-yah	ඔහු කෑවේය
she ate	a-yah kaa-vaah-yah	ඇය කෑවාය
we ate	a-pi kaa-ve-mu	අපි කෑවෙමු
you ate	o-bah-laah kaa-voh-yah	ඔබලා කෑවෝය
they ate	o-vun kaa-voh-yah	ඔවුන් කෑවෝය

TO HAVE

The verb 'to have' doesn't change according to person; however, the forms of the pronouns are different, and, unlike other verbs, the present and future forms are not the same.

I	mah-tah	මට	Present: thi-ye-nah-vaah තියෙනවා
you	o-bah-tah	ඔබට	
he	o-hu-tah	ඔහුට	
she	a-yah-tah	ඇයට	Past: thi-bu-naah තිබුණා
it	eh-yah-tah	ඒයට	
we	ah-pah-tah	අපට	Future: thi-yeh vi තියේවි
you	o-bah-laah-tah	ඔබලාට	
they	o-vun-tah	ඔවුන්ට	

TO BE

There's no equivalent of the verb 'to be' in Sinhala – you just use the noun or the subject pronoun followed by the adjective or noun:

The car is blue.
    kaahr e-kah nil paah-tai   **කාර් එක නිල්**
    (lit: car one blue colour)   **පාටයි**
I'm frightened.
    mah-mah bhah-yai   **මම භයයි**
    (lit: I frightened)
I'm a student.
    mah-mah shish-yah-yek   **මම ශිෂ්‍යයෙක්**
    (lit: I student)

MODALS

Modals are auxiliary verbs used in conjunction with other verbs to express certainty, probability or possibility. In Sinhala, modals come immediately after the verb.

You'll notice that the syllable immediately before -nah (**න**) in the verb takes a final n (**න්**) – providing there isn't one already.

Must/Have To

To create a sense of obligation (must, have to, should, need to etc), mah (**ම**) replaces the final syllable (vaah, **ව**) of the present/future form of the verb and oh-neh (**ඕනෙ**) is placed after the verb:

leave   yah-nah-vaah   **යනවා**

I must leave now.
    mah-mah dhan   **මම දැන් යන්නම**
    yahn-nah-mah oh-neh   **ඕනේ .**
    (lit: I now go-mah must)

Can/To Be Able To

With the modal 'can/to be able', the final syllable (vaah, **වා**) of the present/future form of the verb is dropped and pu-lu-vah-ni (**පුළුවනි**) is placed after the verb:

do   kah-rah-nah-vaah   කරනවා

I can do this.
   meh-kah mah-tah   මේක මට කරන්න
   kah-rahn-nah pu-lu-vah-ni   පුළුවනි .
   (lit: this I do can)

Note, to express 'can't', you don't need pu-lu-vah-ni – just the negative form ba-ha (**බැහැ**), which is placed immediately after the verb:

I can't do this.
   meh-kah mah-tah   මෙක මට කරන්න
   kah-rahn-nah ba-ha   බැහැ .
   (lit: this I do no)

To Like

To form 'to like', the final syllable (vaah, **වා**) of the present/future form of the verb is dropped and ka-mah-thiy (**කැමතියි**) must be placed after the verb:

read   ki-yah-vah-nah-vaah   කියවනවා

I like reading.
   mah-mah ki-yah-vahn-nah   මම කියවන්න
   ka-mah-thiy   කැමතියි .
   (lit: I read like)

ESSENTIAL VERBS

The verbs listed here are given in the present/future tense (spoken language), since this is the form they'll be in in the dictionary.

be able	ha-ki ve-nah-vaah	හැකි වෙනවා
become	ve-nah-vaah	වෙනවා
bring	ge-ne-nah-vaah	ගෙනෙනවා
buy	gahn nah vaah	ගන්නවා
come	e-nah-vaah	එනවා
cost	va-yah ve-nah-vaah	වැය වෙනවා
depart/leave	yah-nah-vaah	යනවා
drink	bo-nah-vaah	බොනවා
eat	kah-nah-vaah	කනවා
give	dhe-nah-vaah	දෙනවා
go	yah-nah-vaah	යනවා
have	thi-yah-nah-vaah	තියනවා
know	dhan-nah-vaah	දන්නවා
like	ka-mah-thi	කැමති
	ve-nah-vaah	වෙනවා
live	jee-vahth ve-nah-vaah	ජීවත් වෙනවා
love	aah-dhah-rah-yah	ආදරය
	kah-rah-nah-vaah	කරනවා
make	hah-dhah-nah-vaah	හදනවා
meet	hah-mu ve-nah-vaah	හමුවෙනවා
need	ah-vahsh-yah	අවශ්‍ය
	ve-nah-vaah	වෙනවා
return	aah-pah-su	ආපසු
	dhe-nah-vaah	දෙනවා
	say ki-yah-nah-vaah	කියනවා
stay	in-nah-vaah	ඉන්නවා
take	gahn-nah-vaah	ගන්නවා
understand	theh-rum gahn-nah-vaah	තෙරුම් ගන්නවා
want	oh-nah kah-rah-nah-vaah	ඕන කරනවා

GRAMMAR

ADVERBS

Adverbs are words that usually derive from adjectives and add information about verbs. They're normally formed by adding an extra syllable to the adjective. Below is a list of some of the common ones:

cheap	laah-bah	ලාභ
cheaply	laah-be-tah	ලාභෙට
close	lahn-gah	ළඟ
closely	lahn-gah-mah	ළඟම
clear	pa-ha-di-li	පැහැදිලි
clearly	pa-ha-di-li-vah	පැහැදිලිව
direct	ke-lin	කෙළින්
directly	ke-lin-mah	කෙළින්ම
free	ni-dhah-hahs	නිදහස්
freely	ni-dhah-hahs-vah	නිදහස්ව
slow	he-min	හෙමින්
slowly	he-min	හෙමින්
quick	ik-mah-n	ඉක්මන්
quickly	ik-mah-nin	ඉක්මනින්

In Sinhala, adverbs always precede the verb:

He bought it very cheaply.
  o-hu eh-kah hah-ri laah-be-tah   ඔහු ඒක හරි
  gahth-theh   ලාභෙට ගත්තේ .
  (lit: he it very cheaply bought)

The dog ran quickly.
  bahl-laah ik-mah-nin   බල්ලා ඉක්මනින්
  dhiv-veh-yah   දිව්වේය .
  (lit: dog quickly ran)

POSSESSIVES

Possessive adjectives and pronouns have the same form in Sinhala so mah-geh (මගේ), for example, is used to express both 'my' and 'mine':

Possessive Adjective/Pronoun		
my/mine	mah-geh	මගේ
your/yours (sg & pl)	o-beh, o-bah-geh	ඔබේ, ඔබගේ
his	o-hu-geh	ඔහුගේ
her/hers	a-(yah)-geh	ඇ(ය)ගේ
its	u-geh, eh-kah	උගේ, ඒකේ
our/ours	ah-peh, ah-pah-geh	අපේ, අපගේ
their/theirs	o-vun-geh	ඔවුන්ගේ

Note that in spoken language, o-beh, 'your/yours' and ah-peh, 'our/ours', are used rather than o-bah-geh and ah-pah-geh, and that a-yah-geh, 'her/hers', is abbreviated to a-geh. In addition, be aware that u-geh, 'its', is used only to refer to animals.

Possessive adjectives come before the noun they possess and possessive pronouns are placed after:

This is my car.
    meh mah-geh kaahr e-kah   මේ මගේ කාර් එක.
    (lit: this my car one)

This car is mine.
    meh kaahr e-kah mah-geh   මේ කාර් එක මගේ.
    (lit: this car one mine)

GRAMMAR

QUESTIONS

Question words usually appear at the end of the sentence, but there's no hard-and-fast rule, so you can place them anywhere and still be understood. You'll notice that -dhah (**ද**), which denotes an inquiry, appears at the end of all question words.

Common question words are listed below. Where two alternatives appear, the first is used in spoken language and the second in written language.

Where?	ko-heh-dhah?	**කොහේද?**
Where's the bank?		
ban-ku-wah ko-heh-dhah?		**බැංකුව කොහේද?**
(lit: bank where?)		
Why?	a-yi/a-yi-dhah?	**ඇයි/ඇයිද?**
Why is the office closed?		
kahn-thoh-ru-wah		**කන්තෝරුව**
vah-hah-laah a-yi?		**වහල ඇයි?**
(lit: office closed why?)		
When?	kah-vah-dhaah-dhah?	**කවදාද?**
When are you coming?		
o-bah en-neh		**ඔබ එන්නේ**
kah-vah-dhaah-dhah?		**කවදාද?**
(lit: you coming when?)		
What?	ku-mahk-dhah?/	**කුමක්ද?/**
	mo-kahk-dhah?	**මොකක්ද?**
What happened?		
ku-mahk-dhah vu-neh?		**කුමක්ද වුණේ?**
(lit: what happened?)		
How?	ko-ho-mah-dhah?	**කොහොමද?**
How did you come? (get here)		
aah-veh ko-ho-mah-dhah?		**ආවේ**
(lit: came how?)		**කොහොමද?**
Who?	kahv-dhah?	**කවිද?**
Who came today?		
ah-dhah kahv-dhah aah-veh?		**අද කවිද ආවේ?**
(lit: today who came?)		

Which?	koi e-kah-dhah?;	කොයි එකද?;
	ku-mahk-dhah?	කුමක්ද?

Which one is mine?
koi e-kah-dhah mah-geh?   කොයි එකද මගේ?
(lit: which one mine?)

As already mentioned, word order in Sinhala questions is very flexible, so the same question can be phrased in a number of different ways. Two common variations are as follows:

What's the time?
veh-laah-vah kee-yah-dhah?   වේලාව කියද?
(lit: time how-much?)
What's the time?
kee-yah-dhah veh-laah-vah?   කියද වේලාව?
(lit: how-much time?)

'Yes/No' Questions

To form a yes/no question, ie a question that elicits a 'yes/no' answer, simply add -dhah (ද) to the end of any sentence – there's no need to change the word order at all.

You're going.
o-bah yah-nah-vaah   ඔබ යනවා.
(lit: you going)
Are you going?
o-bah yah-nah-vaah-dhah?   ඔබ යනවාද?
(lit: you going-dhah?)

NEGATIVES

Negative sentences are formed by changing the verb ending from nah-vaah (නවා) to neh (නේ) and adding an extra n (න්) to the preceding syllable. The negative particle na-ha (නැහැ) is placed immediately after the verb.

I'm going today.
mah-mah ah-dhah yah-nah-vaah   මම අද යනවා.
(lit: I today am-going)

I'm not going today.
　mah-mah ah-dhah yahn-neh na-ha　　මම අද යන්නේ
　(lit: I today go no)　　　　　　　　නැහැ.

For emphasis, you may hear na-ha placed twice in a sentence
– at the beginning, as well as after the verb:

No, I'm not going today.
　na-ha, mah-mah ah-dhah　　　　　නැහැ, මම
　yahn-neh na-ha　　　　　　　　　අද යන්නේ නැහැ.
(lit: no I today go no)

PREPOSITIONS

Sinhalese prepositions are placed after the noun or pronoun
they refer to. The prepositions most commonly used are:

above	u-din	උඩින්
below	pah-hah-lin	පහළින්
beside	ah-yi-neh	අයිනේ
by	lahn-gah	ළඟ
from	si-tah	සිට
in	a-thu-leh	ඇතුළේ
on	mah-thah/u-dah	මත/උඩ
over	u-din	උඩින්
to	tah	ට
under	yah-tah	යට

GRAMMAR

The dog is in the house.
　bahl-laah ge-yah a-thu-leh　　　බල්ලා ගෙය ඇතුළේ.
　(lit: dog house in)

Sit under the tree.
　gah-hah yah-tah　　　　　　　　ගහ යට
　in-dhah gahn-nah　　　　　　　　ඉඳ ගන්න.
　(lit: tree under sit)

Look over your shoulder.
　o-beh u-rah-hi-sah-tah　　　　　ඔබේ උරහිසට
　u-din bah-lahn-nah　　　　　　　උඩින් බලන්න.
　(lit: your shoulder over look)

CONJUNCTIONS

Conjunctions join together sentences or parts of a sentence. The following is a list of the most common conjunctions:

and	sah-hah	සහ
as	ni-saah	නිසා)
because	he-yin	හෙයින්
but	nah-muth	නමුත්
although	voo-vahth	වුවත්
however	e-she-dhah/	එසේද/
	ke-seh-ve-thahth	කෙසේවෙතත්
since	ni-saah	නිසා)

I can't go because I'm sick.
  ah-sah-nee-pah he-yin mah-tah
  yahn-nah ba-ha
  (lit: sick because to-me go not)

අසනීප හෙයින් මට
යන්න බැහැ .

I like it, but it's too expensive for me.
  mah-mah eh-kah-tah
  kah-mah-thiy nah-muth, mi-lah
  va-diy
  (lit: I it like but expensive too)

මම ඒකට කැමතියි
නමුත් , මිළ වැඩියි

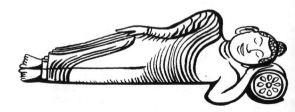

You'll find that a few well-chosen words in Sinhala will go a long way towards enriching your travels in Sri Lanka.

YOU SHOULD KNOW

ඔබ දැන ගත යුතු දේ

Hello./ Goodbye.	aah-yu-boh-wahn	ආයුබෝවන්.
Yes.	o-vu	ඔව්.
No.	na-ha	නැහැ.
Excuse me.	sah-maah-vahn-nah	සමාවන්න.
Excuse me. (to a Buddhist priest)	ah-vah-sah-rah	අවසර.
Please.	kah-ru-naah-kah-rah-lah	කරුණාකරල.
Thank you.	sthoo-thiy	ස්තුතියි.
Thank you very much.	bo-ho-mah sthoo-thiy	බොහොම ස්තුතියි.
Sorry.	kah-nah-gaah-tuy	කණගාටුයි.

GREETINGS & GOODBYES

සුභ පැතීම් සහ සමුගැනීම්

People often greet each other with just a friendly smile – there's no particular word for 'hello' in Sinhala. The nearest equivalent is aah-yu-boh-wahn (ආයුබෝවන්), which is also used for 'goodbye' and literally means 'may you live long'. This is usually accompanied by a slight bow, with the hands joined together in front. If you're greeted in this way, simply return the gesture.

Good morning.	su-bah u-dhaa-sah-nahk	සුභ උදෑසනක්.
Good afternoon.	su-bah dhah-vaah-lahk	සුභ දවාලක්.
Good evening.	su-bah san-dhaa-vahk	සුභ සැන්දෑවක්.
Good night.	su-bah raahth-ri-yahk	සුභ රාත්‍රියක්.

FORMS OF ADDRESS   ආමන්ත්‍රණය කිරීම

There are many different ways of saying 'you' in Sinhala, such as:

o-bah **(ඔබ)**	commonly used, also found in verse and prose
num-bah **(නුඹ)**	old-fashioned
o-yaah **(ඔයා)**	more familiar and colloquial
um-bah **(උඹ)**	usually used when in anger

It can be difficult to know which form to use – there are many to choose from and the one you select will convey how you feel about the person you're talking to. The all-purpose o-yaah and o-bah can be used fairly safely, but it's generally best to stick to names or avoid saying 'you' altogether. Close friends and children often call each other by their first names.

HOW TO HELLO

In more informal situations, you can greet people by asking ko-ho-mah-dah? **(කොහොමද?)**, meaning 'How are you?', and when saying goodbye, use gi-hin en-nahm **(ගිහින් එන්නම්)**, literally 'I'll go and come back'.

Useful titles to be familiar with are:

Mr/Sir	mah-hahth-mah-yaah/	මහත්මයා/
	mah-hah-thaah (inf)	මහතා
Mrs	mah-hahth-mi-yah	මහත්මිය
Miss	me-nah-vi-yah	මෙනවිය
Master	po-di	පොඩි
	mah-hahth-mah-yaah	මහත්මයා
Your Honour	haah-mu-dhu-ru-vah-neh	හාමුදුරුවනේ
thera (Buddhist	swaah-meen-	ස්වාමීන්වහන්ස
priest/monks)	wah-hahn-sah	
policeman	raah-lah-haah-mi	රාළහාමී
shopkeeper	mu-dhah-laah-li	මුදලාලි

Sinhalese titles follow a person's name:

Mr Carl Young
   kaahl yahng mah-hah-thaah   කාල් යං මහතා
   (lit: Carl Young Mr)

Miss Mary Richards
   meh-ri ri-chahds   මේරි රිචඩ්ස්
   me-nah-vi-yah   මෙනවිය
   (lit: Mary Richards Miss)

TALKING   පැවිදි අය
TO MONKS   ආමන්තුන්නාය කිරිමේදි

When greeting or farewelling Buddhist priests or monks, join
your hands together (as if in prayer) and with a bow say: ah-vah-
sah-rah swaah-meen-wah-hahn-sah (අවසර ස්වාමින්වහන්ස),
which means 'Excuse me, priest/monk'. If in conversation you
need to say 'yes', use e-hei (එහෙයි) – not
the more usual word o-vu (ඔව්).

On the following page is a
list of other key words used
when speaking with monks.

Word	Temple Vocabulary	Standard Sinhala
bathing (wash)	pan sa-nah-he-nah-vaah පැන් සැනහෙනව	naah-nah-vaah නානවා
breakfast	heel dhaah-nah-dyah හීල් දානය	u-dheh kaa-mah උදේ කෑම
coming/going	vah-di-nah-vaah වඩිනව	e-nah-vaah එනවා
die	ah-pah-vahth ve-nah-vaah අපවත් වෙනව	ma-re-nah-vaah මැරෙනවා
drinks	gi-lahn pah-sah ගිලන් පස	bee-mah බීම
eating	vah-lahn-dhi-nah-vaah වළඳිනව	kah-nah-vaah කනවා
food	dhaah-nah-yah දානයකෑම	kaa-mah කෑම
garden	mah-lu-wah මළුව	mi-dhu-lah මිදුල
lunch	dhah-vahl dhaah-nah-yah දවල් දානය	dhah-vahl kaa-mah දවල් කෑම
saying	vah-dhaah-rah-nah-vaah වදාරනව	ki-yah-nah-vaah කියනවා
sleeping	sa-thah-pe-nah-vaah සැතපෙනව	ni-dhah-nah-vaah නිදනවා
sweep	ah-mah-dhi-nah-vah අමදිනව	ah-thu-gaah-nah-vah අතුගානවා
wash	dhoh-wah-nah-yah kah-rah-nah-vaah දෝවනය කරනව	soh-dhah-nah-vah සෝදනවා
water	pan පැන්	wah-thu-rah වතුර
yes	e-hei එහෙයි	o-vu ඔව්
you	o-bah vah-hahn-seh ඔබ වහන්සේ	o-bah ඔබ

BODY LANGUAGE ශාරීරික ඉඟියන්

Body language plays an important part in Sinhalese communication. Even the eyes convey meaning – particularly 'thank you' and 'sorry' – far more expressively than words do.

One important gesture not to misunderstand is the shaking of the head from side to side – this is not a negative sign but, in fact, indicates approval of something or a 'yes'.

Waving a hand towards oneself with the palm down signals 'come here'. When the gesture is made in an outward manner, it signals 'go away'.

Generally speaking, public displays of affection between couples are not appreciated, especially by older members of the community.

Avoid blowing your nose in public where possible – Sri Lankans would rather sniff incessantly than blow into a handkerchief.

FIRST ENCOUNTERS පළමු හමුවීම්

When first making conversation with someone, an effective 'kick start' to the process is to ask their name:

What's your name?
o-beh nah-mah mo-kahk-dhah? ඔබේ නම මොකක්ද?
My name is ...
mah-geh nah-mah ... මගේ නම ...
I'm pleased to meet you.
o-bah dha-nah-gan-nah ඔබ දැනගන්න
la-bee-mah sah-thu-tahk ලැබීම සතුටක්.
I'd like to introduce you to ...
...-tah o-bah hah-dhu-naah ...ට ඔබ හඳුනා
dhen-nah mah-mah දෙන්න මම
ka-mah-thiy කැමතියි.

How are you?	ko-ho-mah-dhah?	කොහොමද?
Good, thank you.	hon-dhin in-nah-waah	හොඳින් ඉන්නවා.
Not too bad.	wah-rah-dhahk na-ha	වරදක් නැහැ.
Not too good.	e-thah-rahm hon-dhah na-ha	එතරම් හොඳ නැහැ.

MAKING CONVERSATION

කථාවට මුල පිරිම

Do you live here?
o-bah me-heh-dhah in-neh?

ඔබ මෙහේද ඉන්නේ?

Where are you going?
o-bah ko-heh-dhah yahn-neh?

ඔබ කොහේද යන්නේ?

What are you doing?
o-bah mo-kahk-dah
kah-rahn-neh?

ඔබ මොකක්ද
කරන්නේ?

Can I take a photo (of you)?
mah-tah (o-beh)
pin-thoo-rah-yahk gahn-nah
pu-lu-vahn-dhah?

මට (ඔබේ)
පිංතුරයක් ගන්න
පුළුවන්ද?

Are you here on holiday?
o-bah ni-vaah-du-vah-tah
a-vith-dhah?

ඔබ නිවාඩුවට
ඇවිත්ද?

I'm here ...   mah-mah me-heh
                   in-neh ...

මම මෙහේ
ඉන්නේ ...

for a holiday	ni-vaah-du-vah-kah-tah	නිවාඩුවකට
on business	bis-nahs vah-lah-tah	ඔස්නස් වලට
to study	i-ge-nah gahn-nah	ඉගෙන ගන්න

How long are you here for?
o-bah koch-chah-rah kah-lahk
in-nah-vaah-dhah?

ඔබ කොච්චර
කලක් ඉන්නවාද?

I'm/We're here for ... weeks/days.
mah-mah/ah-pi sah-thi/
dhi-nah ...-k in-nah-vaah

මම/අපි සති/
දින ...ක් ඉන්නවා.

Do you like it here?
o-bah me-heh-tah ka-mah-thi-dhah?

ඔබ මෙහෙට කැමතිද?

I/We like it here very much.
mah-mah/ah-pi me-heh-tah
hah-ri ka-mah-thiy

මම/අපි මෙහෙට
හරි කැමතියි.

I'm here with my partner.
mah-mah me-heh in-neh
mah-geh sah-hah-kah-ru/
sah-hah-kaah-ri-yah ek-kah (m/f)

මම මෙහේ ඉන්නේ
මගේ සහකරු/
සහකාරිය එක්ක.

NATIONALITIES   ජාතින්

When meeting someone, especially for the first time, you're bound to be asked where you come from.

Where are you from?
o-bah ko-hen-dhah?   ඔබ කොහෙන්ද?

Which country are you from?
o-bah mo-nah rah-ten-dhah?   ඔබ මොන රටෙන්ද?

I'm from ...	mah-mah ...	මම ...
We're from ...	ah-pi ...	අපි ...
Africa	ah-pri-kaah-ven	අප්‍රිකාවෙන්
America	ah-meh-ri-kaah-ven	අමෙරිකාවෙන්
Argentina	aahr-jahn-tee-naah-ven	ආර්ජන්ටිනාවෙන්
Australia	ohs-treh-li-yaah-ven	ඕස්ට්‍රේලියාවෙන්
Canada	ka-nah-daah-ven	කැනඩාවෙන්
Dubai	du-bai vah-lin	බායි වලින්
England	en-gah-lahn-thah-yen	එංගලන්තයෙන්
France	prahn-shah-yen	ප්‍රංශයෙන්
Germany	jahr-mah-ni-yen	ජර්මනියෙන්
Holland	oh-lahn-dhah-yen	ඕලන්දයෙන්
India	in-dhi-yaah-ven	ඉන්දියාවෙන්
Ireland	ah-yahr-lahn-thah-yen	අයර්ලන්තයෙන්
Italy	i-thaah-li-yen	ඉතාලියෙන්
Japan	jah-paah-nah-yen	ජපානයෙන්
Malaysia	mah-lah-yah-aah-si-yaah-ven	මලයාසියාවෙන්
New Zealand	nah-vah-see-lahn-thah-yen	නවසි-ලන්තයෙන්
Russia	ru-si-yaah-ven	රුසියාවෙන්
Scotland	s-kot-lahn-thah-yen	ස්කොට්ලන්තයෙන්
South America	dhah-ku-nu ah-meh-ri-kaah-ven	දකුණු අමෙරිකාවෙන්
Spain	spaahn-gna-yen	ස්පාඤ්ඤයෙන්
Thailand	thaai-lahn-thah-yen	තායිලන්තයෙන්
Wales	wehls vah-lin	වේල්ස් වලින්

I live in/at the/a ...	mah-mah in-neh ...	මම ඉන්නේ ...
city	nah-gah-rah-yeh	නගරයේ
countryside	gah-meh/gahm-bah-dah	ගමේ/ගම්බද
mountains	kahn-dhu-kah-rah-yeh	කඳුකරයේ
seaside	mu-hu-dhu-bah-dah	මුහුදුබඩ
village	gah-meh	ගමේ

CULTURAL DIFFERENCES   සංස්කෘතික වෙනස්කම්

Is this a custom in your country?
  meh o-beh rah-teh
  chaah-ri-thrah-yak-dhah?
මේ ඔබේ රටේ
වාරිත්‍රයක්ද?

How do you do this in your country?
  meh-kah o-beh rah-teh
  kah-rahn-neh ko-ho-mah-dhah?
මේක ඔබේ රටේ
කරන්නේ කොහොමද?

I'm not accustomed to this.
  mah-tah meh-kah
  pu-ru-dhu na-ha
මට මේක පුරුදු
නැහැ.

I don't mind watching but
I'd prefer not to participate.
  mah-mah sah-hah-baah-gee
  ven-neh na-ha, nah-muth
  bah-laah in-nahm
මම සහභාගී වෙන්නේ
නැහැ, නමුත් බලා
ඉන්නම්.

I don't want to offend you.
  o-beh hi-thah ri-dhah-vahn-nah
  mah-mah ka-mah-thi na-ha
ඔබේ හිත රිදවන්න
මම කැමති නැහැ.

I'm sorry, it's not the custom
in my country.
  kah-nah-gaah-tuy, mah-geh
  rah-te si-ri-thah eh-kah no-veh
කණගාටුයි, මගේ
රටේ සිරිත එක නොවේ.

I'm sorry, it's against my ...	mah-tah kah-nah-gaah-tuy eh-kah, mah-geh ...-tah vi-rudh_dhai	මට කණගාටුයි එක, මගේ ...ට විරුද්ධයි.
beliefs	a-dhah-heem	ඇදහිම්
culture	sahns-kru-thi-yah	සංස්කෘතිය
religion	aah-gah-mah	ආගම

I'll give it a go.
mah-mah eh-kah
kah-rah-lah bah-lahn-nahm

මම එක
කරල බලන්නම්.

I'll watch.
mah-mah bah-laah in-nahm

මම බලා ඉන්නම්.

AGE

වයස

How old ...?	... vah-yah-sah kee-yah-dhah?	... වයස කියද?
are you	o-bah-geh	ඔබගේ
is your son/	o-bah-geh	ඔබගේ
daughter	pu-thaah-geh/ dhu-wah-geh	පුතාගේ/ දුවගේ

I'm ... years old.
mah-geh vah-yah-sah
ah-vu-ru-dhu ...

මගේ වයස
අවුරුදු ...

For numbers, see page 173.

OCCUPATIONS

රැකියාවන්

What (work) do you do?	o-beh ra-ki-yaah-wah mo-kahk-dhah?	ඔබේ රැකියාව මොකක්ද?
I am a/an ...	mah-mah ...	මම ...
artist	chith-rah shil-pi-yek/ shil-pi-ni-yahk (m/f)	චිතු ශිල්පියෙක්/ ශිල්පිනියක්
author	kah-thu vah-rah-yek/ vah-ri-yahk (m/f)	කතු වරයෙක්/ වරියක්
business-person	ve-lahn-dhah vyaah-paah-ri-kah-yek/vyaah-paah-ri-kaah-vahk (m/f)	වෙළද වනාපාරිකයෙක්/ වනාපාරිකාවක්

MEETING PEOPLE

doctor	vai-dhyah-vah-rah-yek/	වෛද්‍යවරයෙක්/
	vai-dhyah-vah-ri-yahk (m/f)	වෛද්‍යවරියක්
engineer	inji-neh-ru-vek/	ඉංජිනේරුවෙක්/
	inji-neh-ru-vah-ri-yahk (m/f)	ඉංජිනේරුවරියක්
factory worker	kahm-hahl kah-ru-vek/ kaah-ri-yak (m/f)	කම්හල් කරුවෙක්/කාරියක්
farmer	go-vi-yek/go-vi kaahn-thaah-wahk (m/f)	ගොවියෙක්/ ගොවි කාන්තාවක්
journalist	leh-khah-kah-yek/leh-khah-kaah-vi-yahk (m/f)	ලේඛකයෙක්/ ලේඛකාවියක්
lawyer	nee-thee-gnah vah-rah-yek/ vah-ri-yahk (m/f)	නීතිඥ වරයෙක්/ වරියක්
mechanic	kaahr-mi-kah shil-pi-yek/ shil-pi-ni-yahk (m/f)	කාර්මික ශිල්පියෙක්/ ශිල්පිනියක්
musician	sahn-gee-thah-gna-yek/ sahn-gee-thah-gna-vah-ri-yahk (m/f)	සංගීතඥයෙක්/ සංගීතඥවරියක්
nurse	saahth-thu seh-vah-kah-yek/ seh-vi-kaah-vahk (m/f)	සාත්තු සේවකයෙක්/ සේවිකාවක්
office worker	kaahr-yaah-lah seh-vah-kah-yek/ seh-vi-kaah-vahk (m/f)	කාර්යාල සේවකයෙක්/ සේවිකාවක්
scientist	vi-dhyaah-gnah vah-rah-yek/ vah-ri-yahk (m/f)	විද්‍යාඥ වරයෙක්/ වරියක්
secretary	leh-khahm vah-rah-yek/ vah-ri-yahk (m/f)	ලේඛම් වරයෙක්/ වරියක්
student	shish-yah-yek/ shish-yaah-wahk (m/f)	ශිෂ්‍යයෙක්/ ශිෂ්‍යාවක්
teacher	guru-vah-rah-yek/ guru-vah-ri-yahk (m/f)	ගුරුවරයෙක්/ ගුරුවරියක්
waiter	u-pah-tan vah-rah-yek/ vah-ri-yahk (m/f)	උපටැන් වරයෙක්/ වරියක්

I'm retired.
   mah-mah vish-raah-mi-kai   මම විශ්‍රාමිකයි.

I'm unemployed.
   mah-mah ra-ki-yaah-vahk   මම රැකියාවක්
   kah-rahn-neh na-ha   කරන්නේ නැහැ.

I'm self-employed.
   mah-mah swah-yahn   මම ස්වයං රැකියා
   ra-ki-yaah kah-rahn-neh   කරන්නේ.

I stay home doing the housework.
   mah-mah ge-dhah-rah va-dah   මම ගෙදර වැඩ
   kah-rah-ge-nah ge-dhah-rah   කරගෙන ගෙදර
   in-nah-vaah   ඉන්නවා.

Do you enjoy your work?
   o-beh kah-rah-nah ra-ki-yaah-vah   ඔබ කරන රැකියාව
   hon-dhah-dhah?   හොඳද?

How long have you been in the job?
   o-bah koch-chah-rah   ඔබ කොච්චර
   kaah-lah-yak si-tah-dhah   කාලයක් සිටද වැඩ
   va-dah kah-rahn-neh?   කරන්නේ?

What are you studying?
   o-bah mo-nah-wah-dhah   ඔබ මොනවද,
   i-ge-nah gahn-neh?   ඉගෙන ගන්නේ?

I'm studying ...	mah-mah kah-rahn-neh ...	මම කරන්නේ ...
art	chi-thra shil-pah-yah	චිත්‍ර ශිල්පය
business	vyaah-paah-ri-kah	ව්‍යාපාරික
studies	ah-<u>dhy</u>ah-yah-nah-yah	අධ්‍යයනය
education	ah-<u>dhy</u>aah-pah-nah-yah	අධ්‍යාපනය
engineering	in-ji-neh-ru vi-dhyaah-vah	ඉංජිනේරු විද්‍යාව
hospitality	aah-ġahn-thu-kah sahth-kah-rah-nah-yah	ආගන්තුක සත්කරණය
languages	bhaah-shaah-vahn	භාෂාවන්
law	nee-thi vi-dhyaah-vah	නීති විද්‍යාව
medicine	vai-dhyah vi-dhyaah-vah	වෛද්‍ය විද්‍යාව
science	vi-dhyaah-vah	විද්‍යාව

FEELINGS

හැඟීම්

I'm ...	mah-mah ... in-neh	මම ... ඉන්නේ.
afraid	bhah-yen	භයෙන්
angry	thah-rah-hen	තරහෙන්
cold	see-thah-len	සිතලෙන්
happy	sah-thu-tin	සතුටින්
hot	rahs-nen	රස්නෙන්
hungry	bah-dah-gin-neh	බඩගින්නේ
in a hurry	hah-dhis-si-yen	හදිස්සියෙන්
sad	dhu-kin	දුකින්
sleepy	ni-dhi-mah-then	නිදිමතෙන්
thirsty	thi-bah-hen	තිබහෙන්
tired	mah-han-si-yen	මහන්සියෙන්
well	sah-nee-pen	සනීපෙන්
worried	sith tha-vu-len	සිත් තැවුලෙන්

I'm sorry. (apology)
    mah-tah sah-maah-ven-nah

මට සමාවෙන්න.

I'm grateful (to you).
    mah-mah o-bah-tah
    kru-thah-gnah ve-nah-vaah

මම ඔබට කෘතඥ වෙනවා.

I'm happy for you.
    o-bah ga-nah mah-tah
    sahn-thoh-sai

ඔබ ගැන මට සන්තෝෂයි.

I'm worried about you.
    o-bah ga-nah mah-tah
    bhah-yai

ඔබ ගැන මට භයයි.

I'm sorry (for you). (condolence)
    o-bah ga-nah mah-tah dhu-kai

ඔබ ගැන මට දුකයි.

BREAKING THE LANGUAGE BARRIER

භාෂාව පිළිබඳ
බාධක බිඳ හැරීම

Do you speak English?
o-bah in-gree-si kah-thaah
kau-rah-nah-vaah-dhah?

ඔබ ඉංග්‍රීසි කථා
කරනවාද?

Does anyone speak English?
kau-ru hah-ri in-gree-si
kah-thaah kah-rah-nah-vaah-dhah?

කව්රු හරි ඉංග්‍රීසි
කථා කරනවාද?

I am still learning.
mah-mah eh-kah thah-vah-mah
i-ge-nah gahn-nah-vaah

මම ඒක තවම
ඉගෙන ගන්නවා.

Excuse my Sinhala.
mah-geh sin-hah-lah ga-nah
sa-maah ven-nah

මගේ සිංහල ගැන
සමා වෙන්න.

I don't understand you.
mah-tah o-bah-vah theh-rum
gahn-nah ba-ha

මට ඔබව තේරුම්
ගන්න බැහැ.

Could you please repeat that?
kah-ru-naah-kah-rah-lah
eh-kah na-vah-thah ki-yahn-nah
pu-lu-vahn-dhah?

කරුණාකරල ඒක
නැවත කියන්න
පුළුවන්ද?

Could you please write that for me?
kah-ru-naah-kah-rah-lah mah-tah
eh-kah li-yah-lah dhen-nah
pu-lu-vahn-dhah?

කරුණාකරල මට
ඒක ලියලා දෙන්න
පුළුවන්ද?

How would you say ...?
... ki-yahn-neh ko-ho-mah-dhah?

... කියන්නේ කොහොමද?

What does ... mean?
... theh-ru-mah mo-kahk-dhah?

... තේරුම මොකක්ද?

How do you say this word?
meh vah-chah-nah-yah
ki-yahn-neh ko-ho-mah-dhah?

මේ වචනය කියන්නේ
කොහොමද?

What's this called?
meh-kah-tah mo-kahk-dhah
ki-yahn-neh?

මේකට මොකක්ද
කියන්නේ?

MEETING PEOPLE

STAYING IN TOUCH   ඇසුරේ සිටීම

When you're about to leave the country, you may need the following phrases to help you stay in touch:

... is my last day.
  ... mah-geh ahn-thi-mah   ... මගේ අන්තිම
  dhah-vah-sah   දවස .

I'll be leaving on ...
  mah-mah ... yah-nah-vaah   මම ... යනවා .

For Days of the Week, see page 165.

Here's my address.
  men-nah mah-geh li-pi-nah-yah   මෙන්න මගේ ලිපිනය .

Can I have your address please?
  kah-ru-naah-kah-rah mah-tah   කරුණාකර මට ඔබේ
  o-beh li-pi-nah-yah   ලිපිනය දෙනවාද ?
  dhen-nah-vaah-dhah?

If you ever visit ...,
you must come and visit me.
  o-bah kah-vah-dhaah hah-ri   ඔබ කවදා හරි
  ... aah-voth maah ha-mu   ... ආවොත් මා
  ven-nah en-nah oh-neh   හමු වෙන්න එන්න ඕනේ .

Do you have an email address?
  o-bah-tah e-mehl li-pi-nah-yahk   ඔබට ඊමේල්
  thi-yeh-dhah?   ලිපිනයක් තියේද ?

I'll send you copies of the photographs.
  mah-mah o-bah-tah pin-thoo-ru   මම ඔබට පින්තූරු
  vah-lah ko-pi e-vahn-nahm   වල කොපි එවන්නම් .

Don't forget to write.
  li-yum li-yah-nah   ලියුම් ලියන්න
  ah-mah-thah-kah   අමතක කරන්න එපා .
  kah-rahn-nah e-paah

It's been great meeting you.
  o-bah hah-mu-vee-mah   ඔබ හමුවීම
  lo-ku de-yahk   ලොකු දෙයක් .

Keep in touch!
  mah-tah ni-thah-rah li-yahn-nah!   මට නිතර ලියන්න !

Writing Letters   ලිපි ලිවීම

Once you get back home, you may want to write to the people
you met. Here are a few lines to help you:

Dear ...
   හිතවත් ...
I'm sorry it's taken me so long to write.
   මෙපමණ කලකට ලියන්න බැරි වීම ගැන කණගාටුයි. It
was great to meet you.
   ඔබ හමුවීම ගැන මම හරි සන්තෝෂයි.
Thank you so much for your hospitality.
   ඔබ දැක්වූ සත්කාර වලට බොහොම ස්තුතියි.
I miss you. (sg)
   ඔබ නැතුව මට පාළු දැනෙනවා.
I miss you. (pl)
   ඔබලා නැතුව මට පාළු දැනෙනවා.
I had a fantastic time in ...
   ... මම රසවත් කාලයක් ගත කලා.
My favourite place was ...
   ගිය තැන් වලින් මම හුඟාක්ම ආශා වුනේ ...
I hope to visit ... again.
   ...ට යන්න මා නැවත එන්න බලාපොරොත්තු වෙනවා.
Say 'hi' to ... and ... for me.
   ...ට හා ...ට කියන්න මම මතක් කළ බව.
I'd love to see you again.
   මට නැවත ඔබලා බලන්න ආසයි.
Write soon!
   ඉක්මණට ලියුමක් එවන්න!
With love,
   ආදරයෙන්,
Regards,
   සමරනුයේ,

For Addresses, see page 57.

SAY WHAT?

When translated into Sinhala, the expression 'I beg your pardon', becomes a question, mo-kahk-dhah kiv-veh? (මොකක්ද කිව්වේ?), literally meaning 'What did you say?'. Alternatively, you could say sa-maah-ven-nah (සමාවෙන්න), meaning 'sorry'.

USEFUL PHRASES   ප්‍රයෝජන්වත් වාක්‍යපද්

OK.	hon-dhai	හොඳයි.
Sure.	hah-ri	හරි.
Let's go.	yah-mu	යමු.
Careful!	bah-laah-ge-nai!	බලාගෙනයි!
Wait!	oh-ho-mah in-nah!	ඔහොම ඉන්න!
Just a minute.	vi-naah-di-yahk in-nah	විනාඩියක් ඉන්න
Are you ready?	o-bah laas-thi-dhah?	ඔබ ලෑස්තිද?
I'm ready.	mah-mah laas-thiy	මම ලෑස්තියි.
No problem.	prash-nah-yahk na-ha	ප්‍රශ්නයක් නැහැ.

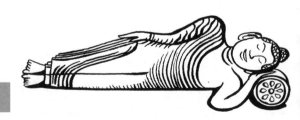

ගමනේ බිමනේ යෙදීම

GETTING AROUND

Sri Lanka has a good network of roads connecting the principal towns and places of interest, as well as a train service linking the island's key tourist destinations.

Cars can be hired with or without drivers, and taxis are available in all the main towns. Taxis usually have meters, but if not, the fare must be negotiated – ideally, before the journey begins. For an open-air experience, try a three-wheeled 'autorickshaw'.

Bus travel is cheap and there's an island-wide service. Express buses run to all principal towns and seats can be booked in advance (except during certain festival seasons).

FINDING YOUR WAY
ගමන් බිමන් යෑමේදි

Where's the ...?	... ko-heh-dhah thi-yen-neh?	... කොහේද තියෙන්නේ?
bus stop	bahs staand e-kah	බස් ස්ටෑනඩ් එක
road to ...	...-tah yah-nah paah-rah	...ට යන පාර
train station	dhum-ri-yah sthaah-nah-yah	දුම්රිය ස්ථානය

What time does the ... leave/arrive?	... pi-tahth ven-neh/ en-neh kee-yah-tah-dhah?	... පිටත් වෙන්නේ/ එන්නේ කියටද?
boat	boht-tu-wah	බෝට්ටුව
bus	bahs e-kah	බස් එක
plane	ah-hahs-yaah thraah-vah	අහස් යාත්‍රාව
train	dhum-ri-yah	දුම්රිය

How do we get to ...?
...-tah yahn-neh
ko-ho-mah-dhah?
...ට යන්නේ
කොහොමද?

55

GETTING AROUND

Is it close by?
dhan lahn-gah-dhah?　　　　　　දැන් ළඟද?

Can we walk there?
ah-pi-tah eh-haah-tah　　　　　අපිට එහාට
a-vi-dhin-nah pu-lu-vahn-dhah?　ඇවිදින්න පුළුවන්ද?

Can you show me
(on the map)?
mah-tah (si-thi-yah-meh)　　　　මට (සිතියමේ)
pen-vahn-nah pu-lu-vahn-dhah?　පෙන්වන්න පුළුවන්ද?

Are there other means of
getting there?
e-haah-tah ve-nah vi-dhi-yah-kin　එහාට වෙන විධියකින්
yahn-nah ba-ri-dhah?　　　　　යන්න බැරිද?

What ... is this?	meh mo-nah ...-dhah?	මේ මොන ...ද?
city	nah-gah-rah-yah	නගරය
street	vee-thi-yah	වීථිය
village	gah-mah	ගම

Directions　　　　　　　මහ සලකුණු

Turn at the ...	... ha-ren-nah	... හැරෙන්න.
next corner	ee-lahn-gah	ඊළඟ
	ko-neh-dhee	කොණේදි
traffic lights	tra-fic lait	ට්‍රැෆික්
	vah-lah-dhee	ලයිට් වලදි
next crossroads	ee-lahn-gah	ඊළඟ
	hahn-dhi-yeh-dhee	හන්දියේදි

Go straight ahead.	ke-lin	කෙළින්
	is-sah-rah-hah-tah	ඉස්සරහට
	yahn-nah	යන්න.
Turn left/right.	vah-mah-tah/	වමට/දකුණට
	dhah-ku-nah-tah	හැරෙන්න.
	ha-ren-nah	

behind	pahs-sah-tah/	පස්සට/
	pahs-sen	පස්සෙන්
in front of	is-sah-rah-hin	ඉස්සරහින්
far	aa-thah	ඈත
near	lan-gah	ළඟ
here	me-thah-nah	මෙතන
there	ah-tha-nah	අතන
opposite	i-di-ri-pah-sah	ඉදිරිපස
north	u-thu-rah	උතුර
south	dhah-ku-nah	දකුණ
east	na-ge-nah-hi-rah	නැගෙනහිර
west	bah-tah-hi-rah	බටහිර

Thank you for showing us the way.

| ah-pah-tah paah-rah | අපට පාර |
| pen-nu-waah-tah sthoo-thiy | පෙන්නුවාට ස්තුතියි . |

ADDRESSES   ලිපිනයන්

Addresses are often written in English, but occasionally they're written in Sinhala – particularly in suburban and rural areas. A written address in Sinhala would give the person's name, the number and street, the suburb and the city. For Colombo addresses usually only the suburb is given, unless the address is in one of the city zones. For example:

සීතා හේරත්	see-thaah heh-rah-th	Seetha Herath
45 නාවල පාර	45 naah-wah-lah paah-rah	45 Nawala Road
නුගේගොඩ	nu-geh-go-dah	Nugegoda

GETTING AROUND

TAXI

කුලී රථ

Is this taxi free?
    yahn-nah pu-lu-vahn-dhah?

යන්න පුළුවන්ද?

Please take me to ...
    kah-ru-naah-kah-rah-lah
    maah-wah ...-tah ge-ni-yahn-nah

කරුණාකරල මාව
...ට ගෙනියන්න.

How much is it to go to ...?
    ...-tah yahn-nah kee-yahk
    gahn-nah-vaah-dhah?

...ට යන්න කියක්
ගන්නවාද?

Do we pay extra for luggage?
    bah-du ge-ni-yah-nah-vaah-tah
    va-di-pu-rah ge-vahn-nah
    oh-ne-dhah?

බඩු ගෙනියනවාට
වැඩිපුර ගෙවන්න
ඕනෙද?

Instructions

නියෝග

Continue!
    no-na-vah-thee yahn-nah!

නොනැවතී යන්න!

Take the next street to the left/right.
    vah-mah-tah/dhah-ku-nah-tah
    a-thi ee-lahn-gah paah-reh
    yahn-nah

වමට/දකුණට
ඇති ඊළඟ පාරේ
යන්න.

Please slow down.
    kah-ru-naah-kah-rah-lah
    he-min yahn-nah

කරුණාකරල
හෙමින් යන්න.

Please wait here.
    kah-ru-naah-kah-rah-lah
    me-thah-nah in-nah

කරුණාකරල
මෙතන ඉන්න.

Stop here.
    me-thah-nah nah-vah-thin-nah

මෙතන නවතින්න.

Stop at the corner.
    ko-ne nah-vah-thin-nah

කොණේ නවතින්න.

BUYING TICKETS

ටිකට් මිළදී ගැනීම

Where can I buy a ticket?
mah-tah ti-kaht e-kahk
gahn-neh ko-hen-dhah?

මට ටිකට් එකක්
ගන්නේ කොහෙන්ද?

We want to go to ...
ah-pah-tah ...-tah yahn-nah
oh-neh

අපට ...ට යන්න
ඕනේ.

Do I need to book?
mah-mah seet ven-kah-rah
gahn-nah oh-neh-dhah?

මම සිට් වෙන්කර
ගන්න ඕනේද?

I'd like to book a seat to ...
mah-tah ...-tah seet e-kahk
buk kah-rahn-nah oh-neh

මට ...ට සිට් එකක්
බුක් කරන්න ඕනේ.

How long does the trip take?
gah-mah-nah-tah
koch-chah-rah ve-laah
gah-thah ve-nah-vaah-dhah?

ගමනට කොච්චර
වෙලා ගත
වෙනවාද?

I'd like a luggage locker.
bah-du dhah-mahn-nah
yah-thu-rahk ek-kah
sehp-pu-wak oh-neh

බඩු දමන්න යතුරක්
එක්ක සේප්පුවක්
ඕනේ.

I'd like (a) ...	mah-tah oh-neh ...	මට ඕනේ ...
one-way	yahn-nah	යන්න
ticket	vi-thah-rahk	විතරක්
	ti-kaht e-kahk	ටිකට් එකක්
return ticket	yahn-nah en-nah	යන්න එන්න
	dhe-kah-tah-mah	දෙකටම
	ti-kaht e-kahk	ටිකට් එකක්
two tickets	ti-kaht dhe-kahk	ටිකට් දෙකක්
1st-class ticket	pah-lah-mu-vah-nah	පළමුවන
	pahn-thi-yeh	පන්තියේ
	ti-kaht e-kahk	ටිකට් එකක්
2nd-class ticket	dhe-vah-nah	දෙවන
	pahn-thi-yeh	පන්තියේ
	ti-kaht e-kahk	ටිකට් එකක්

GETTING AROUND

AIR   ගුවනින්

When's the next flight to ...?
    ...-tah ee-lan-gah flait e-kah   ...ට ඊළඟ ෆ්ලයිට්
    kee-yah-tah-dhah?   එක කියටද?

What time do I have to check
in at the airport?
    mah-mah e-yaah-poht   මම එයාපෝට්
    e-kah-tah en-nah oh-neh   එකට එන්න
    kee-yah-tah-dhah?   ඕනේ කියටද?

I'd like a seat in the non-smoking area.
    dum-bee-mah thah-hah-nahm   දුම්බීම තහනම්
    pa-th-theh seet e-kah-kah-tah   පැත්තේ සීට් එකකට
    mah-mah ka-mah-thiy   මම කැමතියි.

I'd like vegetarian meals.
    mah-mah ka-mah-thi mahs   මම කැමති මස් මාළු
    maah-lu na-thi kaa-mah   නැති කෑම.

I'd like to cancel my reservation.
    mah-geh seet e-kah can-sahl   මගේ සීට් එක කැන්සල්
    kah-rahn-nah ka-mah-thiy   කරන්න කැමතියි.

I'd like to make change my
reservation.
    mah-mah buk kah-lah   මම බුක් කළ සීට්
    seet e-kah ve-nahs   එක වෙනස්
    kah-rahn-nah ka-mah-thiy   කරන්න කැමතියි.

My luggage hasn't arrived.
    mah-geh bah-du thah-vah-mah   මගේ බඩ තවම
    a-vith na-ha   ඇවිත් නැහැ.

SIGNS	
බඩ ලබා ගැනීම්	BAGGAGE CLAIM
රේගුව	CUSTOMS
අභ්‍යන්තර	DOMESTIC
ජාත්‍යන්තර	INTERNATIONAL
ගමන් බලපත්‍ර කටයුතු	PASSPORT CONTROL

At Customs
රේගුවේදි

I have nothing to declare.
mah-tah pen-vahn-nah
ki-si-vahk na-ha
මට පෙන්වන්න
කිසිවක් නැහැ.

I have something to declare.
mah-tah pen-vahn-nah
yah-mahk thi-yah-nah-vaah
මට පෙන්වන්න යමක්
තියනවා.

Although the translation of 'to declare' is prah-kaah-shah, in the above context you would say pen-vahn-nah, meaning 'to show'.

This is all my luggage.
meh ok-kah-mah bah-du
mah-geh
මේ ඔක්කම
බ මගේ.

That's not mine.
eh-kah mah-geh no-veh
ඒක මගෙ නොවේ.

I didn't know I had to declare it.
eh ga-nah ki-yahn-nah
oh-neh ki-yaah mah-mah
dha-nah-ge-nah hi-ti-yeh na-ha
ඒ ගැන කියන්න
ඕනේ කියා මම
දැනගෙන හිටියේ නැහැ.

In this last example, although 'to declare' is prah-kaah-shah, ki-yahn-nah, 'to tell', is more suitable in this context.

THEY MAY SAY ...	
seet na-ha	It's full.

BOAT
බෝට්ටු

Where does the boat leave from?
boht-tu-wah ko-hen-dhah
pi-thahth ven-neh?
බෝට්ටුව කොහෙන්ද
පිටත් වෙන්නේ?

What time does the boat arrive?
boht-ti-wah en-neh
kee-yah-tah-dhah?
බෝට්ටුව
එන්නේ කියටද?

GETTING AROUND

BUS බස් රථ

Where's the bus stop?
bahs e-kah nah-vaht-vahn-neh
ko-thah-nah-dhah?
බස් එක නවත්වන්නේ
කොතනද?

Does this bus go to ...?
meh bahs e-kah ...-tah
yah-nah-vaah-dhah?
මේ බස් එක ...ට
යනවාද?

How often do buses come?
koch-chah-rah
veh-laah-vah-kah-tah
va-thaah-vahk-dhah bahs en-neh?
කොච්චර වෙලාවකට
වතාවක්ද බස්
එන්නේ?

What time's	... bahs eh-kah	... බස් එක
the ... bus?	kee-yah-tah-dhah?	කියටද?
first	pah-lah-mu	පළමු
last	ahn-thi-mah	අන්තිම
next	ee-lahn-gah	ඊළඟ

Could you let me know
when we get to ...?
...-tah gi-yaah-mah mah-tah
ki-yah-nah-vaah-dhah?
...ට ගියාම මට
කියනවාද?

Where do I get the bus for ...?
...-tah bahs e-kah gahn-neh
ko-thah-nin-dhah?
...ට බස් එක
ගන්නේ කොතනින්ද?

TRAIN

දුම්රිය/කෝච්චිය

Which station is this?
meh mo-nah
steh-shah-mah-dhah?

මේ මොන
ස්ටේෂමද?

What's the next station?
ee-lahn-gah steh-shah-mah
mo-kahk-dhah?

ඊළඟ ස්ටේෂම
මොකක්ද?

Does this train stop at ...?
meh koch-chi-yah
... nah-thah-rah
kah-rah-nah-vaah-dhah?

මේ කෝච්චිය
... නතර
කරනවාද?

The train is delayed/cancelled.
koch-chi-yah [prah-maah-dhai;
dhu-vahn-neh na-ha]

කෝච්චිය[පුමාදයි;
දුවන්නේ නැහැ] .

Do I have to change?
ah-tha-rah mah-gah maah-ru
ven-nah oh-ne-dhah?

අතර මඟ මාරු
වෙන්න ඕනෙද?

Is that seat taken?
meh seet e-keh kau-ru hah-ri
in-nah-vaah-dhah?

මේ සීට් එකේ කවුරු
හරි ඉන්නවාද?

I want to get off in (Kandy).
mah-tah (nu-wah-rin)
bah-hin-nah oh-neh

මට (නුවරින්)
බහින්න ඕනේ.

CAR

කාර් එක

When hiring a car in Sri Lanka, you can either drive yourself or
hire a car with a driver. Hiring a car and driver is a popular option,
as most drivers are happy to provide you with local knowledge
and act as a tour guide.

Where can I hire a car (and driver)?
kaahr e-kahk
(sah-hah drai-vah ke-nek)
hah-yahr kah-rahn-neh
ko-hen-dhah?

කාර් එකක්
(සහ ඩුයිවර් කෙනෙක්)
හයර් කරන්නේ
කොහෙන්ද?

GETTING AROUND

How much is it daily/weekly?
dhah-vah-sah-kah-tah/
sah-thi-yah-kah-tah
kee-yah-dhah?

දවසකට/
සතියකට
කියද?

Does that include insurance/
mileage?
meh rakh-sha-nah/sa-thah-pum
gah-nah-nah ek-kah-dhah?

මේ රක්ෂණ/සැතපුම්
ගණන එක්කද?

Where's the next petrol station?
ee-lahn-gah pet-rohl
sta-shah-mah ko-heh-dhah?

ඊළඟ පෙට්‍රෝල්
ස්ටේෂම කොහේද?

Please fill the tank.
kah-ru-naah-kah-rah-lah
tan-ki-yah pu-rah-vahn-nah

කරුණාකරල ටැංකිය
පුරවන්න.

Does this road lead to ...?
meh paah-rah ...
yah-nah-vaah-dhah?

මේ පාර ...
යනවාද?

Please check	kah-ru-naah-kah-rah-lah	කරුණාකරල
the ...	... bah-lahn-nah	... බලන්න.
oil	thel	තෙල්
tyre pressure	hu-lahng	හුළං
water	wah-thu-rah	වතුර

SIGNS

අන්තරාදායකයි	DANGER
ඉඩ දෙන්න	GIVE WAY
නතර කිරීම තහනම්	NO PARKING
ඒකිය ධාවනය	ONE WAY
පාර අළුත්වැඩියා කෙරේ	ROADWORKS
සෙමින් පදවන්න	SLOW DOWN
නතර වෙන්න	STOP

air	hu-lahng	හුළං
battery	ba-tri-yah	බැට්‍රිය
brakes	brehk	බ්‍රේක්
clutch	klahch e-kah	ක්ලච් එක
drivers licence	lai-sahn e-kah	ලයිසන් එක
lights	lait	ලයිට්
... petrol (gas)	... pet-rohl	... පෙට්‍රෝල්
leaded	led ek-kah	ලෙඩ් එක්ක
regular	saah-maan-yah	සාමාන්‍ය
unleaded	led na-thi	ලෙඩ් නැති
puncture	tah-yahr e-keh hu-lahng	ටයර් එකේ හුළං
	gi-hil-laah	ගිහිල්ලා
radiator	reh-di-yeh-tah-rah-yah	රේඩියේටරය
seatbelt	seet belt e-kah	සීට් බෙල්ට් එක
tyres	tah-yahr	ටයර්
windscreen	vin skreen e-kah	වින් ස්ක්‍රීන් එක

BICYCLE බයිසිකලය

Is it within cycling distance?
bai-si-kah-lah-yen yah-nah
dhu-rah-dhah?
බයිසිකලයෙන්
යන දුරද?

Where can I hire a bicycle?
bai-si-kah-lah-yahk
ku-li-yah-tah gahn-neh
ko-hen-dhah?
බයිසිකලයක්
කුලියට ගන්නේ
කොහෙන්ද?

How much is it for ...?	... gaah-nah kee-yah-dhah?	... ගාන කියද?
an hour	pa-yah-kah-tah	පැයකට
the morning	u-dheh-tah	උදේට
the afternoon	hah-vah-sah-tah	හවසට
the day	dhah-vah-sah-tah	දවසට

I have a flat tyre.
mah-geh tah-yahr e-keh
hu-lahng ba-ha-laah
මගේ ටයර් එකේ
හුළං බැහැලා.

GETTING AROUND

bike	bai-si-kah-la-yah	බයිසිකලය
handlebars	han-dhahl baahr e-kah	හැන්ඩල් බාර් එක
helmet	hel-maht e-kah	හෙල්මට් එක
inner tube	a-thu-leh ti-yub e-kah	ඇතුළේ ටියුබ් එක
lights	lait	ලයිට්
padlock	ib-baah	ඉබ්බා
pump	pom-pah-yah	පොම්පය
puncture	tah-yahr e-keh hu-lahng gi-hil-laah	ටයර් එකේ හුළං ගිහිල්ලා
saddle	sa-dah-lah-yah	සැඩලය
wheel	roh-dhah	රෝද

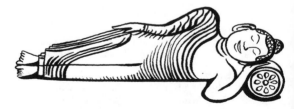

Sri Lanka has a wide variety of accommodation options, ranging from family homes, guesthouses and rest houses to hotels, motels, lodges and tourist resorts.

FINDING ACCOMMODATION
නවාතැන් සොයා ගැනීම

I'm looking	mah-mah	මම
for a ...	so-yahn-neh ...	සොයන්නේ ...
guesthouse	gest hah-vus e-kahk	ගෙස්ට් හවුස් එකක්
hotel	hoh-tah-lah-yahk	හෝටලයක්
motel	mo-tehl e-kahk	මොටේල් එකක්
youth hostel	thah-ru-nah-yahn-geh nah-vaah-tha-nahk	තරුණයන්ගේ නවාතැනක්

Where can I find a ... hotel?	mah-tah ... hoh-tah-lah-yahk so-yaah gahn-neh ko-hen-dhah?	මට ... හෝටලයක් සොයා ගන්නේ කොහෙන්ද?
clean	pi-ri-si-du	පිරිසිදු
good	hon-dhah	හොඳ

Where's the ... hotel?	... hoh-tah-lah-yah thi-yen-neh ko-heh-dhah?	... හෝටලය තියෙන්නේ කොහේද?
best	hon-dhah-mah	හොඳම
cheapest	laah-bah-mah	ලාභම
nearest	lahn-gah-mah	ළඟම

SIGNS

නවාතැන් නැත	NO VACANCIES
නවාතැන් ඇත	ROOMS AVAILABLE

What's the address?

e-keh li-pi-nah-yah   ඒකේ ලිපිනය
mo-kahk-dhah?   මොකක්ද?

Could you write the address, please?

kah-ru-naah-kah-rah-lah   කරුණාකරල ලිපිනය
lipi-nah-yah li-yah-laah dhen-nah?   ලියලා දෙන්න?

BOOKING AHEAD   කලින් වෙන්කරවා ගැනීම

I'd like to book a (single/double)
room, please.

kah-ru-naah-kah-rah-lah mah-tah   කරුණාකරල මට
(thah-ni/dhen-ne-ku-tah)   (තනි/දෙන්නෙකුට)
kaah-mah-rah-yahk   කාමරයක් ගන්න
gahn-nah ha-ki-dhah?   හැකිද?

For (three) nights.

raa (thu-nah-)kah-tah   රෑ (තුන)කට.

How much for ...?	... kee-yah-dhah?	... කියද?
one night	e-kah ra-yah-kahk	එක රැයක්
a week	e-kah	එක
	sah-thi-yah-kah-tah	සතියකට
two people	dhen-ne-ku-tah	දෙන්නෙකුට

Is there a discount for children/students?

lah-mun-tah/shish-yah-yahn-tah   ළමුන්ට/ශිෂ්‍යයන්ට
mi-lah ah-du-dhah?   මිළ අඩුද?

I'll/We'll be arriving at ...

mah-mah/ah-pi ... e-nah-vaah   මම/අපි ... එනවා.

My name's ...

mah-geh nah-mah ...   මගේ නම ...

Can I pay by credit card?

kaahd e-ken ge-vahn-nah   කාඩ් එකෙන්
ha-ki-dhah?   ගෙවන්න හැකිද?

ACCOMMODATION

CHECKING IN

පැමිණීමේදි

Do you have any rooms/beds available?
kaah-mah-rah/a-dahn
thi-yeh-dhah?

කාමර/ඇදන්
තියේද?

Do you have a room with two beds?
a-dahn dhe-keh kaah-mah-rah
thi-yeh-dhah?

ඇදන් දෙකේ කාමර
තියේද?

Do you have a room with
a double bed?
dah-bahl an-dahk ek-kah
kaah-mah-rah-yak thi-yeh-dhah?

ඩබල් ඇදක් එක්ක
කාමරයක් තියේද?

I'd like ...	mah-mah	මම
	ka-mah-thiy ...	කැමතියි ...
to share a dorm	ni-dhah-nah	නිදන
	shaah-laah-vah-kah	ශාලාවක
	hah-vu-leh in-nah	හවුලේ ඉන්න
a single room	thah-ni	තනි
	kaah-mah-rah-yahk	කාමරයක්

I/We want a room	mah-tah/ah-pi-tah	මට/අපට
with a ...	oh-neh ... ek-kah	ඕනේ ...
	kaah-mah-rah-yahk	එක්ක කාමරයක් .
bathroom	naah-nah	නාන
	kaah-mah-rah-yahk	කාමරයක්
shower	shah-vahr e-kahk	ෂවර් එකක්
TV	tee-vee e-kahk	ටි.වී. එකක්
window	jah-neh-lah-yahk	ජනේලයක්

ACCOMMODATION

THEY MAY SAY ...

kah-nah-gaah-tuy kaah-mah-rah na-ha
Sorry, we're full.

ACCOMMODATION

Can I see it?
mah-tah bah-lahn-nah
ha-ki-dhah?

මට බලන්න
හැකිද?

Are there any others?
ve-nah kaah-mah-rah
thi-yeh-dhah?

වෙන කාමර
තියේද?

It's fine. I'll take it.
eh-kah hon-dhai. mah-mah
eh-kah gahn-nam

එක හොඳයි. මම
එක ගන්නම්.

REQUESTS & QUERIES

ඉල්ලීම් හා
විමසීම්

Where's the bathroom?
naah-nah kaah-mah-rah-yah
ko-heh-dhah?

නාන කාමරය
කොහේද?

Where's breakfast served?
u-dheh kaa-mah gahn-neh
ko-heh-dhah?

උදේ කෑම ගන්නේ
කොහේද?

Is there somewhere to wash clothes?
an-dum soh-dhaah gahn-nah
tha-nahk thi-yeh-dhah?

ඇඳුම් සෝදා ගන්න
තැනක් තියේද?

Is there hot water all day?
dhah-vah-sah pu-raah u-nu
wah-thu-rah thi-yeh-dhah?

දවස පුරා උණු
වතුර තියේද?

Can we use the kitchen?
a-pah-tah kus-si-yah
paah-vich-chi kah-rahn-nah
ha-ki-dhah?

අපට කුස්සිය
පාච්චිච් කරන්න
හැකිද?

Can we use the telephone?
a-pah-tah te-li-fohn e-kah
paah-vich-chi
kah-rahn-nah ha-ki-dhah?

අපට ටෙලිෆෝන්
එක පාච්චිච් කරන්න
හැකිද?

Do you have a safe where I can
leave my valuables?
    mah-geh vah-ti-naah bah-du
    thi-yahn-nah ha-ki
    sehp-pu-wahk thi-yeh-dhah?

මගේ වටිනා ඔ
තියන්න හැකි
සේප්පුවක් තියේද?

Could I have a receipt for them?
    eh-vah-tah ri-seet e-kahk
    gahn-nah ha-ki-dhah?

ඒවාට රිසිට් එකක්
ගන්න හැකිද?

Do you change money here?
    o-bah sahl-li maah-ru
    kah-rah-nah-vaah-dhah?

ඔබ සල්ලි මාරු
කරනවාද?

Do you arrange tours?
    o-bah sahn-chaah-rah gah-mahn
    laas-thi kah-rah-nah-vaah-dhah?

ඔබ සංචාර ගමන්
ලැස්ති කරනවාද?

Can I leave a message?
    mah-tah pah-ni-vu-dah-yak
    thi-yahn-nah ha-ki-dhah?

මට පණිවුඩයක්
තියන්න හැකිද?

Is there a message for me?
    mah-tah pah-ni-vu-dah-yak
    thi-yeh-dhah?

මට පණිවුඩයක්
තියේද?

Please wake us at (seven).
    kah-ru-naah-kah-rah-lah
    ah-pah-vah (hah-thah-tah)
    ah-vah-di kah-rahn-nah

කරුණාකරල අපව
(හතට) අවදි
කරන්න.

Please change the sheets.
    kah-ru-naah-kah-rah-lah
    sheet maah-ru kah-rahn-nah

කරුණාකරල මිට්
මාරු කරන්න.

The room needs to be cleaned.
    kaah-mah-rah-yah pi-ri-si-du
    kah-rahn-nah oh-neh

කාමරය පිරිසිදු
කරන්න ඕනේ.

I need a/another ...
    mah-tah thah-vahth ... oh-neh

මට තවත් ... ඕනේ.

ACCOMMODATION

Could	ah-pah-tah …	අපට ...
we have …?	gahn-nah	ගන්න පුළුවන්ද?
	pu-lu-vahn-dhah?	
an extra	va-di-pu-rah	වැඩිපුර
blanket	blan-kaht e-kahk	බ්ලැන්කට් එකක්
a mosquito net	mah-dhu-ru dha-lahk	මදුරු දැලක්
our key	ah-peh yah-thu-rah	අපේ යතුර

I've locked myself out of my room.

yah-thu-rah kaah-mah-rah-yah
a-thu-leh dhah-mah-laah
mah-mah dho-rah vah-hah-lah

යතුර කාමරය
ඇතුළේ දමලා මම
දොර වහලා.

We left the key at reception.

ah-pi yah-thu-rah is-sah-rah-hah
kaun-tah-reh thib-baah

අපි යතුර ඉස්සරහ
කවුන්ටරයේ තිබ්බා.

COMPLAINTS   පැමිණිලි

I can't open/close the window.

mah-tah jah-neh-lah-yah
ah-rin-nah/vah-hahn-nah
ba-ha

මට ජනේලය
අරින්න/වහන්න
බැහැ.

I don't like this room.

mah-mah meh
kaah-mah-rah-yah-tah
ka-mah-thi na-ha

මම මේ කාමරයට
කැමති නැහැ.

The toilet won't flush.

toi-laht e-kah va-dah
kah-rahn-neh na-ha

ටොයිලට් එක වැඩ
කරන්නේ නැහැ.

Can I change to another room?

mah-tah ve-nah
kaah-mah-rah-yah-kah-tah
yahn-nah ha-ki-dhah?

මට වෙන
කාමරයකට යන්න
හැකිද?

It's too ...	meh-kah hu-gaahk ...	මේක හුභාක් ...
cold	see-thah-lai	සිතලයි
dark	kah-lu-vah-rai	කළුවරයි
expensive	gah-nahn va-diy	ගණන් වැඩියි
light/bright	e-li-yah va-diy	එළිය වැඩියි
noisy	shahb-dhah va-diy	ශබ්ද වැඩියි
small	po-di va-diy	පොඩි වැඩියි

This ... is not clean.	meh ... pi-ri-si-du na-ha	මේ ... පිරිසිදු නැහැ.
blanket	blan-kaht e-kah	බ්ලැන්කට් එක
pillow	kot-tah-yah	කොට්ටය
pillowcase	kot-tah u-rah-yah	කොට්ට උරය
sheet	sheet e-kah	ශීට් එක

ACCOMMODATION

CHECKING OUT

බැහැරව යෑම

What time do we have to check out?
ah-pah i-vahth-vah yahn-nah
oh-neh kee-yah-tah-dhah?

අප ඉවත්ව යන්න ඕනේ කියටද?

I'm/We're leaving now.
mah-mah/ah-pi dhan
yah-nah-vaah

මම/අපි දැන් යනවා.

We had a great stay, thank you.
ah-pah sah-thu-tin
hi-ti-yeh sthoo-thiy

අප සතුටින් හිටියේ ස්තූතියි.

Thank you for all your help.
kah-lah u-dhahv vah-lah-tah
sthoo-thiy

කළ උදව් වලට ස්තූතියි.

The room was perfect.
kaah-mah-rah-yah ni-yah-mah-yi

කාමරය නියමයි.

We hope we can return some day.
na-vah-thah kah-vah-dhaah
hoh en-nah ah-pi
bah-laah-po-roth-thu
ve-nah-vaah

නැවත කවදා හෝ එන්න අපි බලාපොරොත්තු වෙනවා.

ACCOMMODATION

I'd like to pay the bill.
mah-tah bi-lah ge-vahn-nah
oh-neh

මට බිල ගෙවන්න
ඕනේ.

Can I pay with a travellers cheque?
tra-vah-lahs chek e-kah-kin
ge-vahn-nah-dah?

ටැවලර්ස් චෙක්
එකකින් ගෙවන්නද?

There's a mistake in the bill.
bi-leh vah-rah-dhahk
thi-ye-nah-vaah

බිලේ වරදක්
තියෙනවා.

Can I leave my backpack
here until tonight?
ah-dhah raa vah-nah
thu-ru mah-geh bak-pak
e-kah me-heh thi-yahn-nah
ha-ki-dhah?

අද රෑ වන තුරු
මගේ බැක්පැක් එක
මෙහේ තියන්න
හැකිද?

We'll be back in (three) days.
ah-pi dhah-vas (thu-nah)
kin aah-pah-su e-nah-vaah

අපි දවස් (තුන)
කින් ආපසු එනවා.

Can you call a taxi for me?
mah-tah tak-si e-kahk
kah-thaah kah-rah-lah
dhe-nah-vaah-dhah?

මට ටැක්සි එකක්
කථා කරල
දෙනවාද?

RENTING

කුලියට ගැනීම

Renting in Sri Lanka is another accommodation option, with many people renting out individual rooms or even part of their house on a short- or long-term basis.

I'm here about your advertisement for a room to rent.

kaah-mah-rah-yahk ku-li-yah-tah
dhee-mah-tah a-thi dhan-vee-mah
ga-nai mah-mah aah-veh

කාමරයක් කුලියට
දීමට ඇති දැන්වීම
ගැනයි මම ආවේ .

I'm looking for a flat to rent for (two) months.

maah-sah (dhe-kah)-kah-tah
ku-li-yah-tah gahn nah po-di
ge-yak mah-mah
so-yah-nah-vaah

මාස (දෙක)කට
කුලියට ගන්න
පොඩි ගෙයක් මම
සොයනවා .

ACCOMMODATION

I'm looking for something close to the …	mah-mah so-yahn-neh …-tah kit-tu-ven	මම සොයන්නේ ...ට කිට්ටුවෙන් .
beach	mu-hu-du ve-rah-lah	මුහුදු වෙරළ
city centre	nah-gah-rah mah-<u>dhy</u>ah-yah	නගර මධ්‍යය
train station	dhum-ri-yah s<u>th</u>aah-nah-yah	දුම්රිය ස්ථානය

Could I see it?

mah-tah bah-lahn-nah   මට බලන්න හැකිද?
ha-ki-dhah?

How much is it   ... kee-yah-dhah?   ... කියද?
per ...?

week   sah-thi-yah-kah-tah   සතියකට
month   maah-sah-yah-kah-tah   මාසයකට

Is there anything cheaper?

mi-lah ah-du ve-nah   මිළ අඩු වෙන
ki-si-vahk thi-yeh-dhah?   කිසිවක් තියේද?

Do you need a deposit?

a-pah mu-dhahl oh-ne-dhah?   ඇප මුදල් ඕනෙද?

I'd like to rent it for (a month).

(maah-sah-yah-kah-tah)   (මාසයකට) කූලියට
ku-li-yah-tah gahn-nah   ගන්න මම කැමතියි.
mah-mah ka-mah-thiy

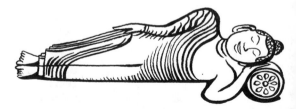

AROUND TOWN

In many of the major cities, you'll find that English is widely understood. However, in the suburbs or country you may have to rely on Sinhala, so it's best to familiarise yourself with commonly used terms and phrases before venturing out onto the streets. Besides, your efforts to communicate in Sinhala will be much appreciated.

LOOKING FOR ...

... සොයා බැලීම

Where's a/an/the ...?	... ko-heh-dhah thi-yen-neh?	... කොහේද තියෙන්නේ?
art gallery	kah-laah bhah-vah-nah-yah	කලා භවනය
bank	ban-ku-wah	බැංකුව
cinema	si-nah-maah shaah-laah-wah	සිනමා ශාලාව
city centre	nah-gah-rah-yah	නගරය
... consulate	... kon-sahl kaahr-yaah-lah-yah	... කොන්සල් කායඹලය
... embassy	... thaah-naah-pah-thi kaahr-yaah-lah-yah	... තානාපති කායඹලය
... hotel	... hoh-tah-lah-yah	... හෝටලය
market	ve-lahn-dhah po-lah	වෙළඳ පොළ
museum	mu-se-um e-kah; kau-thu-kaah-gaah-rah-yah	මඟුසියම් එක; කෞතුකාගාරය
police station	po-lee-si-yah	පොලිසිය
post office	tha-pal kahn-thoh-ru-wah	තැපැල් කන්තෝරුව
public telephone	po-dhu te-li-foh-nah-yah	පොදු ටෙලිෆෝනය
public toilet	po-dhu va-si-ki-li-yah	පොදු වැසිකිළිය
telephone centre	te-li-fohn mah-dhya-sthaah-nah-yah	ටෙලිෆෝන් මධඟස්ථානය
temple	pahn-sah-lah	පන්සල

AT THE BANK   බැංකුවේදි

No doubt, at some stage during your visit to Sri Lanka, you'll
need to visit a bank. Again, any attempts you make at Sinhala
will be appreciated and, as you tour the more remote parts of the
country, you'll find it a necessity.

I want to change (a) ...	mah-tah ... maah-ru-kah-rahn-nah oh-neh	මට ... මාරු-කරන්න ඕනේ.
cash/money	mu-dahl/sahl-li	මුදල්/සල්ලි
cheque	chek e-kahk	වෙක් එකක්
travellers cheque	tra-vah-lahs chek e-kahk	ට්‍රැවලර්ස් වෙක් එකක්

What time does the bank open?
  ban-ku-wah ah-rin-neh
  kee-yah-tah-dhah?
බැංකුව අරින්නේ කියටද?

Can I use my credit card to
withdraw money?
  sahl-li gahn-nah mah-geh kaahd
  e-kah paah-vich-chi
  kah-rahn-nah ha-ki-dhah?
සල්ලි ගන්න මගේ කාඩ් එක පාච්චිව් කරන්න හැකිද?

The automatic teller machine
(ATM) swallowed my card.
  te-lah me-shin e-kah mah-geh
  kaahd e-kah gahth-thaah
ටෙල මෙෂින් එක මගේ කාඩ් එක ගත්තා.

Can I exchange money here?
  mah-tah me-thah-nah sahl-li
  maah-ru kah-rahn-nah
  ha-ki-dhah?
මට මෙතන සල්ලි මාරු කරන්න හැකිද?

How many rupees per dollar?
  dor-lah e-kah-kah-tah
  ru-pi-yahl kee-yahk
  la-be-nah-vaah-dhah?
ඩොලර් එකකට රූපියල් කියක් ලැබෙනවාද?

What's your commission?
  sahl-li maah-ru kah-rahn-nah
  ko-mis kee-yah-dhah?
සල්ලි මාරු කරන්න කොමිස් කියද?

Please write it down.
    kah-ru-naah-kah-rah-lah mah-tah
    eh-kah li-yaah dhen-nah

කරුණාකරල මට
එක ලියා දෙන්න .

Can I have smaller notes?
    mah-tah ah-du gah-nah-neh
    noht-tu dhe-nah-vaah-dhah?

මට අ ගණනේ
නෝට්ටු දෙනවාද?

Can I transfer money here from
my bank?
    mah-geh ban-ku-wen
    me-haah-tah sahl-li maah-ru
    kah-rahn-nah pu-lu-vahn-dhah?

මගේ බැංකුවෙන්
මෙහාට සල්ලි මාරු
කරන්න පුළුවන්ද?

How long will it take to arrive?
    me-haah-tah la-ben-nah
    koch-chah-rah kah-lahk
    yaah-vi-dhah?

මෙහාට ලැබෙන්න
කොච්චර කලක්
යාවිද?

Has my money arrived yet?
    mah-geh sahl-li dhan a-vith
    ath-dhah?

මගේ සල්ලි දැන්
ඇවිත් ඇත්ද?

Can I transfer money overseas?
    sahl-li pi-tah-rah-tah
    yah-vahn-nah mah-tah
    ha-ki veh-dhah?

සල්ලි පිටරට යවන්න
මට හැකි වේද?

Where do I sign?
    ko-heh-dhah mah-mah
    ahth-sahn kah-rahn-neh?

කොහේද මම
අත්සන් කරන්නේ?

SIGNS

වසා ඇත	CLOSED
ඇතුල්වීම	ENTRANCE
පිටවීම	EXIT
තොරතුරු	INFORMATION
විමසීම	INQUIRIES
ඇතුල්වීම තහනම්	NO ENTRY
දුම් බීම තහනම්	NO SMOKING
විවෘතව ඇත	OPEN

AT THE POST OFFICE

තැපැල් කන්තෝරුවේදී

I want to buy ...	mah-tah ... gahn-nah oh-neh	මට ... ගන්න ඕනේ.
postcards	pohst kaahd; tha-pal pahth	පෝස්ට් කාඩ්; තැපැල් පත්
stamps	mudh-dhah-rah	මුද්දර

I want to send a ...	mah-tah ... yah-vahn-nah oh-neh	මට ... යවන්න ඕනේ.
fax	faks e-kahk	ෆැක්ස් එකක්
letter	li-yu-mahk/ li-pi-yahk	ලියුමක්/ ලිපියක්
parcel	paahr-sah-lah-yahk	පාර්සලයක්
postcard	pohst kaahd e-kahk; tha-pal pah-thahk	පෝස්ට් කාඩ් එකක්; තැපැල් පතක්

Please send it by air.
kah-ru-naah-kah-rah-lah, e-yaah-mehl e-ken yah-vahn-nah
කරුණාකර, එයාමේල් එකෙන් යවන්න.

Please send it by surface.
kah-ru-naah-kah-rah-lah, saah-maahn-yah tha-paa-len yah-vahn-nah
කරුණාකර, සාමානa තැපෑලෙන් යවන්න.

How much is it to send this to ...?
meh-kah ...-tah yah-vahn-nah kee-yahk ve-nah-vaah-dhah?
මේක ...ට යවන්න කියක් වෙනවාද?

Where's the poste restante section?
tha-pal bhaah-rah dhe-nah tha-nah ko-heh-dhah?
තැපැල් භාර දෙන තැන කොහේද?

Is there any mail for me?
mah-tah li-yum thi-yah-nah-vaah-dhah?
මට ලියුම් තියෙනවාද?

AROUND TOWN

aerogram	gu-wahn tha-pal	ගුවන් තැපැල්
	li-pi ko-lah-yah	ලිපි කොළය
air mail	e-yaah mehl	එයා මේල්
envelope	li-yum kah-vah-rah-yah	ලියුම් කවරය
express mail	see-grah-gaah-mi tha-pal	සීසුගාමි තැපැල්
mail box	tha-pal pet-ti-yah	තැපැල් පෙට්ටිය
parcel	paahr-sah-lah-yah	පාර්සලය
pen	paa-nah	පෑන
postcode	tha-pal sahn-keh-thah	තැපැල් සංකේත
registered mail	li-yaah-pah-dhin-chi tha-pal	ලියාපදිංචි තැපැල්
surface mail	saah-maahn-yah tha-pal	සාමාන්‍ය තැපැල්

TELECOMMUNICATIONS   විදුලි සංදේශ

In Sri Lanka, you can only use public phones to call locally. If you want to call overseas, you have to go to a post office or private communication bureau. All calls, including local calls, are charged by the minute.

Where's the nearest public phone?
lahn-gah-mah a-thi po-dhu
teli-fohn e-kah ko-heh-dhah
thi-yen-neh?

ළඟම ඇති පොදු
ටෙලිෆෝන් එක
කොහේද තියෙන්නේ?

Could I please use the telephone?
mah-tah te-li-fohn korl
e-kahk gahn-nah
pu-lu-vahn-dhah?

මට ටෙලිෆෝන්
කෝල් එකක් ගන්න
පුළුවන්ද?

I want to speak for (three) minutes.
mah-tah vi-naah-di
(thu-nah)-kah-tah kah-<u>thaah</u>
kah-rahn-nah oh-neh

මට විනාඩි
(තුන)කටකටා
කරන්න ඕනේ.

How much does a (three)-minute
call cost?
vi-naah-di (thu-nah)-kah
korl e-kahk kee-yahk
vei-dhah?

විනාඩි (තුන)ක
කෝල් එකක් කියක්
වෙයිද?

How much does each minute cost?
vi-naah-di-yah-kah-tah kee-yahk
ah-yah kah-rah-nah-vaah-dhah?

විනාඩියකට කියක්
අය කරනවාද?

The number is ...
ahn-kah-yah ...

අංකය ...

What's the area code for ...?
...(-veh) tha-pal
sahn-keh-thah-yah
mo-kahk-dhah?

...(වේ) තැපැල්
සංකේතය
මොකක්ද?

I want to make a long-distance
call to (Australia).
mah-tah (ohs-treh-li-yaah-wah)-tah
dhu-rah a-mah-thum korl e-kahk
gahn-nah oh-neh

මට (ඕස්ට්‍රේලියාව)ට
දුර ඇමතුම් කෝල්
එකක් ගන්න ඕනේ.

I want to make a reverse-charges/
collect call.
ah-yah-ki-reem a-mah-thum
lah-bahn-naah-tah
ah-yah-vahn-nah korl e-kahk
gahn-nah oh-neh

අයකිරීම් ඇමතුම්
ලබන්නාට
අයවන්න කෝල්
එකක් ගන්න ඕනේ.

It's engaged.
eh-kah gahn-nah ba-ha

ඒක ගන්න බැහැ.

I've been cut off.
maah-wah ka-pu-nah

මාව කැපුණා.

mobile phone;	moh-bail e-kahk;	මෝබයිල් එකක්;
cell phone	sel-tel e-kahk	සෙල්ටෙල් එකක්
operator	or-pah-reh-tah	ඔපරේට
phone book	te-li-fohn po-thah	ටෙලිෆෝන් පොත
phone box	te-li-fohn booth e-kah	ටෙලිෆෝන් බූත් එක
phonecard	fohn kaahd	ෆෝන් කාඩ්
telephone	te-li-fohn e-kah	ටෙලිෆෝන් එක
urgent	hah-dhi-siy	හදිසියි

Internet අන්තර්ජාලය

Is there a local Internet cafe?
me-heh in-tah-net bah-lah-nah
tha-nahk thi-yeh-dhah?
මෙහේ ඉන්ටර්නෙට්
බලන තැනක් තියේද?

I'd like to get Internet access.
in-tah-net pah-hah-su-kahm
lah-bah-nah mah-mah
ka-mah-thiy
ඉන්ටනෙට් පහසුකම්
ලබන්න මම
කැමතියි.

I'd like to check my email.
mah-geh e-mehl bah-lahn-nah
mah-mah ka-mah-thiy
මගේ ඊමේල් බලන්න
මම කැමතියි.

I'd like to send an email.
mah-tah e-mehl e-kahk
yah-vahn-nah oh-neh
මට ඊමේල්
එකක් යවන්න ඕනේ.

computer	com-pi-yu-tah-rah-yah	කොම්පියුටරය
fax	faks e-kah	ෆැක්ස් එක
modem	moh-dahm e-kah	මෝඩම් එක

Making a Call

දුරකථන ඇමතුම් ගැනීම

Hello, is ... there?
he-loh ... in-nah-vaah-dhah?

හෙලෝ ... ඉන්නවාද?

Hello. (answering a call)
he-loh

හෙලෝ.

Can I speak to ...?
mah-tah ...-tah kah-<u>thaah</u>
kah-rahn-nah pu-lu-vahn-dhah?

මට ...ට කථා
කරන්න පුළුවන්ද?

Who's calling?
kau-dhah kah-<u>thaah</u>
kah-rahn-neh?

කවුද කථා
කරන්නේ?

It's ...
meh ...

මේ ...

One moment (please).
mo-ho-thahk in-nah
(ka-ru-naah-kah-rah-lah)

මොහොතක් ඉන්න
(කරුණාකරල).

I'm sorry, he's/she's not here.
kah-nah-gaah-tuy, e-yaah na-ha

කණගාටුයි, එයා නැහැ.

What time will he/she be back?
e-yaah koi ve-laah-veh-dhah
aah-pah-su en-neh?

එයා කොයි වෙලාවෙද
ආපසු එන්නේ?

Can I leave a message?
mah-tah pah-ni-vu-dah-yahk
thi-yahn-nah pu-lu-vahn-dhah?

මට පණිවුඩයක්
තියන්න පුළුවන්ද?

Please tell ... I called.
ka-ru-naah-kah-rah-lah
...-tah ki-yahn-nah mah-mah
kah-<u>thaah</u> kah-laah ki-yah-lah

කරුණාකරල ...ට
කියන්න මම කථා
කළා කියල.

My number is ...
mah-geh nom-mah-rah-yah ...

මගේ නොම්බරය ...

I don't have a contact number.
aah-pah-su kah-<u>thaah</u>
kah-rahn-nah ha-ki
nom-mah-rah-yahk
mah-tah na-ha

ආපසු කථා කරන්න
හැකි නොම්බරයක්
මට නැහැ.

I'll call back later.
mah-mah pahs-seh kah-<u>thaah</u>
kah-rahn-nahm

මම පස්සේ කථා
කරන්නම්.

AROUND TOWN

SIGHTSEEING

සංචාර ගමන්

Where's the tourist office?
tu-wah-rist kahn-thoh-ru-wah
ko-heh-dah thi-yen-neh?

ටුවරිස්ට් කන්තෝරුව
කොහේද තියෙන්නේ?

Do you have a local map?
o-bah lahn-gah meh
pah-laah-theh si-thi-yah-mahk
thi-ye-nah-vaah-dhah?

ඔබ ළඟ මේ
පළාතේ සිතියමක්
තියනවාද?

Do you have a guidebook in English?
o-bah lahn-gah in-gree-si
gaid buk e-kahk
thi-ye-nah-vaah-dhah?

ඔබ ළඟ ඉංග්‍රීසි
ගෙඩ් බුක්
එකක් තියෙනවාද?

What are the main attractions?
vah-daahth sith gahn-naah
dheh-vahl mo-nah-vaah-dhah
thi-yen-neh?

වඩාත් සිත් ගන්නා
දේවල් මොනවාද
තියෙන්නේ?

We only have [one day; two days].
ah-pah-tah thah-vah
thi-yen-neh [e-kah dhah-vah-sai;
dhah-vahs dhe-kai]

අපට තව තියෙන්නේ
[එක දවසයි;
දවස් දෙකයි].

I'd like to see ...
mah-tah ... bah-lahn-nah aah-sai

මට ... බලන්න ආසයි.

Can we take photographs?
ah-pah-tah pin-thoo-ru
gahn-nah ha-ki-dhah?

අපට පින්තූර ගන්න
හැකිද?

Could you take a photograph of me?
o-bah-tah pu-lu-vahn-dhah
mah-geh pin-thoo-rah-yahk
gahn-nah?

ඔබට පුළුවන්ද මගේ
පින්තුරයක්
ගන්න?

AROUND TOWN

SIGNS

අල්ලන්න එපා	DO NOT TOUCH
නො මිළයේ ඇතුල්වීම	FREE ADMISSION
තණකොළ මඟ හරින්න	KEEP OFF THE GRASS
වෙන් කර ඇත	RESERVED
වැසිකිළි	TOILETS

What time does it open/close?
eh-kah ah-rin-neh/wah-han-neh
kee-yah-tah-dhah?

එක අරින්නේ/
වහන්නේ කියටද?

Is there an admission charge?
a-thul-vee-meh gaahs-thu-vahk
thi-yah-nah-vaah-dhah?

ඇතුල්වීමේ ගාස්තුවක්
තියනවාද?

The Sights   දර්ශනයන්

What's that building?
ah-rah go-dah-na-gil-lah
mo-kahk-dhah?

අර ගොඩනැගිල්ල
මොකක්ද?

What's this monument?
meh smaah-rah-kah-yah
mo-kahk-dhah?

මේ ස්මාරකය
මොකක්ද?

What's that?
ah-rah mo-kahk-dhah?

අර මොකක්ද?

How old is it?
eh-kah koch-chah-rah
pah-rah-nah-dhah?

එක කොච්චර
පරණද?

church	pahl-li-yah/dhev-ma-dhu-rah	පල්ලිය/දෙවිමැදුර
cinema	si-nah-maah shaah-laah-wah	සිනමා ශාලාව
museum	kah-tu-ge-yah/	කටුගෙය/
	kau-thu-kaah-gaah-rah-yah	කෞතුකාගාරය
park	u-dhyaah-nah-yah	උද්‍යානය
ruins	nah-tah-bun	නටබුන්
statue	pi-li-mah-yah	පිළිමය
temple	pahn-sah-lah	පන්සල
university	vish-vah vi-dhyaah-lah-yah	විශ්ව විද්‍යාලය

COLOMBO SIGHTS

Changing Guard (at President's Residence)	jah-naah-di-pah-thi mahn-dee-rah-yeh mu-rah-kaah-vahl maah-ru-wah	ජනාධිපති මන්දිරයේ මුරකාවල් මාරුව
Clock Tower	o-rah-loh-su kah-nu-wah	ඔරලෝසු කණුව
Fort Train Station	ko-tu-wah dhum-ri-yah sthaah-nah-yah	කොටුව දුම්රිය ස්ථානය
Galle Buck	gaah-lu mu-vah-dho-rah	ගාලු මුවදොර
Lighthouse	ek-tam-ge-yah	එක්ටැම්ගෙය
New Parliament House	nah-vah paahr-li-mehn-thu-wah	නව පාර්ලිමේන්තුව
Old Parliament House	pa-rah-ni paahr-li-mehn-thu-wah	පැරණි පාර්ලිමේන්තුව
Port (of Colombo)	ko-lom-bah vah-raah-yah	කොළඹ වරාය
President's Residence	jah-naah-dhi-pah-thi mahn-dhee-rah-yah	ජනාධිපති මන්දිරය
'Temple-Trees' (Prime Minister's residence)	ah-rah-li-yah gah-hah mahn-dhee-rah-yah (ah-gah-ma-thi ni-lah ni-vah-sah)	අරලිය ගහ මන්දිරය (අගමැති නිල නිවස)

AROUND TOWN

Tours
චාරිකා

Are there regular tours we can join?
ah-pah-tah yaah ha-ki
chaah-ri-kaah ni-thah-rah
thi-yeh-dhah?
අපට යා හැකි
චාරිකා නිතර
තියේද?

Can we hire a guide?
gaid ke-nek ah-pah-tah
lah-baah gah-thah
ha-ki-veh-dhah?
ගයිඩ් කෙනෙක්
අපට ලබා ගත
හැකිවේද?

How much is [the tour; a guide]?
[san-chaah-rah-yah-tah;
gaid ke-nek-tah] kee-yahk
ge-vahn-nah oh-ne-dhah?
[සංචාරයට; ගයිඩ්
කෙනෙක්ට] කියක්
ගෙවන්න ඕනෙද?

How long is the tour?
san-chaah-rah-yah-tah
ko-pah-mah-nah
veh-laah gah-thah-veh-dhah?
සංචාරයට කොපමණ
වේලා ගතවේද?

Will we have free time?
ah-pah-tah vi-veh-kah
kaah-lah-yahk thi-yeh-dhah?
අපට විවේක
කාලයක් තියේද?

What time should we be back?
ah-pi aah-pah-su en-nah
oh-neh kee-yah-tah-dhah?
අපි ආපසු එන්න
ඕනේ කියටද?

The guide [has paid; will pay].
gaid gev-vaah/ge-vai
ගයිඩ් ගෙව්වා/ගෙවෙයි.

I'm with them.
mah-mah eh ah-yah ek-kai
මම ඒ අය එක්කයි.

I've lost my group.
mah-mah kahn-daah-yah-men
mah-gah ha-ri-lah
මම කණ්ඩායමෙන්
මග හැරිල.

Have you seen a group of (Australians)?
o-bah (ohs-treh-li-yaah-nu)
kahn-daah-yah-mahk
dhak-kah-dhah?
ඔබ (ඕස්ට්‍රේලියානු)
කණ්ඩායමක්
දැක්කද?

PAPERWORK කඩදාසි සම්පූර්ණ කිරීම

Most of the paperwork in Sri Lanka is trilingual (Sinhala, Tamil and English), but you may need to be familiar with the following terms and phrases:

name	nah-mah	නම
address	li-pi-nah-yah	ලිපිනය
date of birth	u-pahn dhi-nah-yah	උපන් දිනය
place of birth	u-pahn sthaah-nah-yah	උපන් ස්ථානය
age	vah-yah-sah	වයස
sex	sthree/pu-ru-shah	ස්ත්‍රී/පුරුෂ
	bhaah-vah-yah	භාවය
nationality	jaah-thi-kahth-vah-yah	ජාතිකත්වය
religion	aah-gah-mah	ආගම
profession/work	vruth-thee-yah/	වෘත්තිය/
	ra-ki-yaah-vah	රැකියාව
marital status	vi-vaah-hah-kah	විවාහක
	thahth-vah-yah	තත්වය
single	ah-vi-vaah-hah-kai	අවිවාහකයි
married	vi-vaah-hah-kai	විවාහකයි
divorced	dhik-kah-saah-dhai	දික්කසාදැයි
widow/widower	van-dhah-bu-wah	වැන්දඹුව
identification	han-dhu-nu-mah	හැඳුනුම
passport number	gah-mahn	ගමන් බලපත්‍ර
	bah-lah-path-rah	අංකය
	ahn-kah-yah	
visa	aah-gah-mah-nah	ආගමන
	ah-vah-sah-rah-yah;	අවසරය;
	vee-saah	විසා
baptismal	bau-this-mah	බෝතිස්ම
certificate	sah-hah-thi-kah-yah	සහතිකය
drivers licence	ri-yah-dhu-ru	රියදුරු
	bah-lah-pahth-rah-yah	බලපත්‍රය
customs	reh-gu kah-tah-yu-thu	රේගු කටයුතු
immigration	aah-gah-mah-nah	ආගමන
	kah-tah-yu-thu	කටයුතු

AROUND TOWN

purpose of visit	(me-rah-tah-tah)	(මෙරටට)
	eh-mah-tah heh-thu	එමට හේතු
reason for travel	gah-mah-nah-tah	ගමනට
	heh-thu	හේතු
business	bis-nahs vah-lah-tah	බිස්නස් වලට
holiday	ni-vaah-du	නිවාඩු
visiting	naa-dhaa-yahn	නෑදෑයන්
relatives	bah-lahn-nah	බලන්න
visiting the	mau-rah-tah-tah	මව්රටට
homeland	yaah-mah	යාම

$#@*?!

Swearing isn't as common in Sri Lanka as it is in Western countries, so it generally has a greater impact. Some swear words, which correspond to the more common English swear words, are:

Bastard!

ah-vah-jaah-thah-kah-yaah   අවජාතකයා

Son of a bitch!

bal-li-geh pu-thaah   බැල්ලිගේ පුතා

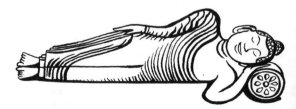

වினோදය තකා එළියට යෑම

GOING OUT

There are various cinemas and theatres in Sri Lanka, catering for all tastes. Concerts and operas are also popular and the nightlife is fast catching up with that of European countries.

WHERE TO GO

යා හැකි තැන්

What's there to do in the evenings?
san-dhaa-veh mo-nah-vaah-dhah
kah-lah ha-ki vahn-neh?

සැන්දෑවේ මොනවාද
කළ හැකි වන්නේ?

Where can I find out what's on?
mo-nah-vaah thi-yeh-dhah
mah-mah dha-nah gahn-neh
ko-ho-mah-dhah?

මොනවා තියේද මම
දැන ගන්නේ
කොහොමද?

What's on tonight?
ah-dhah raa-tah mo-nah-vah-dhah
thi-yehn-neh?

අද රැට මොනවද
තියෙන්නේ?

I feel like	mah-tah	මට
going to	hi-the-nah-vaah	හිතෙනවා
a/the ...	... yahn-nah	... යන්න .
bar/pub	baahr e-kah-tah;	බාර් එකට;
	tha-baa-ru-mah-tah	තැබෑරුමට
concert	kon-sahrt e-kah-kah-tah	කොන්සර්ට් එකකට
nightclub	raah-three sah-maah-jah	රාතූ සමාජ
	shaah-laah-vah-kah-tah	ශාලාවකට
restaurant	aah-pah-nah	ආපන
	shaah-laah-vah-kah-tah	ශාලාවකට

I feel like ...	mah-tah ...	මට
	hi-the-nah-vaah	හිතෙනවා ...
a stroll	a-vi-din-nah yahn-nah	ඇවිදින්න යන්න
dancing	baahl na-tu-mah-kah-tah	බාල් නැටුමකට
	yahn-nah	යන්න
going for a	koh-pi/bee-mah e-kahk	කෝපි/බීම එකක්
coffee/drink	bon-nah yahn-nah	බොන්න යන්න

GOING OUT

91

INVITATIONS

ආරාධනා

What are you doing this evening/weekend?

ah-dhah hah-vah-sah/sah-thi
ahn-thah-yeh o-bah mo-kah-dhah
kah-rahn-neh?

අද හවස/සති
අන්තයේ ඔබ
මොකද කරන්නේ?

Would you like to go for a drink/meal?

[bee-mah e-kahk bon-nah;
kaa-mah e-kahk kahn-nah]
yahn-nah o-bah ka-mah-thi-dhah?

[බීම එකක් බොන්න;
කෑම එකක් කන්න]
යන්න ඔබ කැමතිද?

It's my shout. (I'll buy)

mah-geh vaah-rah-yah

මගේ වාරය.

Do you want to come to the variety
show with me?

maah ek-kah vi-vi-dhah
prah-sahn-gah-yah-tah yahn-nah
o-bah ka-mah-thi-dhah?

මා එක්ක විවිධ
පුසංගයට යන්න
ඔබ කැමතිද?

RESPONDING
TO INVITATIONS

ආරාධනා සඳහා
පුතිචාරය දැක්ම

Yes, I'd love to.

o-vu. mah-mah hah-ri aah-sai

ඔව්. මම හරි ආසයි.

Where shall we go?

ah-pi ko-heh-dhah
yahn-neh?

අපි කොහේද
යන්නේ?

No, I'm afraid I can't.

ba-ha. mah-tah ba-ri-ve-yi

බැහැ. මට බැරිවෙයි.

What about tomorrow?

he-tah ko-ho-mah-dhah?

හෙට කොහොමද?

NIGHTCLUBS & BARS

රාත්‍රී සමාජ ශාලා සහ බීම හල්

Are there any good nightclubs?
   hon-dhah raah-three
   sah-maah-jah shaah-laah ki-si-vahk
   thi-yah-nah-vaah-dhah?

හොඳ රාත්‍රී සමාජ ශාලා කිසිවක් තියනවාද?

Do you want to dance?
   o-bah-tah nah-tan-nah
   ka-mah-thi-dhah?

ඔබට නටන්න කැමතිද?

Do you want to go to a karaoke bar?
   ka-ri-oh-ki sahn-gee-thah-yah
   a-thi tha-nah-kah-tah o-bah
   yahn-nah ka-mah-thi-dhah?

කැරිඕකි සංගීතය ඇති තැනකට ඔබ යන්න කැමතිද?

Do you have to pay to enter?
   a-thul vee-mah-tah ge-vahn-nah
   oh-neh-dhah?

ඇතුළ විමට ගෙවන්න ඕනේද?

No, it's free.
   na-ha. e-kah no-mi-leh.

නැහැ. එක නොමිලේ.

Yes, it's ...
   o-vu. e-kah ...

ඔව්. එක ...

I'm having a great time!
   mah-tah hah-ri vi-noh-dhai!

මට හරි විනෝදයි!

I don't like the music here.
   me-thah-nah
   sahn-gee-thah-yah-tah mah-mah
   ka-mah-thi na-ha

මෙතන සංගීතයට මම කැමති නැහැ.

It's great here.
   ni-yah-mai me-thah-nah

නියමයි මෙතන.

Shall we go somewhere else?
   ah-pi ve-nah tha-nah-kah-tah
   yah-mu-dhah?

අපි වෙන තැනකට යමුද?

GOING OUT

STATEMENT TO QUESTION

Adding -dhah (ද) to the end of a statement, transforms it into a question.

ARRANGING TO MEET

හමුවීමට යොදා ගැනීම

What time shall we meet?
ah-pi kee-yah-tah-dhah
hah-mu vahn-neh?

අපි කියටද හමු
වන්නේ?

Where will we meet?
ah-pi ko-heh-dhah
hah-mu vahn-neh?

අපි කොහේද හමු
වන්නේ?

Let's meet at (eight o'clock) at the (...).
ah-pi (ah-tah-tah)
hah-mu-ve-mu (...-dhee)

අපි (අටට)
හමුවෙමු (...දී).

OK. I'll see you then.
hon-dhai. e-thah-ko-tah
hah-mu-ve-mu

හොඳයි. එතකොට
හමුවෙමු.

I'll come over at (six).
mah-mah (hah-yah-tah) en-nahm

මම (හයට) එන්නම්.

I'll try to make it.
mah-mah en-nah bah-lahn-nahm

මම එන්න බලන්නම්.

See you later/tomorrow.
pahs-seh/he-tah hah-mu-ve-mu

පස්සේ/හෙට හමුවෙමු.

Sorry I'm late.
kah-nah-gaah-tuy mah-mah
pah-rahk-kuy

කණගාටුයි මම
පරක්කුයි.

Never mind.
kah-mahk na-ha

කමක් නැහැ.

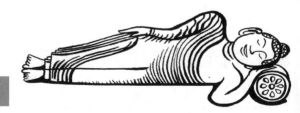

GOING OUT

FAMILY

In Sri Lanka, people place great importance on family life. When visiting friends or relatives, the whole family goes together. Parents would be insulted if they were invited somewhere without their children, and probably wouldn't go.

QUESTIONS   ප්‍රශ්න

Are you married?
  o-bah vi-vaah-hah-kah-dhah?   ඔබ විවාහකද?

Do you have a girlfriend/boyfriend?
  o-bah-tah pem-vah-thi-yahk/
  pem-vah-thek si-tee-dhah?   ඔබට පෙම්වතියක්/
  පෙම්වතෙක් සිටීද?

How many children do you have?
  o-bah-tah lah-mai kee
  dhe-nek in-nah-vaah-dhah?   ඔබට ළමයි කී
  දෙනෙක් ඉන්නාද?

How many brothers/sisters
do you have?
  o-bah-tah sah-hoh-dhah-rah/
  sah-hoh-dhah-ri-yahn
  kee dhe-nek
  in-nah-vaah-dhah?   ඔබට සහෝදර/
  සහෝදරියන්
  කී දෙනෙක්
  ඉන්නාද?

How old are they?
  o-vun-geh yah-sah
  kee-yah-dhah?   ඔවුන්ගේ වයස
  කියද?

Do you live with your family?
  o-bah jee-vahth vehn-neh
  o-beh pah-vu-leh ah-yah
  ek-kah-dhah?   ඔබ ජීවත් වෙන්නේ
  ඔබේ පවුලේ අය
  එක්කද?

FAMILY

REPLIES පිළිතුරු

I'm ...	mah-mah ...	මම ...
single	ah-vi-vaah-hah-kai	අවිවාහකයි
married	vi-vaah-hah-kai	විවාහකයි
separated	ven-ve-laah	වෙන්වෙලා
divorced	dhik-kah-saah-dhai	දික්කසාදයි
widowed	van-dhah-bhu-yi	වැන්දඹුයි

I have a partner.

mah-tah sah-hah-kah-ru-vek/ මට සහකරුවෙක්/
sah-hah-kaah-ri-yahk (m/f) සහකාරියක්
in-nah-vaah ඉන්නවා.

We live together but we're
not married.

ah-pi e-kah-tah අපි එකට ජීවත්
jee-vahth ve-nah-vaah වෙනවා නමුත්,
nah-muth ah-pi kah-saah-dhah අපි කසාද බැඳල
ban-dhah-laah na-ha නැහැ.

I don't have any children.

mah-tah lah-mai මට ළමයි
kah-vu-ruth na-ha කවුරුත් නැහැ.

I have a daughter/son.

mah-tah e-kah dhu-wek/ මට එක දුවෙක්/
pu-thek in-nah-vaah පුතෙක් ඉන්නවා.

I live with my family.

mah-geh pah-vu-leh ah-yah මගේ පවුලේ අය
ek-kai mah-mah in-neh එක්කයි මම ඉන්නේ.

'TIL DEATH DO US PART

Unless horoscopes can confirm a couple's compatibility,
it's thought their marriage will not last.

FAMILY පවුල

aunt	nan-dhaah	නැන්දා
	(father's sister)	
	lo-ku ahm-maah	ලොකු අම්මා
	(mother's older sister)	
	pun-chi ahm-maah	පුංචි අම්මා
	(mother's younger sister)	
baby	lah-dhah-ru-waah/	ළදරුවා/
	bah-baah	බබා
boy	pi-ri-mi lah-mah-yaah	පිරිමි ළමයා
brother	ai-yaah (older)	අයියා
	mahl-lee (younger)	මල්ලි
	so-ho-yu-raah	සොහොයුරා
	(refers to either)	
brother-in-law	mahs-si-naah	මස්සිනා
dad	thaahth-thaah	තාත්තා
daughter	dhu-wah	දුව
daughter-in-law	leh-lee	ලේලි
family	pah-vu-lah	පවුල
family name	vaah-sah-gah-mah	වාසගම
father	pi-yaah	පියා
father-in-law	maah-maah	මාමා
girl	ga-ha-nu	ගැහැණු
	lah-mah-yaah	ළමයා
given name	pah-lah-mu nah-mah	පළමු නම
grandfather	see-yaah	සීයා
grandmother	aahch-chee	ආච්චි
husband	sa-mi-yaah/	සැමියා/
	swaah-mi-yaah	ස්වාමියා
mother	mah-vah	මව
mother-in-law	nan-dhahm-maah	නැන්දම්මා
mum	ahm-maah/ahm-mee	අම්මා/අම්මි

FAMILY

nickname	vi-kah-tah nah-mah	විකට නම
sister	ak-kaah (older)	අක්කා
	nahn-gee (younger)	නංගී
	so-ho-yu-ri-yah	සොහොයුරිය
	(refers to either)	
sister-in-law	naa-naah	නෑනා
son	pu-thaah	පුතා
son-in-law	baa-naah	බෑනා
uncle	maah-maah	මාමා
	(mother's brother)	
	mah-hap-paah	මහප්පා
	(father's older brother)	
	baahp-paah	බාප්පා
	(father's younger brother)	
wife	bi-rin-dhah/	බිරිඳ/
	bhaahr-yaah-wah	භාර්යාව

INTERESTS & ACTIVITIES

COMMON INTERESTS පොදුවේ කැමති දේ

What do you do in your spare time?

o-beh vi-veh-kah kaah-lah-yeh	ඔබේ විවේක කාලයේ
o-bah mo-kah-dhah	ඔබ මොකද
kah-rahn-neh?	කරන්නේ?

Do you like ...?	o-bah ka-mah-thi-dhah	ඔබ කැමතිද
	... vah-lah-tah?	... වලට?
I (don't) like ...	mah-mah ... vah-lah-tah	මම ... වලට
	ka-mah-thi (na-ha)	කැමති (නැහැ).
dancing	na-tum	නැටුම්
gardening	wahth-theh	වත්තේ
	va-dah-tah	වැඩට
travelling	gah-mahn yahn-nah	ගමන් යන්න
I like to ...	mah-mah ka-mah-thiy ...	මම කැමතියි ...
cook	u-yahn-nah	උයන්න
draw	an-dhee-mah-tah	ඇදීමට
paint	pin-thaah-ru	පින්තාරු
	kah-rahn-nah	කරන්න
take	chaah-yaah-roo-pah	ජායාරූප
photographs	gahn-nah	ගන්න

99

MUSIC

සංගීතය

INTERESTS & ACTIVITIES

Do you like listening to music?
sahn-gee-thah-yah-tah
sah-vahn dhee-mah-tah
o-bah ka-mah-thi-dhah?

සංගීතයට
සවන් දීම ඔබ
කැමතිද?

What music do you like?
o-bah mo-nah
sahn-gee-thah-yah-tah-dhah
ka-mah-thi?

ඔබ මොන
සංගීතයටද
කැමති?

I really like (reggae).
mah-mah hun-gaahk ka-mah-thiy
(re-geh) sahn-gee-thah-yah-tah

මම හුඟාක් කැමතියි
(රෙගේ) සංගීතයට.

Which bands do you like?
o-bah mo-nah vaah-dhah-kah
mahn-dah-lah vah-lah-tah-dhah
ka-mah-thi?

ඔබ මොන වාදක
මණ්ඩල වලටද
කැමති?

I like ...
mah-mah ka-mah-thi ...

මම කැමති ...

Have you heard the latest record by ...?
...-geh ah-luth tha-ti-yah
a-hu-vaah-dhah?

... ගේ අළුත්
තැටිය ඇහුවද?

Where can you hear traditional
music around here?
sahm-prah-dhaah-yee
sahn-gee-thah-yah
ah-hahn-nah pu-lu-vahn
ko-heh-dhah?

සම්ප්‍රදායි සංගීතය
අහන්න පුළුවන්
කොහේද?

Shall we sit or stand?
ah-pi in-dhah-gahn-nah-dhah
hi-tah gahn-nah-dhah?

අපි ඉදගන්නද
හිට ගන්නද?

What a fantastic concert!
is-thah-rahm kon-saht e-kah!

ඉස්තරම් කොන්සට් එක

It's terrible!
hah-ri-mah pahl eh-kah! හරිම පල් එක!

This singer is brilliant.
gaah-yah-kah-yaah ගායකයා
vi-shish-tai විශිෂ්ඨයි.

CINEMA & THEATRE සිනමාව සහ තියටරය

I feel like going to a/an/the ...	... mah-tah yahn-nah hi-the-nah-vaah	... මට යන්න හිතෙනවා.
ballet	ba-leh e-kah-kah-tah; na-tu-mah-kah-tah	බැලේ එකකට; නැටුමකට
comedy	haahs-yah jah-nah-kah naah-tyah-kah-tah	හාසය ජනක නාට්යයකට
film	chi-thrah-pah-ti-yah-kah-tah	චිත්රපටියකට
opera	or-pah-raah e-kah-kah-tah	ඔපරා එකකට
play	naah-tyah-kah-tah	නාට්යයකට

INTERESTS & ACTIVITIES

What's on at the cinema tonight?
si-nah-maah shaah-laah-vah-lah සිනමා ශාලාවල
ah-dhah pen-vahn-neh අද පෙන්වන්නේ
mo-nah-vaah-dhah? මොනවාද?

Are there any tickets for ...?
...-tah ti-kaht thi-yeh-dhah? ...ට ටිකට් තියේද?

Sorry, we're sold out.
kah-nah-gaah-tuy, කණගාටුයි, ටිකට්
ti-kaht na-ha නැහැ.

Is it in English?
eh-kah in-gree-si-yen-dhah? ඒක ඉංග්රීසියෙන්ද?

Does it have English subtitles?
eh-keh in-gree-si ඒකේ ඉංග්රීසි
u-pah-sheer-shah thi-yeh-dhah? උපශීර්ෂ තියේද?

INTERESTS & ACTIVITIES

OPINIONS   අදහස්

Did you like the ...?	...-tah o-bah ka-mah-thi vu-naah-dhah?	...ට ඔබ කැමති වුනාද?
film	chi-thrah-pah-ti-yah	චිත්‍රපටිය
performance	rahn-gah dhak-mah	රඟ දැක්ම
play	naaht-yah-yah	නාට්‍යය

I liked it very much.
mah-mah eh-kah-tah   මම ඒකට හුඟාක්
hun-gaahk ka-mah-thi vu-naah   කැමති වුනා.

I didn't like it very much.
mah-mah eh-kah-tah va-di-yah   මම ඒකට වැඩිය
ka-mah-thi vu-neh na-ha   කැමති වුනේ නැහැ.

I thought it was ...	mah-mah hi-thu-veh eh-kah ... ki-yah-lah	මම හිතුවේ ඒක ... කියල.
It's ...	eh-kah ...	ඒක ...
awful	ahn-thi-mai	අන්තිමයි
beautiful	lahs-sah-nai	ලස්සණයි
boring	nee-rah-sai	නීරසයි
dramatic	vish-mah-yah jah-nah-kai	විශ්මය ජනකයි
entertaining	vi-noh-dhaath-mah-kai	විනෝදාත්මකයි
excellent	hun-gaahk hon-dhai	හුඟාක් හොඳයි
great	bo-ho-mah hon-dhai	බොහොම හොඳයි
incomprehensible	theh-rum gah-thah no-ha-ki	තේරුම් ගත නොහැකි
interesting	sith gahn-naah su-luy	සිත් ගන්නා සුළුයි
OK	hon-dhai	හොඳයි
too expensive	mi-lah va-di	මිල වැඩි
unusual	ah-saah-maahn-yai	අසාමාන්‍යයි

TYPES OF SPORT   විවිධ ක්‍රීඩා

What sport do you play?

o-bah mo-nah kree-daah-dhah
sel-lahm kah-rahn-neh?

ඔබ මොන ක්‍රීඩාද
සෙල්ලම් කරන්නේ?

I play/practise ...   mah-mah   මම
                           kah-rahn-neh ...   කරන්නේ ...

aerobics	ridh-mah-yaah-nu-koo-lah vi-yaah-yaah-mah	රිද්ම-යානුකුල ව්‍යායාම
athletics	vi-yaah-yaah-mi-kah kree-dhaah	ව්‍යායාමික ක්‍රීඩා
basketball	baahs-kaht-bawl	බාස්කට්බෝල්
cricket	kri-kaht	ක්‍රිකට්
cycling	bai-si-kaahl pa-dee-mah	බයිසිකල් පැදීම
diving	ki-mi-dee-mah	කිමිදීම
football (soccer)	paah-pahn-du	පාපන්දු
hockey	hoh-ki	හොකි
rowing	o-ru pa-dhee-mah	ඔරු පැදීම
rugby	rah-gah	රගර්
swimming	pi-hi-nee-mah	පිහිනීම
tennis	te-nis	ටෙනිස්
volleyball	vo-li-bawl	වොලිබෝල්

For trekking terms, see In the Country, page 137.

INTERESTS & ACTIVITIES

CALMER ACTIVITIES   සන්සුන් ක්‍රියාකාරකම්

meditation	bhaa-vah-naah ki-ree-mah	භාවනා කිරීම
Tai Chi	taai chi	ටායි චි
yoga	yoh-gaah	යෝගා

INTERESTS & ACTIVITIES

TALKING ABOUT SPORT

ක්‍රීඩා ගැන
කථා කිරීම

Do you like sport?
o-bah kree-dhaah vah-lah-tah
ka-mah-thi-dhah?

ඔබ ක්‍රීඩා වලට
කැමතිද?

Yes, very much.
o-vu, bo-hoh-mah ka-mah-thiy

ඔව්, බොහොම කැමතියි.

No, not at all.
na-ha, ko-hehth-mah na-ha

නැහැ, කොහේත්ම
නැහැ.

I like watching it.
mah-mah ka-mah-thiy
eh-kah bah-lahn-nah

මම කැමතියි ඒක
බලන්න.

What sports do you follow?
o-bah bah-lahn-neh mo-nah
kree-dhaah-vah-dhah?

ඔබ බලන්නේ
මොන ක්‍රීඩාවද?

I follow ...
mah-mah bah-lahn-neh ...

මම බලන්නේ ...

Who's your favourite ...?	o-beh pri-yah-thah-mah ... kau-dhah?	ඔබේ ප්‍රියතම ... කව්ද?
player	kree-dhah-kah-yaah	ක්‍රීඩකයා
sportsperson	kree-dhaah shil-pi-yah	ක්‍රීඩා ශිල්පියා

Which team do you support?
o-bah koi
kahn-dhaah-yah-mah-dhah
sah-poht kah-rahn-neh?

ඔබ කොයි
කණ්ඩායමද
සපෝට් කරන්නේ?

I support ...
mah-mah sah-poht
kah-rahn-neh ...

මම සපෝට්
කරන්නේ ...

Do you play (tennis)?
o-bah (te-nis)
gah-hah-nah-vaah-dhah?

ඔබ (ටෙනිස්)
ගහනවාද?

GOING TO A MATCH

තරහයක බලන්නට යඳම්

Would you like to go to a (cricket) match?
o-bah (cri-kaht) thah-rahn-gah-yahk bah-lahn-nah-tah yahn-nah ka-mah-thi-dhah?

ඔබ (ක්‍රිකට්) තරහයක් බලන්නට යන්න කැමතිද?

Where is it being held?
ko-heh-dhah eh-kah thi-yen-neh?

කොහේද ඒක තියෙන්නේ?

How much are the tickets?
ti-kaht mi-lah kee-yah-dhah?

ටිකට් මිල කියද?

What time does it start?
eh-kah pah-tan gahn-neh kee-yah-tah-dhah?

ඒක පටන් ගන්නේ කියටද?

Who's playing?
kau-dhah gah-hahn-neh?

කවිද ගහන්නේ?

Who do you think will win?
kau-ru dhi-nai ki-yaah-dhah hi-then-neh?

කව්රු දිනයි කියාද හිතන්නේ?

Which team is winning/losing?
koi kahn-daah-yah-mah-dhah dhi-nahn-neh/pah-rah-dhin-neh?

කොයි කණ්ඩායමද දිනන්නේ/පරදින්නේ?

What's the score?
lah-ku-nu thahth-vah-yah ko-ho-mah-dhah?

ලකුණු තත්වය කොහොමද?

What a great performance!
hah-ri is-thah-rahm!

හරි ඉස්තරම්!

INTERESTS & ACTIVITIES

KEEPING FIT

හොඳ ශරීර සෞඛ්‍යයෙන් සිටීම

Where's the best place to
jog/run around here?
[jog kah-rahn-nah;
dhu-wahn-nah] hon-dhah-mah
tha-nah meh kit-tu-wah
ko-heh-dhah thi-yen-neh?

[ජෝග් කරන්න; දුවන්න]
හොඳම තැන මේ
කිට්ටුව කොහේද
තියෙන්නේ?

Do you feel like (going for a run)?
o-bah-tah (dhu-whan-nah)
yahn-nah hi-the-nah-vaah-dhah?

ඔබට (දුවන්න) යන්න
හිතෙනවාද?

Would you like to play (tennis)?
o-bah (te-nis) gah-hahn-nah
ka-mah-thi-dhah?

ඔබ (ටෙනිස්)
ගහන්න කැමතිද?

Where's the nearest ...?	lahn-gah-mah a-thi ... ko-heh-dhah thi-yen-neh?	ළඟම ඇති ... කොහේද තියෙන්නේ?
gym	jim e-kah	ජිම් එක
(swimming) pool	(swi-ming) pool e-kah	(ස්විමිං) පූල් එක
tennis court	te-nis pit-tah-ni-yah	ටෙනිස් පිට්ටනිය

GIVE IT SOME STICK!

Long before present-day sports became popular,
Sri Lankans enjoyed other sporting activities, such as
gu-du (ගු). This game involves two or more players and
two sticks – one short and one long. The short stick is
placed on two blocks or stones and the long stick is
used to hit the short one as far as possible. The long
stick is then used to score by measuring the distance
the short stick has been hit. In villages and more rural
areas, gu-du is still popular.

Do I have to be a member to attend?
  sah-hah-bhaah-gi ven-nah
  mah-mah saah-maah-ji-kah-yah-ku
  ven-nah oh-ne-dhah?

සහභාගි වෙන්න මම
සාමාජිකයකු
වෙන්න ඕනෙද?

Where are the changing rooms?
  an-dhum maah-ru kah-rah-nah
  kaah-mah-rah ko-heh-dhah
  thi-yen-neh?

ඇඳුම් මාරු කරන
කාමර කොහේද
තියෙන්නේ?

TALKING ABOUT
TRAVELLING

ගමන්-බීමන් ගැන
කථා කිරීම

Have you travelled much?
  o-bah hun-gahk gah-mahn
  kah-rah ath-dhah?

ඔබ හුඟාක් ගමන්
කර ඇත්ද?

How long have you been travelling?
  o-bah koch-chah-rah kah-lahk
  this-seh sahn-chaah-rah-yah
  kah-rah-nah-vaah-dhah?

ඔබ කොච්චර කලක්
තිස්සේ සංචාරය
කරනවාද?

I've been travelling for (two) months.
  mah-mah maah-sah (dhe-kahk)
  this-seh sahn-chaah-rah-yah
  kah-rah-nah-vaah

මම මාස
(දෙකක්) තිස්සේ
සංචාරය කරනවා.

Where have you been?
  o-bah ko-heh ko-heh-dhah
  gi-yeh?

ඔබ කොහේ
කොහේද ගියේ?

I've been to ...
  mah-mah ...-tah gi-yaah

මම ...ට ගියා.

What did you think of (Athens)?
  o-bah (a-thahns) ga-nah
  mo-nah-vah-dhah hi-thu-veh?

ඔබ (ඇතන්ස්) ගැන
මොනවද හිතුවේ?

People are really friendly there.
  e-heh mi-nis-su hah-ri
  yah-hah-luy

එහේ මිනිස්සු හරි
යහළුයි.

INTERESTS & ACTIVITIES

INTERESTS & ACTIVITIES

There are too many tourists there.
e-heh sahn-chaah-rah-kah-yin
bo-hoh-mah va-diy

එහි සංචාරකයින්
බොහොම වැඩියි.

Not many people speak (English).
(in-gree-si) kah-<u>thaah</u>
kah-rahn-neh bo-ho-ma
ti-kah dhe-nai

(ඉංග්‍රීසි) කථා
කරන්නේ බොහොම
ටික දෙනයි.

I was ripped off in (...).
(...) vah-lah maah-vah
gah-saah kaa-vaah

(...) වල
මාව ගසා කෑවා.

What's there to do in (Brussels)?
(brah-sahls)-vah-lah
mo-nah-vah-dhah
kah-rahn-nah thi-yen-neh?

(බ්‍රසල්ස්)වල
මොනවද කරන්න
තියෙන්නේ?

The best time to go is in (December).
e-heh yahn-nah hon-dhah-mah
kaah-lah-yah (dhe-sam-bahr)
vah-lah

එහෙ යන්න හොඳම
කාලය (දෙසැම්බර්)
වල.

Is it safe for women travellers on
their own?
sahn-chaah-rah-kah ga-ha-nu
ah-yah thah-ni-vah yaa-mah
aah-rahk-shaah sah-hi-thah-dhah?

සංචාරක ගැහැණු
අය නනිව යෑම
ආරක්ෂා සහිතද?

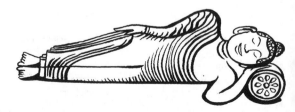

SOCIAL ISSUES

POLITICS   දේශපාලනය

Although Sri Lankans enjoy discussing politics, they're very cautious about where they speak and with whom.

Did you hear about ...?		
... ga-nah aah-rahn-chi-dhah?	... ගැන ආරංචිද?	
What do you think of the current government?		
dhan pah-vah-thi-nah rah-jah-yah ga-nah o-bah mo-na-vaah-dhah hi-thahn-neh?	දැන් පවතින රජය ගැන ඔබ මොනවද හිතන්නේ?	

I (don't) agree with their policy on (the) ...	... ga-nah o-vun-geh prah-thi-pahth-thi ek-kah mah-mah e-kahn-gah ven-neh (na-ha)	... ගැන ඔවුන්ගේ ප්‍රතිපත්ති එක්ක මම එකහ වෙන්නේ (නැහැ).
drugs	mahth-dhrah-vyah	මත්ද්‍රව්‍ය
economy	aahr-thi-kah-yah	ආර්ථිකය
education	ah-dhyaah-pah-nah-yah	අධ්‍යාපන
environment	vaah-thaah-vah-rah-nah-yah	වාතාවරණය
globalisation	goh-lee-kah-rah-nah-yah	ගෝලිකරණය
military service	hah-mu-dhaah seh-vah-yah	හමුදා සේවය
privatisation	pudh-gah-lee-kah-rah-nah-yah	පුද්ගලි-කරණය
social welfare	sah-maah-jah su-bhah saah-dhah-nah-yah	සමාජ සුභ සාධනය

SOCIAL ISSUES

I support the	mah-mah ...	මම
... party.	pahk-shah-yah	...පක්‍ෂය
	path-theh	පැත්තේ.
I'm a member of	mah-mah ...	මම ...
the ... party.	pahk-shah-yeh	පක්‍ෂයේ
	saah-maah-ji-kah-yek	සාමාජිකයෙක්.

Communist	kah-mu-nist	කොමියුනිස්ට්
People's Alliance	po-dhu	පොදු
	pe-rah-mu-nah	පෙරමුණ
People's Liberation	jaah-thi-kah	ජාතික
Front	vi-muk-thi	විමුක්ති
	pe-rah-mu-nah	පෙරමුණ
Social Democratic	sah-maah-jah-vaah-dhi	සමාජවාදි
	prah-jaah-thahn-thri-kah	ප්‍රජාතන්ත්‍රික
Socialist	sah-maah-jah-vaah-dhee	සමාජවාදී
Sri Lanka Freedom	sree lahn-kaah	ශ්‍රී ලංකා
	ni-dhah-hahs	නිදහස්
	pahk-shah-yah	පසය
United National	ek-sath jaah-thi-kah	එක්සත් ජාතික

I'm an abstainer.

   mah-mah chahn-dhah-yen   මම ජන්දයෙන්
   va-lah-kee si-tin-ne-ki   වැළකි සිටින්නෙකි.

In my country we have a
(socialist) government.

   ah-peh rah-the ath-theh   අපේ රටේ ඇත්තේ
   (sah-maah-jah-vaah-dhi)   (සමාජවාදි)
   rah-jah-yahk   රජයක්.

candidate's speech	chahn-dhah	ජන්ද
	dhaah-yah-kah-yaah-geh	දායකයාගේ
	kah-thaah-vah	කථාව
corrupt	dhoo-shah-nah	දූෂණ
counting of votes	chahn-dhah gah-nahn	ජන්ද ගණන්
	ki-ree-mah	කිරීම
democracy	prah-jaah-thahn-	පුජාතන්-
	thrah-vaah-dhah-yah	තුවාදය
demonstration	pe-lah-paah-li-yah	පෙළපාලිය
election	chahn-dhah	ජන්ද
	vi-mah-see-mah	විමසීම
legislation	vyaah-vahs-thah	වෳාවස්ථා
legalisation	nee-thyaah-nu-koo-lah	නිතෳානුකූල
	ki-ree-mah	කිරීම
parliament	paahr-	පාර්-
	li-mehn-thu-wah	ලිමේන්තුව
policy	pra-thi-pahth-thi	පුතිපත්ති
polls	chahn-dhah	ජන්ද
	vi-mah-see-mah	විමසීම
president	jah-naah-dhi-pah-thi	ජනාධිපති
prime minister	ah-gah-ma-thi	අගමැති
rally	ras-vee-mah	රැස්වීම
sexism	lin-gi-kahth-vah-yah	ලිංගිකත්වය
strike	va-dah vahr-jah-nah-yah	වැඩ
		වර්ජනය
term of office	ni-lah kaah-lah-yah	නිල
		කාලය
trade union	vruth-thee-yah	වෳත්තීය
	sah-mi-thi-yah	සමිතිය
unemployment	ra-ki-yaah	රැකියා
	vi-rah-hi-tha kah-mah	විරහිත කම
vote	chahn-dhah-yah	ජන්දය

SOCIAL ISSUES

SOCIAL ISSUES   සමාජීය කරුණු

How do people feel about ...?
... ga-nah   ... ගැන මහජනයාගේ
mah-hah-jah-nah-yaah-geh   හැඟීම් මොනවාද?
ha-geem mo-nah-vaah-dhah?

What do you think about ...?
... ga-nah o-bah   ... ගැන ඔබ
mo-nah-vaah-dhah   මොනවාද
hi-thahn-neh?   හිතන්නේ?

I'm [in favour   ... ga-nah mah-mah   ... ගැන
of; against] ...   e-kahn-gai/   මම   එකහයි/
                    vi-rudh-dhai   විරුද්ධයි.

abortion	gahb-saah ki-ree-mah	ගබ්සා කිරීම
animal rights	sahth-vah hi-mi-kahm	සත්ව හිමිකම්
equal	sah-maah-nah	සමාන
opportunity	ah-vahs-thaah-wah	අවස්ථාව
euthanasia	ah-naah-yaah-sah	අනායාස
	mah-rah-nah-yah	මරණය
immigration	aah-gah-mah-ni-kah	ආගමනික
racism	jaah-thi bheh-dhah-yah	ජාති හේදය
tax	bah-dhu	බදු
unions	sah-mi-thi	සමිති

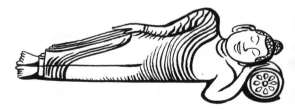

SHOPPING

Sri Lanka offers various shopping experiences, from tiny corner shops to vast shopping centres. Look out for the street vendors set up along the pavements – they're a colourful and popular part of Sri Lankan culture.

LOOKING FOR ...   ... සොයා යාම

Where can I buy ...?
   mah-tah ... gahn-nah
   pu-lu-vahn ko-hen-dhah?

මට ... ගන්න
පුළුවන් කොහෙන්ද?

Where's the nearest ...?
   lahn-gah-mah a-thi ...
   ko-heh-dhah thi-yehn-neh?

ළඟම ඇති ... කෝදේ
තියෙන්නේ?

bank	ban-ku-wah	බැංකුව
barber	baah-bahr saahp-pu-wah	බාබර් සාප්පු
bookshop	poth saahp-pu-wah	පොත් සාප්පුව
camera shop	ka-mah-raah saahp-pu-wah	කැමරා සාප්පුව
chemist	in-gree-si be-heth vi-ku-nahn-naah	ඉංග්‍රීසි බෙහෙත් විකුනන්නා
clothing store	an-dhum saahp-pu-wah	ඇඳුම් සාප්පුව
craft shop	ahth-va-dah saahp-pu-wah	අත්වැඩ සාප්පුව
department store	vi-vi-dhah bah-du saahp-pu-wah	විවිධ බඩු සාප්පුව
general store	po-dhu saahp-pu-wah	පොදු සාප්පුව
launderette	lon-dah-ri-yah	ලොන්ඩරිය
market	maah-kaht e-kah	මාකට් එක
music shop	sahn-gee-thah tha-ti saahp-pu-wah	සංගීත තැටි සාප්පුව
optician	as kahn-naah-di saah-dhahn-naah	ඇස් කන්නාඩි සාදන්නා
pharmacy	in-gree-si be-heth saahp-pu-wah	ඉංග්‍රීසි බෙහෙත් සාප්පුව

shoe shop	sah-pahth-thu	සපත්තු
	saahp-pu-wah	සාප්පුව
souvenir shop	sah-mah-ru bah-du	සමරු බ
	saahp-pu-wah	සාප්පුව
stationers	li-pi-dhrah-vyah	ලිපිදවය
	saahp-pu-wah	සාප්පුව
supermarket	su-pah maah-kaht e-kah	සුපර් මාකට් එක
travel agency	sahn-chaah-rah-kah	සංචාරක
	eh-jahn-si-yah	ඒජන්සිය

MAKING A PURCHASE

යමක් මිලට ගැනීම

I'm just looking.
   mah-mah ni-kahng
   bah-lah-nah-vaah

මම නිකං බලනවා.

How much is this?
   meh-kah kee-yah-dhah?

මේක කියද?

Can you write down the price?
   gah-nah-nah li-yaah
   dhen-nah pu-lu-vahn-dhah?

ගණන ලියා දෙන්න
පුළුවන්ද?

I'd like to buy ...
   mah-mah ka-mah-thiy ...
   gahn-nah

මම කැමතියි
... ගන්න.

Do you have any others?
   ve-nah mo-nah-vaah-dhah
   thi-yen-neh?

වෙන මොනවද
තියෙන්නේ?

Can I look at it?
   mah-tah eh-kah bah-lahn-nah
   pu-lu-vahn-dhah?

මට එක බලන්න
පුළුවන්ද?

I don't like it.
   mah-mah eh-kah-tah
   ka-mah-thi na-ha

මම එකට කැමති
නැහැ.

Do you accept credit cards?
   kaahd e-ken ge-vahn-nah
   pu-lu-vahn-dhah?

කාඩ් එකෙන්
ගෙවන්න පුළුවන්ද?

Could I have a receipt please?
mah-tah ri-seet e-kahk
gahn-nah ha-ki-dhah?

මට රිසිට් එකක්
ගන්න හැකිද?

Does it have a guarantee?
eh-kah vah-gah-kee-mahk
ek-kah-dhah en-neh?

ඒක වගකිමක්
එක්කද එන්නේ?

Can I have it sent overseas?
mah-tah eh-kah pi-tah-rah-tah
yah-vahn-nah pu-lu-vahn-dhah?

මට ඒක පිටරට
යවන්න පුළුවන්ද?

Please wrap it.
kah-ru-naah-kah-rah-lah
mah-tah eh-kah o-thah-lah
dhe-nah-vaah-dhah?

කරුණාකරල
මට ඒක ඔතල
දෙනවාද?

I'd like to return this please.
meh-kah aah-pah-su
dhen-nah ge-naah-veh

මේක ආපසු දෙන්න
ගෙනාවේ.

It's faulty.
eh-keh vah-rah-dhahk
thi-yah-nah-vaah

ඒකෙ වරදක්
තියනවා.

It's broken.
eh-kah ka-di-laah

ඒක කැඩිල.

I'd like my money back.
mah-geh sahl-li mah-tah
aah-pah-su oh-neh

මගේ සල්ලි මට
ආපසු ඕනේ.

BARGAINING   කෙවල් කිරීම

Bargaining is very common in Sri Lanka – especially at road-side stalls, where shoppers are expected to haggle. In shopping centres, however, bargaining is generally not welcome.

I think it's too expensive.
mah-mah hi-thahn-neh eh-kah
gah-nahn va-di ki-yah-laah

මම හිතන්නේ ඒක
ගණන් වැඩි කියල.

The price is too high.
gah-nah-nah
hun-gaahk va-diy

ගණන හුඟාක්
වැඩියි.

It's too much for us.
ah-pi-tah eh-kah
gah-nahn va-di

අපිට එක
ගණන් වැඩියි.

Can you lower the price?
gah-nah-nah ti-kahk ah-du
kah-rahn-nah pu-lu-vahn-dhah?

ගණන ටිකක් අ
කරන්න පුළුවන්ද?

Do you have something cheaper?
mee-tah vah-daah laah-bhah
e-kahk thi-yah-nah-vaah-dhah?

මීට වඩා ලාභ
එකක් තියනවාද?

Really?
ath-thah-tah?

ඇත්තටa?

I'll give you ...
mah-mah o-bah-tah ...
dhen-nahm

මම ඔබට
... දෙන්නම්.

No more than ...
...-tah va-di-yah ne-mei

...ට වැඩිය නෙමෙයි.

ESSENTIAL GROCERIES

අත්‍යාවශ්‍ය
සිල්ලර බ

Where can I find ...?	... gahn-nah pu-lu-vahn ko-hen-dhah?	... ගන්න පුළුවන් කොහෙන්ද?
I'd like (a/some) ...	mah-tah oh-neh ...	මට ඕනේ ...
batteries	ba-tah-ri	බැටරි
bread	paahn	පාන්
butter	bah-tah	බටර්
candles	i-ti-pahn-dhahm	ඉටිපන්දම්
cheese	chees	චීස්
chocolate	chok-laht	චොක්ලට්
eggs	bith-thah-rah	බිත්තර
flour	pi-ti	පිටි
gas cylinder	gaas si-lin-dah-rah-yah	ගෑස් සිලින්ඩරය
ham	ham	හැම්
honey	pa-ni	පැණි
margarine	maah-jah-reen	මාජරීන්
matches	gi-ni-pet-ti	ගිනිපෙට්ටි

SHOPPING

milk	ki-ri	කිරි
mosquito coil	mah-dhu-ru koil/	මදුරු දහර/
	dhahn-gah-rah	කොයිල්
pepper	gahm-mi-ris	ගම්මිරිස්
salt	lu-nu	ලුණු
shampoo	sham-poo	ෂැම්පූ
soap	sah-bahn	සබන්
sugar	see-ni	සීනි
toilet paper	toi-laht	ටොයිලට්
	kah-dah-dhaah-si	කඩදාසි
toothpaste	dhath-be-heth	දත්බෙහෙත්
washing powder	sah-bahn ku-du	සබන් කු
yogurt	yoh-gaht	යෝගට්

CLOTHING   ඇහලුම්

boots	boot sah-paht-thu	බූට් සපත්තු
clothing	an-gah-lum	ඇහලුම්
coat	koht e-kah; kah-baah-yah	කෝට් එක; කබාය
dress	gah-vu-mah	ගවුම
jacket	ja-kaht	ජැකට් කෝට්
	koht e-kah	එක
jeans	jeens/kah-li-sah-mah	ජීන්ස්/කලිසම
jumper	jam-pah-rah-yah	ජම්පරය
(sweater)	(swee-tah-rah-yah)	(ස්විටරය)
pants	kah-li-sah-mah	කලිසම
raincoat	wa-hi kah-baah-yah	වැහි කබාය
shirt	kah-mi-sah-yah	කමිසය
shoes	sah-paht-thu	සපත්තු
socks	mehs	මේස්
swimsuit	swim soot e-kah	ස්විම් සූට් එක
T-shirt	tee shaht e-kah	ටි ෂර්ට් එක
underwear	yah-tah an-dhum	යට ඇදුම්

DARK BUSINESS!

No shopkeeper or vendor will sell salt or needles after
dusk, as it's believed to bring bad luck on the business.

SHOPPING

Can I try it on?
 mah-mah an-dhah-lah   මම ඇදල බලන්නද?
 bah-lahn-nah-dhah?
My size is ...
 mah-geh sais e-kah ...   මගේ සයිස් එක ...
It doesn't fit.
 meh-kah hah-ri na-ha   මෙක හරි නැහැ.

It's too ... meh-kah hun-gaahk ... මෙක හුඟාක් ...
 big   lo-kuy   ලොකුයි
 small po-diy   පොඩියි
 short ko-tai   කොටයි
 long dhi-gai   දිගයි
 tight thah-dhai   තදයි
 loose bu-rul   බුරුල්

SOUVENIRS

සමරු භාණ්ඩ

batiks	bah-thik	බතික්
brassware	pith-thah-lah bah-du	පිත්තල බ
cane ware/	weh-wal [bah-du;	වේවැල් [බ;
furniture	gru-hah bhaahn-dah]	ගෘහ භාණ්ඩ]
handicraft	ahth-va-dah	අත්කම් වැඩ
items made of ...	... vah-lin	... වලින්
	saa-doo bah-du	සෑදූ බ
bamboo	bahm-bu	බම්බු
ebony	kah-lu-vah-rah	කළුවර
satin	bu-ru-thah	බුරුත
shell	sip-pi kah-tu	සිප්පි කටු
straw	pi-du-ru	පිදුරු
wood	lee	ලී
Sri Lankan tea	sree lahn-kaah theh	ශී ලංකා තේ
woodcarved	lee ka-tah-yahm	ලී කැටයම් රූප
figure	roo-pah	

MATERIALS

දුවු

brass	pith-thah-lah	පිත්තල
ceramic	pi-gahn gah-dol	පිහන් ගඩොල්
cotton	kah-pu	කපු
glass	vee-dhu-ru	වීදුරු
gold	rahth-rahn	රත්තුන්
handmade	ah-thin ni-mah voo	අතින් නිමවූ
leather	hahm	හම්
lycra	lik-raah	ලිකුරා
metal	loh-hah	ලෝහ
plastic	plaahs-tik	ප්ලාස්ටික්
silk	silk	සිල්ක්
silver	ri-dee	රිදී
stainless steel	su-dhu yah-kah-dah	සුදු යකඩ
synthetic	kru-three-mah	කෘතිම
wood	lee	ලී
wool	loh-mah	ලෝම

COLOURS පාට

dark ...	thah-dhah ...	තද ...
light ...	laah ...	ලා ...
black	kah-lu	කළු
blue	nil	නිල්
brown	dhum-bu-ru	දුඹුරු
green	ko-lah	කොළ
grey	ah-lu	අළු
orange	tham-bi-li	තැඹිලි
pink	roh-sah	රෝස
purple	dhahm	දම්
red	rah-thu	රතු
white	su-dhu	සුදු
yellow	kah-hah	කහ

TOILETRIES ශරීර ශුද්ධිය සඳහා අවශාතා

bath/shower gel	baahth/shah-wah jel	බාත්/ෂවර් ජෙල්
comb	pah-naah-wah	පනාව
condoms	kon-dom pah-thah	කොන්ඩොම් පට
dental floss	dhahn-thah muk-thah	දන්ත මුක්ත
	ken-di	කෙඳි
deodorant	dhu-gahn-dhah	දුහඳ
	nahs-nah-yah	නස්නයන්
hairbrush	kon-daah	කොණ්ඩා
	bu-ru-su-wah	බුරුසුව
moisturiser	aah-leh-pah-yah	ආලේපය
pregnancy test	ghahr-bhah-nee	ගර්භණී
kit	pah-reek-shah-nah	පරීක්ෂණ
	kaht-tah-lah-yah	කට්ටලය
razor	dha-li-pi-hi-yah	දැලිපිහිය
razor blades	blehd thah-lah	බ්ලේඩ් තල
sanitary napkins	o-sahp veem	ඔසප් වීම්
	an-dhah-kah-dah	අඳකඩ
shampoo	sham-poo	ෂැම්පූ
shaving cream	shehv kreem; ra-vu-lah	ෂේව් ක්‍රීම්; රැවුල
	kah-pah-nah kreem	කපන ක්‍රීම්
soap	sah-bahn	සබන්

SHOPPING

sunblock	av aah-vah-rah-nah aah-leh-pah-yah	අව් ආවරණ ආලේපය
tissues	ti-shoo (mu-hu-nah pis-nah-yahn)	ටිෂු (මුහුණ පිස්නයන්)
toilet paper	toi-laht kah-dah-dhaah-si	ටොයිලට් කඩදාසි
toothbrush	dhahth bu-ru-su-wah	දත් බුරුසුව
toothpaste	dhahth be-he-th	දත් බෙහෙත්

FOR THE BABY   ළදරුවාට

baby powder	lah-dhah-ru pi-yah-rah	ළදරු පියර
bib	bib e-kah	බිබ් එක
disposable nappies	i-vah-thah-lah-nah na-pi	ඉවතලන නැපි
dummy/pacifier	soop-pu-wah	සූප්පුව
feeding bottle	ki-ri boh-thah-lah-yah	කිරි බෝතලය
nappies/diapers	na-pi	නැපි
nappy rash cream	na-pi dhah-dhah kreem e-kah	නැපි දද කුීම් එක
powdered milk	pi-ti ki-ri	පිටි කිරි
rubber duck	rah-bahr thaah-raah-wah	රබර් තාරාවා
teat	soop-pu	සූප්පු
tinned baby food	tin kah-lah lah-dhah-ru aah-haah-rah	ටින් කළ ළදරු ආහාර

STATIONERY & PUBLICATIONS   ලිපිදුව්‍ය හා පුකාශන

Is there an English-language bookshop nearby?
in-gree-si poth saahp-pu-wahk meh lahn-gah pah-hah-thah ath-dhah?

ඉංගීුසි පොත් සාප්පුවක් මේ ළඟ පහත ඇත්ද?

Is there an English-language section?
in-gree-si bhaah-shaah-wah-tah ve-nah-mah ko-tah-sahk thi-yeh-dhah?

ඉංගීුසි භාෂාවට වෙනම කොටසක් තියේද?

Do you sell ...?	o-bah ... vi-ku-nah-nah-vaah-dhah?	ඔබ ... විකුණනවාද?
dictionaries	shahb-dhah-koh-shah	ශබ්දකෝෂ
envelopes	li-pi kah-vah-rah	ලිපි කවර
maps...	... si-thi-yahm	... සිතියම්
city	nah-gah-rah-yeh	නගරයේ
regional	praah-dheh-shee-yah	පාදේශීය
road	maahr-gah	මාර්ග
magazines	sahn-gah-raah	සඟරා
newspapers	(in-gree-si)	(ඉංගීසි)
(in English)	pu-wahth-pahth	පුවත්පත්
paper	kah-dah-dhaah-si	කඩදාසි
pens	paan	පෑන්
postcards	pohst kaahd	පෝස්ට් කාඩ්
stamps	mudh-dhah-rah	මුද්දර

MUSIC සංගීතය

I'm looking for a ... CD.
mah-mah so-yahn-neh
... see-dee e-kahk
මම සොයන්නේ ... සි.ඩි. එකක්.

Do you have any (traditional) music?
o-bah lahn-gah
(sahm-prah-dhaah-yee)
sahn-gee-thah mu-kuth
thi-ye-nah-vaah-dhah?
ඔබ ළඟ (සම්පදායි) සංගීත මුකුත් තියෙනවාද?

I heard a band/singer called ...
... nahm vaah-dhah-kah
mahn-dah-lah-yah-kah-tah/
gaah-yah-kah-ye-ku-tah
mah-mah sah-vahn dhun-naah
... නම් වාදක මණ්ඩලයකට/ ගායකයෙකුට මම සවන් දුන්නා.

Can I listen to this CD here?
meh see-dee e-kah mah-tah
ah-hahn-nah ha-ki-dhah?
මේ සි.ඩි. එක මට අහන්න හැකිද?

I need a blank tape.
mah-tah his tehp e-kahk
oh-neh
මට හිස් ටේප් එකක් ඕනේ.

PHOTOGRAPHY

ජායාරූප ශිල්පය

How much is it to develop this film?
   meh pi-too-rah sudh-dhah
   kah-rahn-nah kee-yah-dhah?

මේ පින්තූර සුද්ද
කරන්න කියද?

When will it be ready?
   e-kah laas-thi ven-neh
   kah-vah-dhaah-dhah?

එක ලෑස්ති වෙන්නේ
කවදාද?

I'd like a film for this camera.
   mah-tah meh ka-mah-raah-vah-tah
   rohl e-kahk oh-neh

මට මේ කැමරාවට
රෝල් එකක ඕනේ.

battery	ba-tah-ri e-kah	බැටරි එක
B&W film	kah-lu su-du rohl e-kahk	කළු සුදු රෝල් එකක්
camera	ka-mah-raah-vah	කැමරාව
colour film	kah-lah rohl e-kahk	කලර් රෝල් එකක්
film	film rohl e-kah	ෆිල්ම් රෝල් එක
flash	flash e-kah	ෆ්ලෑෂ් එක
lens	kahn-naah-di-yah	කන්නාදිය
light meter	lait mee-tah-rah-yah	ලයිට් මීටරය
slides	slaid pah-ti	ස්ලයිඩ් පටි
videotape	vee-di-yoh pah-ti	විඩියෝ පටි

SMOKING

දුම්බීම

A packet of cigarettes, please.
   kah-ru-naah-kah-rah-lah
   si-gah-raht pa-kaht e-kahk
   dhen-nah

කරුණාකරල සිගරට්
පැකට් එකක් දෙන්න.

Do you have a light?
   o-bah lahn-gah gi-ni
   pet-ti-yahk thi-yeh-dhah?

ඔබ ළඟ ගිනි පෙට්ටියක්
තියේද?

Do you mind if I smoke?
   mah-mah dhum biv-vaah-tah
   kah-mahk nadh-dhah?

මම දුම් බිව්වාට
කමක් නැද්ද?

Please don't smoke.
   kah-ru-naah-kah-rah-lah
   dhum bon-nah e-paah

කරුණාකරල දුම්
බොන්න එපා.

SHOPPING

SIZES & COMPARISONS

ප්‍රමාණ සහ සැසඳුම්

a little bit	ti-kahk	ටිකක්
also	thah-vah-dhah	තවද
big	lo-kuy	ලොකුයි
enough	a-thi	ඇති
heavy	bah-rai	බරයි
light	sa-hal-luy	සැහැල්ලුයි
little (amount)	pod-dai/ti-kai	පොඩ්ඩයි/ටිකයි
many	go-dai	ගොඩයි
more	thah-vahth	තවත්
small	pun-chi	පුංචි
too much/many	go-daahk; bo-hoh va-di	ගොඩාක්; බොහෝ වැඩි

WEIGHTS & MEASURES

කිරුම් සහ මිනුම්

millimetre	mi-li-mee-tah-rah-yah	මිලිමීටරය
centimetre	sen-ti-mee-tah-rah-yah	සෙන්ටිමීටරය
metre	mee-tah-rah-yah	මීටරය
kilometre	ki-loh-mee-tah-rah-yah	කිලෝමීටරය
litre	ee-tah-rah-yah	ලිටරය
gram	graam e-kah	ග්‍රෑම් එක
100 grams	graam see-yahk	ග්‍රෑම් සීයක් kilo-
gram	ki-loh-graam e-kah	කිලෝග්‍රෑම් එක
half a kg	ki-loh-graam baah-gah-yahk	කිලෝග්‍රෑම් භාගයක්

Sri Lankan food is generally hot and spicy, but can be made less so (or even spiceless) on request. Traditionally, meat dishes are preferred, but there's a growing number of vegetarian options, thanks largely to the Hindu and Indian influence. Seafood is a great favourite, particularly along the south coast. Other popular cuisines include Chinese, Malaysian, Indonesian and Indian.

THROUGH THE DAY   දවස පුරා

Lunch is the main meal of the day and typically consists of rice and a meat or fish curry with one or two vegetables, a salad and/ or a green leafy vegetable.

At dinner, the family gets together for a sit-down meal followed by a chat. This may also be a rice and curry meal but people often choose common breakfast foods. Other dinner-time favourites include pasta, noodles and Western cuisine.

breakfast	u-dheh kaa-mah	උදේ කෑම
lunch	dhah-vahl kaa-mah	දවල් කෑම
dinner	raa kaa-mah	රෑ කෑම

Breakfast Food   උදේ කෑමට ගන්නා දේ

Popular breakfast choices include:

hoppers	aahp-pah	ආප්ප

like a flat pancake with crusty edges and a soft centre

kiribath	ki-ri-bahth	කිරිබත්

rice cooked in coconut milk, often cut into diamond-shaped portions

pittu	pit-tu	පිට්ටු

cylindrical cake of rice flour and grated coconut, steamed (usually in a bamboo mould)

roti	ro-tee	රොටී

doughy pancake that is fried without oil, often served wrapped around a variety of fillings

string hoppers	in-di aahp-pah	ඉදි ආප්ප

noodle-like strands of dough, tangled up to form a flat circle

125

FOOD

Other breakfast food includes:

boiled legumes/ yams	thahm-bah-pu a-tah/ ah-lah jaah-thi	තම්බපු ඇට/ අල ජාති
bread	paahn	පාන්
buns	bah-nis	බනිස්
rolls	rohls	රෝල්ස්

SNACKS අතුරුපස

Usually eaten mid-morning and mid-afternoon, snacks may be cakes, biscuits, pastries or other homemade delicacies.

biscuits	vis koh-thu	විස්කෝතු
cake	kehk	කේක්
cutlets (savouries)	kaht-lis	කට්ලිස්
patties	pa-tees	පැටිස්
rice cakes (deep-fried, sweet)	ka-vun	කැවුම්
muscat (sweet, made with ghee)	mahs-kaht	මස්කට්

EATING OUT පිට ගොස් ආහාර කෑම

Table for (five), please.
kah-ru-naah-kah-rah-lah
(pahs) dhe-ne-ku-tah
meh-sah-yahk oh-neh

කරුණාකරල (පස්)
දෙනෙකුට
මේසයක් ඕනේ.

May we see the menu?
me-noo e-kah bah-lahn-nah
pu-lu-vahn-dhah?

මෙනු එක බලන්න
පුළුවන්ද?

Could you recommend something?
mo-nah-vah-dhah hon-dhah
ki-yah-lah o-bah-tah
ki-yahn-nah pu-lu-vahn-dhah?

මොනවද හොඳ
කියල ඔබට
කියන්න පුළුවන්ද?

I'll have what they're having.
eh ah-yah kah-nah dheh
mah-mahth gahn-nahm

ඒ අය කන දේ
මමත් ගන්නම්.

What's in that dish?
eh dhee-si-yeh mo-nah-vah-dhah
thi-yen-neh?

ඒ දිසියේ මොනවද
තියෙන්නේ?

Please bring some ...

kah-ru-naah-kah-rah-lah	කරුණාකරල
... ti-kahk gehn-nah	... ටිකක් ගේන්න .

Do I get it myself or do they bring it to us?

e-kah mah-mah ah-rah-ge-nah	එක මම අරගෙන
en-nah oh-ne-dhah, nath-nahm	එන්න ඕනේද,
ah-pi lahn-gah-tah	නැත්නම් අපි
geh-nah-vaah-dhah?	ළඟට ගේනවාද?

FOOD

Please bring	kah-ru-naah-kah-rah-lah	කරුණාකරල
a/the ...	... gehn-nah	... ගෙනෙන්න .
bill	bi-lah	බිල
fork	gaa-rahp-pu-vahk	ගෑරප්පුවක්
glass of water	vah-thu-rah	වතුර
	vee-dhu-ru-vahk	විදුරුවක්
with ice	ais ek-kah	අයිස් එක්ක
without ice	ais na-thu-vah	අයිස් නැතුව
knife	pi-hi-yahk	පිහියක්
plate	pi-gaah-nahk	පිඟානක්

No ice in my drink, please.

kah-ru-naah-kah-rah-lah	කරුණාකරල මගේ
mah-ghe bee-mah e-kah-tah	බීම එකට අයිස්
ais dhah-mahn-nah e-paah	දමන්න එපා .

Is service included in the bill?

seh-vaah gaahs-thu	සේවා ගාස්තු බිලට
bi-lah-tah a-thu-lahth-dhah?	ඇතුළත්ද?

I love this dish.

meh vaahn-jah-nah-yah-tah	මේ වෑන්ජනයට මම
mah-mah hah-ri ka-mah-thiy	හරි කැමතියි .

We love the local cuisine.

me-heh kaa-mah vah-lah-tah	මෙහේ කෑම වලට
ah-pi hah-ri ka-mah-thiy	අපි හරි කැමතියි .

That was delicious!

eh-kah hah-ri-mah rah-sai!	ඒක හරිම රසයි!

Our compliments to the chef.

ah-rahk-ka-mi-tah	අරක්කැමිට අපේ
ah-peh prah-shahn-saah-wah	ප්‍රශංසාව .

FOOD

TYPICAL DISHES   විශේෂ ආහාර
kah-hah bahth   කහ බත්
'yellow rice', as it is commonly known, is rice cooked in a spicy coconut milk broth with a pinch of saffron or turmeric

bah-tu moh-ju   බටු මෝජු
fried eggplant, diced onion and green chillies cooked in a moderately sweet ground mustard vinaigrette

kah-ju kah-ri-yah   කජු කරිය
cashew nuts cooked in a thick white coconut sauce

po-los kah-ri-yah   පොළොස් කරිය
jackfruit cooked in a mild but spicy coconut sauce

am-bul-thi-yahl   ඇඹුල් තියල්
tuna braised in a gravy with go-rah-kaah (ගොරකා, an acidic fruit), which adds a tangy flavour

mahs ba-du-mah   මස් බැදුම
sliced beef boiled in vinaigrette, shallow-fried and served with onion rings and slit green chillies in a broth

mahs kah-ri-yah   මස් කරිය
diced meat (any type) in a rich, hot and spicy coconut sauce with lemongrass

ba-dhah-pu maah-lu   බැදපු මාළු
deep-fried fish, particularly Spanish mackerel, served with a dash of fresh lime/lemon juice

VEGETARIAN & SPECIAL MEALS

එළවළුමය සහ විශේෂ කෑම

FOOD

I'm vegetarian.
mah-mah e-lah-vah-lu
vi-thah-rai kahn-neh

මම එළවළු විතරයි කන්නේ.

I don't eat meat.
mah-mah mahs kahn-neh na-ha

මම මස් කන්නේ නැහැ.

I can't eat dairy products.
mah-tah ki-ri vah-lin ha-doo
kaa-mah kahn-nah ba-ha

මට කිරි වලින් හැදු කෑම කන්න බැහැ.

I don't eat chicken, fish or ham.
mah-mah ku-kul mahs,
maah-lu, hoh ham
kahn-neh na-ha

මම කුකුල් මස්, මාළු හෝ හැම් කන්නේ නැහැ.

Do you have any vegetarian dishes?
e-lah-vah-lu kaa-mah mu-kuth
thi-yeh-dhah?

එළවළු කෑම මුකුත් තියේද?

Does this dish contain eggs/meat?
meh-keh bith-thah-rah/mahs
thi-ye-nah-vaah-dhah?

මේකේ බිත්තර/මස් තියෙනවාද?

Can I get this without meat?
meh-kah mahs na-thu-vah
mah-tah gahn-nah ba-ri-dhah?

මේක මස් නැතුව මට ගන්න බැරිද?

I'm allergic to (peanuts).
mah-tah (rah-tah-kah-ju)
ah-pahth-ya-yi

මට (රටකජු) අපතයයි.

DON'T GO EMPTY-HANDED

When people visit each other in Sri Lanka, they take something along, eg, cake, biscuits or chocolate, or a gift for the child of the family – they never go empty-handed. Foreign visitiors should do the same.

FOOD

SELF-CATERING
In the Delicatessen

ස්වයං සේවා
ශීතකළ මස් මාංශ
අලෙවි හළ

Deli products, including local varieties of cheese and butter, are usually available in supermarkets. Some pharmacies and grocery shops carry a limited range as well.

How much is (a kilo of cheese)?
   (chees ki-loh e-kahk)
   kee-yah-dhah?

(චීස් කිලෝ එකක්)
කියද?

Do you have anything cheaper?
   mee-tah vah-daah mi-lah
   ah-du yah-mahk
   thi-ye-nah-vaah-dhah?

මීට වඩා මිළ
අ යමක්
තියෙනවාද?

What's the local speciality?
   me-heh vi-sheh-shah-yen
   hah-dhah-nah dheh
   mo-nah-vah-dhah?

මෙහේ විශේෂයෙන්
හදන දේ
මොනවාද?

Can I taste it?
   mah-mah rah-sah
   bah-lahn-nah-dhah?

මම රස බලන්නද?

Give me (half a kilo) please.
   kah-ru-naah-kah-rah
   mah-tah ki-loh
   (baah-gah-yahk) dhen-nah

කරුණාකර මට
කිලෝ (භාගයක්)
දෙන්න.

I'd like (six slices of ham).
   mah-tah (ham kaa-li hah-yahk)
   gah-thah ha-ki-dhah?

මට (හැම් කෑලි
හයක්) ගත හැකිද?

AT THE MARKET
Meat & Poultry

මාකට් එකේදී
මස සහ කුකුළු මස්

beef	hah-rahk mahs	හරක් මස්
chicken	ku-kul mahs	කුකුල් මස්
chop	mahs pe-thi	මස් පෙති
cured ham	pah-dahm kah-lah ham	පදම් කළ හැම්
elk meat	goh-nah mahs	ගෝන මස්
goat	e-lu mahs	එළු මස්

lamb	ba-tah-lu mahs	බැටළු මස්
meat	hah-rahk mahs	හරක් මස්
meatballs	mahs boh-lah	මස් බෝල
pork	oo-ru mahs	ඌරු මස්
rabbit	haah mahs	හා මස්
sausage	lin-gus	ලිංගුස්
steak	ba-dhu-mah-tah mahs	බැදුමට මස්
	pe-thi	පෙති
turkey	kah-lu-ku-maah	කලුකුමා
veal	vah-hu mahs	වහු මස්
venison	mu-wah mahs	මුව මස්
wild boar	vahl oo-ru mahs	වල් ඌරු මස්

Seafood මුහුදු මත්සායන්

clams	bel-laah	බෙල්ලා
fish	maah-lu	මාළු
lobster	po-ki-ris-saah	පොකිරිස්සා
mussels	math-ti-yaah	මට්ටියා
oysters	mu-thu bel-laah	මුතු බෙල්ලා
prawns	is-saah	ඉස්සා
shrimp	koo-nis-saah	කුනිස්සා

FOOD

VEG OUT!

dhahm-bah-lah	දඹල
dambala, frilled beans	
go-tu-ko-lah	ගොටුකොළ
gotu kola, leafy, similar to watercress	
kahn-kun	කන්කුන්
kankun, similar to watercress, but with long slim leaves	
kah-thu-ru mu-run-gaah	කතුරු මුරුංගා
katuru murunga, leafy vegetable	
kah-thu-ru mu-run-gaah mahl	කතුරු මුරුංගා මල්
katuru murunga mal, flower of katuru murunga	
ko-hi-lah	කොහිල
kohila, stringy root vegetable	
ko-hi-lah dhah-lu	කොහිල දළු
kohila, leaf of kotila dalu	
mahn-gnok-kaah	මඤ්ඤොක්කා
manioc, yam, similar to sweet potato	
mu-ku-nu-wan-nah	මුකුනුවැන්න
mukunuwenna, very similar to watercress	
thahm-pah-laah	තම්පලා
thampala, leafy vegetable, like spinach	

Vegetables   එළවළු

artichoke	ah-lu	අළු
	soo-ri-yah-kaahn-thah	සූරියකාන්ත
ash plantain	a-lu ke-sel	අළු කෙසෙල්
asparagus	as-pa-rah-gahs	එස්පැරගස්
aubergine	wahm-bah-tu	වම්බටු
(green) beans	bohn-chi	බෝංචි
	(ko-lah paah-tah)	(කොළ පාට)
beetroot	beet-root	බීට්රූට්
bitter gourd	kah-rah-wi-lah	කරවිල
breadfruit	dhel	දෙල්

FOOD

butter beans	bah-tahr bohn-chi	බටර් බෝංචි
cabbage	goh-waah	ගෝවා
(red/green)	(rah-thu/ko-lah)	(රතු/කොළ)
capsicum	maah-lu mi-ris	මාළු මිරිස්
carrot	ka-raht	කැරට්
cauliflower	mahl goh-waah	මල් ගෝවා
celery	sal-dhi-ri	සැල්දිරි
cucumber	pi-pin-gnaah	පිපිඤ්ඤා
drumsticks	mu-run-gaah	මුරුංගා
eggplant	wam-bah-tu	වම්බටු
leeks	leeks	ලීක්ස්
lettuce	sah-laah-dhah ko-lah	සලාද කොළ
long beans	maa-kah-tah	මෑකරල්
mushrooms	hah-thu	හතු
okrah	bahn-dahk-kaah	බණ්ඩක්කා
onion	loo-nu	ලූනු
peas	pees-a-tah	පිස් ඇට
potato	ah-lah	අල
snake gourd	pah-thoh-lah	පතෝල
spinach	ni-vi-thi	නිවිති
spring onion	loo-nu-ko-lah	ලූණුකොළ
sweet potato	bah-thah-lah	බතල
tomato	thahk-kaah-li	තක්කාලි
zucchini	su-kee-ni	සුකිනී

Fruit   පලතුරු

Tropical fruits are in abundance in Sri Lanka and are enjoyed by both locals and tourists.

apple	a-pahl	ඇපල්
avocado	ah-li-peh-rah	අලිපේර
banana	ke-sel	කෙසෙල්
coconut	pol	පොල්
grapes	mi-dhi	මිදි
lemon	dhe-hi	දෙහි
mango	am-bah	අඹ

FOOD

mangosteen	man-gos-teen	මැන්ගොස්ටින්
melon	ko-mah-du	කොමො
orange	dho-dham	දොඩම්
pear	pe-yaahs	පෙයාස්
pineapple	an-naah-si	අන්නාසි
sapadila	sa-pah-dhil-laah	සැපදිල්ලා
strawberry	straw-be-rees	ස්ට්‍රෝබෙරිස්
watermelon	pa-ni ko-mo-du	පැණි කොමො

Nuts මදැ'ති ගෙඩි

almond	rah-tah kot-than	රට කොට්ටන්
blanched	sud-dah kah-rah, ka-abh-li	ශුද්ධ කර, කැබලි
	vah-lah-tah ka-doo	වලට කැඩූ
raw	ah-mu	අමු
roasted	rohst kah-lah	රෝස්ට් කළ
cashew nut	kah-ju pu-hu-lahn	කජු පුහුලන්
peanut	rah-tah kah-ju	රට කජු

GOING BANANAS!

Don't go ape over by the many varieties of banana in Sri Lanka:

aah-nah-maah-lu ආනමාළු
  long, dark green and not very sweet
koh-li-kut-tu කෝලිකුට්ටු
  short, fat and yellow
am-bun ඇම්බුන්
  long, light green and not very sweet
see-ni සිනි
  small, yellow and sweet
rah-bahr රබර්
  similar to see-ni, but rubbery
su-vahn-del සුවඳැල්
  tiny and yellow, with medicinal properties
poo-vaah-lu සුවාළු
  medium, yellow and not very sweet
am-bul ඇඹුල්
  medium, yellow and sweet (most common)
rath ke-hel රත් කෙහෙල්
  red in colour, thick and not very sweet

FOOD

Pulses　ධාන්‍ය වර්ග

cereal	see-ri-yahl	සිරියල්
chickpeas	kah-dah-lah	කඩල
kidney beans	maa a-tah	මෑ ඇට
lentils	pah-rip-pu	පරිප්පු
lima beans	lee-mah bohn-chi	ලිමා බෝංචි
rice	haahl	හාල්

Spices & Condiments　කුළුබඩු සහ තුනපහ

chillies	mi-ris	මිරිස්
coriander	koth-thah-mahl-lee	කොත්තමල්ලි
cummin	soo-dhu-ru	සුදුරු
fennel	mah-hah-dhu-ru	මහදුරු
fenugreek	u-lu-haahl	උළුහාල්
garlic	su-dhu-loo-nu	සුදුළුණු
ginger	in-gu-ru	ඉඟුරු
salt	lu-nu	ලුනු

DRINKS　බීම වර්ග
Non-Alcoholic Drinks　අමද්‍යප බීම වර්ග

Sri Lankans are great tea-drinkers and are renowned for having many cups of tea throughout the day.

coffee	koh-pi	කෝපි
cocoa	ko-koh	කොකෝ
ginger beer	jin-jah bi-yah	ජින්ජර් බියර්
lemonade	le-mah-nehd	ලෙමනේඩ්
orange barley	or-rehn-j baah-li	ඔරේන්ජ් බාර්ලි
portello (fizzy drink)	poh-te-loh	පෝටෙලෝ
(cup of) tea	theh (kohp-pah-yahk)	තේ (කෝප්පයක්)
with/without milk	ki-ri ek-kah/ na-thu-wah	කිරි එක්ක/ නැතුව
with/without sugar	see-ni ek-kah/ na-thu-wah	සිනි එක්ක/ නැතුව

FOOD

water	wah-thu-rah	වතුර
boiled water	u-thu-raah-gahth	උතුරාගත්
	wah-thu-rah	වතුර
mineral water	si-sil bee-mah	සිසිල් බීම

Alcoholic Drinks මද්‍යප බීම වර්ග

beer	bi-yahr	බියර්
brandy	bran-di	බ්‍රැන්ඩි
champagne	sham-pehn	ෂැම්පේන්
cocktail	kok-tehl	කොක්ටේල්
rum	rahm	රම්
toddy	raah	රා
whisky	wis-ki	විස්කි

a bottle/glass	... wain	... වයින්
of ... wine	boh-thah-lah-yahk/	බෝතලයක්/
	vee-du-ru-wahk	වීදුරුවක්
red	rah-thu	රතු
rose	rohs	රෝස්
sparkling	bu-bu-lu nahn-vah-nah	බුබුළු නංවන
sweet	pa-ni rah-sah	පැණි රස
white	su-dhu	සුදු

a ... of beer	bi-yahr ...	බියර් ...
small bottle	po-di boh-thah-lah-yahk	පොඩි බෝතලයක්
large bottle	lo-ku boh-thah-layahk	ලොකු බෝතලයක්
small glass	po-di vee-dhu-ru-wahk	පොඩි වීදුරුවක්
tall glass	u-sah vee-dhu-ru-vahhk	උස වීදුරුවක්
jug	jog-gu-waks	ජෝග්ගුවක්

| a shot | wis-ki ah-di-yahk | විස්කි අඩියක් |
| of whisky | | |

IN THE COUNTRY

Some of Sri Lanka's most beautiful spots are in the country – if you have the time, head out of the cities and into nature.

CAMPING කඳවුරු බැඳි නවාතැන්

Is there a campsite nearby?
kahn-dhah-vu-ru ban-dhah
in-nah tha-nahk lahn-gah
ath-dhah?
කඳවුරු බැඳ
ඉන්න තැනක් ළඟ
ඇතද?

Do you have any sites available?
his bhoo-mi sthaah-nah
ki-si-vahk thi-yeh-dhah?
හිස් භූමි ස්ථාන
කිසිවක් තියේද?

How much is it per ...?	... kee-yahk veh-dhah?	... කියක් වේද?
person නකුට	ek ke-ne-ku-tah	එක් කෙ
tent mah-kah-tah කුඩාරමකට	tent koo-daah-rah-	koo-daah-rah-
vehicle	vaah-hah-nah-yah-kah-tah	වාහනයකට

Where can I hire a tent?
koo-daah-rah-mahk ku-li-yah-tah
gahn-nah pu-lu-vahn
ko-hen-dhah?
කුඩාරමක්
කුලියට ගන්න
පුළුවන් කොහෙන්ද?

Are there shower facilities?
naahn-nah pah-hah-su-kahm
thi-yeh-dhah?
නාන්න පහසුකම්
තියේද?

Can we camp here?
ah-pah-tah me-thah-nah
kahn-dhah-vu-ru ban-dhah
gahn-nah pu-lu-vahn-dhah?
අපට මෙතන
කඳවුරු බැඳ ගන්න
පුළුවන්ද?

IN THE COUNTRY

HIKING　　　　　　　පා ගමනින් යෑම

Although hiking isn't particularly popular with Sri Lankans, it's becoming increasingly popular with tourists.

Getting Information　　තොරතුරු ලබාගැනීම

Where can I find out about hiking
trails in the region?
   pah-laah-theh paah gah-mahn　　පළාතේ පා ගමන් මාර්ග
   maahr-gah ga-nah mah-mah　　ගැන මම දැනගන්නේ
   dha-nah-gahn-neh ko-hen-dhah?　　කොහෙන්ද?

Do we need a guide?
   gaid ke-nek ah-pah-tah　　ගයිඩ් කෙනෙක් අපට
   oh-neh veh-dhah?　　ඕනේ වේද?

How long is the trail?
   meh maahr-gah-yah　　මේ මාර්ගය
   koch-chah-rah dhu-rah-dhah?　　කොච්චර දුරද?

Is the track (well-)marked?
   mah-gah sah-lah-ku-nu　　මහ සලකුණු (හොඳට)
   (hon-dhah-tah) kah-rah ath-dhah?　　කර ඇත්ද?

How high is the climb?
   nag-mah koch-chah-rah　　නැග්ම කොච්චර උසද?
   u-sah-dhah?

Which is the easiest route?
   pah-hah-su-mah maahr-gah-yah　　පහසුම මාර්ගය
   mo-kahk-dhah?　　මොකක්ද?

Is the path open?
   eh maahr-gah-yah　　ඒ මාර්ගය ඇරලද?
   a-rah-lah-dhah?

When does it get dark?
   kah-lu-vah-rah ven-neh　　කළුවර වෙන්නේ
   koi veh-laah-vah-tah-dhah?　　කොයි වේලාවටද?

Where can we buy supplies?
   ah-pah-tah ah-vahsh-yah　　අපට අවශ්‍ය බ
   bah-du gahn-neh ko-hen-dhah?　　ගන්නේ කොහෙන්ද?

On the Path

මහ තොටදි

Where have you come from?
o-bah ko-heh si-tah-dhah
aah-veh?

ඔබ කොහේ සිටද
ආවේ?

How long did it take you?
o-bah-tah koch-chah-rah
ve-laah gahth-thah-dhah?

ඔබට කොච්චර
වෙලා ගත්තද?

Does this path go to ...?
meh paah-rah ...-tah
yah-nah-vah-dhah?

මේ පාර ...ට
යනවද?

I'm lost.
mah-mah ah-thah-rah-mahng
ve-laah

මම අතරමං වෙලා.

IN THE COUNTRY

NEEDLES & PINS

Don't pass pins or needles directly to anyone, as it's believed it will affect your friendship adversely. If you need to give anyone a pin or a needle, just place it in front of them.

Where can we spend the night?
ah-pi raa gah-thah kah-rahn-neh
ko-heh-dhah?

අප රෑ ගත
කරන්නේ කොහේද?

Can I leave some things here for a while?
mah-geh bah-du ti-kahk ti-kah
ve-laah-vah-kah-tah me-heh
thi-yahn-nah pu-lu-vahn-dhah?

මගේ බඩු ටිකක්
ටික වෙලාවකට
මෙහේ තියන්න
පුළුවන්ද?

Can we go through here?
meh hah-rah-haah ah-pi-tah
yah-nah pu-lu-vahn-dhah?

මේ හරහා අපට
යන්න පුළුවන්ද?

Is the water OK to drink?
meh wah-thu-rah bon-nah
hon-dhah-dhah?

මේ වතුර බොන්න
හොඳද?

AT THE BEACH

මුහුදු වෙරළේදි

Can we swim here?
ah-pah-tah me-thah-nah
pi-hi-nahn-nah pu-lu-vahn-dhah?
අපට මෙතන
පිහිනන්න පුළුවන්ද?

Is it safe to swim here?
me-thah-nah pi-hi-nahn-nah
aah-rahk-shaah sah-hi-thah-dhah?
මෙතන පිහිනන්න
ආරක්ෂා සහිතද?

What time is high/low tide?
wah-dah-dhi-yah/baah-dhi-yah
a-thi vahn-neh
koi veh-laah-vah-lah-dhah?
වඩදිය/බාදිය ඇති
වන්නේ කොයි
වේලාවලද?

Is there a beach near here?
mu-hu-du ve-rah-lahk
meh kit-tu-wah ath-dhah?
මුහුදු වෙරළක්
මේ කිට්ටුව ඇත්ද?

How much for a/an ...?	...-tah gah-nah-nah kee-yah-dhah?	...ට ගණන කියද?
chair	pu-tu-wah	පුටුව
hut	pal-pah-thah	පැල්පත
umbrella	ku-dah-yah	කුඩය

beach	ve-rah-lah	වෙරළ
coast	ve-rah-lah-bah-dah	වෙරළබඩ
coral	hi-ri-gah	හිරිගල්
fishing	maah-lu baa-ma	මාළු බෑම
lagoon	kah-lah-pu-wah	කලපුව
ocean	saah-gah-rah-yah	සාගරය
reef	gahl pah-rah	ගල් පර
rock	gahl pahr-wah-thah	ගල් පර්වත
sand	wa-li	වැලි
sea	mu-hu-dhah	මුහුද
sunglasses	ahv-kahn-naah-di	අව්කන්නාඩි
surf	rah-la pe-nah	රළ පෙණ
surfing	rah-lah pa-dhee-mah	රළ පැදීම
swimming	pi-hi-nee-mah	පිහිනීම
towel	thu-waah-yah	තුවාය
waves	rah-lah	රළ

Diving

කිමිදීම්

Are there good diving sites here?
ki-mi-dhen-nah hon-dah
thahn me-heh thi-yeh-dhah?

කිමිදෙන්න හොඳ
තැන් මෙහේ තියේද?

Can we hire a diving boat/guide?
ki-mi-dhen-nah yahn-nah
boht-tu-wahk/
u-pah-dheh-sahh-kah-yek
ah-pah-tah gahn-nah
pu-lu-vahn-dhah?

කිමිදෙන්න යන්න
බෝට්ටුවක්/
උපදේශකයෙක්
අපට ගන්න
පුළුවන්ද?

We'd like to hire diving equipment.
ki-mi-dhum u-pah-kah-rah-nah
ku-li-yah-tah gahn-nah
ah-pah-tah pu-lu-vahn-dhah?

කිමිදුම් උපකරණ
කුලියට ගන්න
අපට පුළුවන්ද?

I'm interested in exploring wrecks.
sun-bun gah-veh-shah-nah-yah
kah-rahn-nah mah-mah
ka-mah-thiy

සුන්බුන් ගවේෂණය
කරන්න මම
කැමතියි.

IN THE COUNTRY

Aquatic Creatures

ජලජ සත්වයන්

crab	kah-ku-lu-waah	කකුළුවා
dolphin	dol-fin	ඩොල්ෆින්
	mahth-syah-yaah	මත්සයයා
eel	aahn-dhaah	ආදා
fish (pl)	maah-lu	මාළු
lobster	po-ki-ris-sa	පොකිරිස්සා
ray	reh mahth-syah-yaah	රේ මත්සයයා
seal	seel mahth-syah-yaah	සිල් මත්සයයා
shark	moh-raah	මෝරා
shellfish	kah-bah-lu	කබලු
	mahth-syah-yaah	මත්සයයා
turtle	kas-baa-waah	කැස්බෑවා
whale	thahl-mah-hah	තල්මහ

IN THE COUNTRY

WEATHER දේශගුණය

What's the weather like?
dheh-shah-gu-nah-yah
ko-ho-mah-dah?

දේශගුණය
කොහොමද ?

Today it's ...	ah-dhah nahm ...	අද නම් ...
cloudy	kah-lu kah-rah-lah	කළු කරල
cold	see-thah-lai	සීතලයි
hot	rahs-nei	රස්නෙයි
warm	ush-nai	උෂ්ණයි
windy	hu-lahn-gai	හුළහයි

Will it be ... tomorrow?	he-tah ...-dhah?	හෙට ...ද ?
cloudy	kah-lu kah-raah-vi	කළු කරාවි
cold	see-thah-lah-veh	සීතලවේ
hot	rahs-neh-veh	රස්නේ
warm	ush-nah-veh	උෂ්ණාවේ
windy	hu-lahn-gah thi-yeh	හුළහ තියේ

It's raining.
dhan vah-hi-nah-vaah

දැන් වහිනවා .

The weather is fine/bad today.
ah-dhah kaah-lah-gu-nah-yah
hon-dhai/nah-rah-kai

අද කාලගුණය
හොඳයි/නරකයි .

It's sunny.
dhan av-vai

දැන් අව්වයි .

Tomorrow it's supposed to be cooler.
he-tah vah-daaht
see-thah-lai-lu

හෙට වඩාත්
සීතලයිලු .

bright	hah-ri e-li-yai	හරි එළියයි
cold	see-thah-lai	සීතලයි
cloudy	vah-laah-ku-len va-hi-laah	වලාකුලෙන් වැහිලා
dry season	vi-yah-li kaah-lah-yah	වියළි කාලය

floods	gahn wah-thu-rah	ගං වතුර
foggy	mee-dhu-men va-hi-laah	මීදුමෙන් වැහිලා
frosty	hi-mah sah-hi-thai	හිම සහිතයි
misty	mee-dhum sah-hi-thai	මීදුම් සහිතයි
monsoon season	moh-sahm kaah-lah-yah	මෝසම් කාලය
overcast	ah-hah-sah kah-lu kah-rah-lah	අහස කළු කරල
raining	vah-hi-nah-vaah	වහිනවා
rainy season	vas-sah kaah-leh	වැස්ස කාලේ
snowing	hi-mah va-te-nah-vaah	හිම වැටෙනවා
spitting	po-dah gah-hah-nah-vaah	පොද ගහනවා
storm	ku-naah-tu-wah	කුණාටුව
sun/sunny	av-wah/av-vai	අව්ව/අව්වයි
typhoon	su-li-su-lahng	සුළිසුළං
windy	hu-lahn-gai	හුළඟයි

GEOGRAPHICAL TERMS   භූගෝලික වචන

bridge	paah-lah-mah	පාලම
cave	gu-haah-wah	ගුහාව
cliff	kahn-du prah-paah-thah-yah	කඳු ප්‍රපාතය
earthquake	bhoo-mi kahm-paah-wah	භූමි කම්පාව
farm	go-vi-pah-lah	ගොවිපළ
footpath	ah-di paah-rah	අඩි පාර
forest	ka-laa-wah	කැලෑව
harbour	wah-raah-yah	වරාය
hill	kahn-dhah	කන්ද
hot springs	u-nu dhi-yah ling	උණු දිය ලිං
island	dhi-vah-yi-nah	දිවයින
lake	wa-wah	වැව
mountain	kahn-dhah	කන්ද
peak	mu-dhu-nah	මුදුන
river	gahn-gah	ගඟ
sea	mu-hu-dhah	මුහුද
valley	tha-ni-thah-laah-wah	තැනිතලාව
waterfall	dhi-yah al-lah	දිය ඇල්ල

IN THE COUNTRY

IN THE COUNTRY

FAUNA

සත්ව වර්ගයා

What animal is that?
  ah-rah mo-nah sah-thaah-dhah?   අර මොන සතාද?

What do you call that animal?
  ah-rah sah-thaah-tah
  mo-kaahk-dhah ki-yahn-neh?   අර සතාට මොකක්ද
  කියන්නේ?

Domestic Creatures ගෘහස්ත සතුන්

bird	ku-rul-laah	කුරුල්ලා
buffalo	mee hah-rah-kaah	මී හරකා
calf	wah-hu pa-ti-yaah	වහු පැටියා
cat	bah-lah-laah/poo-saah	බළලා/පූසා
chicken	ku-ku-lu pa-ti-yaah	කුකුළු පැටියා
cow	e-lah-dhe-nah	එළදෙන
dog	bahl-laah	බල්ලා
donkey	boo-ru-waah	බූරුවා
duck	thaah-raah-waah	තාරාවා
goat	e-lu-waah	එළුවා
hen	ki-ki-lee	කිකිළී
horse	ahsh-wah-yaah	අශ්වයා
ox	hah-rah-kaah/go-naah	හරකා/ගොනා
pig	oo-raah	ඌරා
rooster	ku-ku-laah	කුකුළා
sheep	ba-tah-lu-waah	බැටළුවා

Wildlife වන සතුන්

ant	koom-bi-yaah	කුම්බියා
bee	mee mas-saah	මී මැස්සා
bird	ku-rul-laah	කුරුල්ලා
butterfly	sah-mah-nah-lah-yaah	සමනළයා
cockroach	ka-rah-poth-thaah	කැරපොත්තා
crocodile	kim-bu-laah	කිඹුලා
deer	mu-vaah	මුවා
elephant	ah-li-yaah	අලියා
elk	goh-naah	ගෝනා
fish	maah-lu	මාළු
fly	mas-saah	මැස්සා
frog	gem-baah	ගෙම්බා
game (animals)	dha-dah mas	දඩ මස්
hare	haah-vaah	හාවා
iguana	thah-lah-go-yaah	තලගොයා
leech	koo-dal-laah	කූඩැල්ලා

IN THE COUNTRY

leopard	dhi-vi-yaah	දිවියා
lion	sin-hah-yaah	සිංහයා
monkey	wahn-dhu-raah	වඳුරා
mosquito	mah-dhu-ru-waah	මදුරුවා
mouse	mee-yaah	මියා
snail	go-lu-bel-laah	ගොළුබෙල්ලා
snake	nah-yaah	නයා
spider	mah-ku-lu-waah	මකුළුවා
squirrel	leh-naah	ලේනා
tiger	ko-ti-yaah	කොටියා
wild boar	vahl-oo-raah	වල් ඌරා

FLORA & AGRICULTURE

ගස් කොළං සහ කෘෂිකර්මය

What tree/plant/flower is that?
    eh mo-nah gah-hahk-dhah/
    pa-lah-yahk-dhah/mah-lahk-dhah?
ඒ මොන ගහක්ද/
පැලයක්ද/මලක්ද?

What's it used for?
    eh-kah paah-vich-chi
    kah-rahn-neh mo-kah-tah-dhah?
ඒක පාවිච්චි
කරන්නේ මොකටද?

Can you eat the fruit?
    eh ge-di kahn-nah
    pu-lu-vahn-dhah?
ඒ ගෙඩි කන්න
පුළුවන්ද?

coconut	pol	පොල්
date	rah-tah in-di	රට ඉඳි
eucalyptus	yoo-kah-lip-tahs	යුකලිප්ටස්
camphor	kah-pu-ru	කපුරු
oak	sin-doo-rah	සින්දුර
palm	thahl	තල්
pine	pain gahs	පයින් ගස්

Herbs, Flowers & Crops

ඖෂධ, මල් සහ වගා

agriculture	kru-shi-kahr-mah-yah	කෘෂිකර්මය
arecanut	pu-wahk	පුවක්
bougainvillea	boh-gahn-wi-laah	බෝගන්විලා
cardamom	e-nah-saahl	එනසාල්
cinnamon	ku-run-dhu	කුරුඳු
cloves	kah-raah-bu na-ti	කරාබු නැටි
cocoa	ko-koh	කොකෝ
coconut palm	pol	පොල්
coffee	koh-pi	කෝපි
corn	i-rin-gu	ඉරිඟු
crops	vah-gaah	වගා
flower	mahl	මල්
grapevine	mi-dhi va-lah	මිදි වැල
harvest (noun)	ahs-van-nah	අස්වැන්න
irrigation	vaah-ri-maahr-gah	වාරිමාර්ග
jasmine	pich-chah	පිච්ච
kitul palm	ki-thul	කිතුල්
lavender	sa-van-dhah-raah	සැවැන්දරා
leaf	ko-lah-yah	කොළය
lemon tree	dhe-hi gah-hah	දෙහි ගහ
orchard	pah-lah-thu-ru	පළතුරු
orange tree	dho-dhahm gah-hah	දොඩම් ගහ
planting/sowing	si-tu-vee-mah/ va-pi-ree-mah	සිටුවීම/ වැපිරීම

IN THE COUNTRY

MILK OF THE GODS

When planted in the front garden, trees that release milky substances are said to bring good fortune to the house and its inhabitants.

IN THE COUNTRY

palm trees	thaah-lah	තාල වර්ගයේ
	vahr-gah-yeh gahs	ගස්
pepper	gahm-mi-ris	ගම්මිරිස්
rice field/paddy	kum-bu-rah	කුඹුර
sunflower	soo-ri-yah kaahn-thah	සූරිය කාන්ත
sugar cane	uk-gahs	උක්ගස්
talipot palm	thahl	තල්
tea	theh	තේ
tea estate	theh wahth-thah	තේ වත්ත
terraced land	te-rahs i-dahm	ටෙරස් ඉඩම්
tobacco	dhum-ko-lah	දුම්කොළ
tree	gah-hah	ගහ
vineyard	mi-dhi wahth-thah	මිදි වත්ත
wheat	thi-rin-gu	තිරිඟු

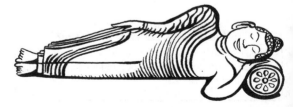

Western-style medicine is practised throughout Sri Lanka and public hospitals offer free service to all. Private hospitals can also be found, and some hospitals function both privately and publicly.

AT THE DOCTOR   වෛද්‍ය ශලාපාගාරයේදී

I'm sick.
mah-tah sah-nee-pah na-ha
(lit: to-me well not) — මට සනීප නැහැ.

My friend is sick.
mah-geh yah-hah-lu-waah-tah
sah-nee-pah na-ha — මගේ යහළුවාට සනීප නැහැ.

I need a doctor (who speaks English).
(in-gree-si kah-thaah kah-rah-nah)
dhos-thah-rah ke-nek mah-tah
oh-neh — (ඉංග්‍රීසි කථා කරන) දොස්තර කෙනෙක් මට ඕනේ.

Could the doctor come here?
dhos-thah-rah-tah me-heh
en-nah pu-lu-vahn-dhah? — දොස්තරට මෙහේ එන්න පුළුවන්ද?

Where's the nearest ...?	lahn-gah-mah a-thi ... ko-heh-dhah thi-yen-neh?	ළඟම ඇති ... කොහේද තියෙන්නේ?
chemist	in-gree-si be-heth saahp-pu-wah	ඉංග්‍රීසි බෙහෙත් සාප්පුව
dentist	dhahth dos-thah-rah	දත් දොස්තර
doctor	dhos-thah-rah	දොස්තර
hospital	roh-hah-lah	රෝහල

AILMENTS   අසනීප

I'm ill.
mah-tah ah-sah-nee-pai — මට අසනීපයි.

I've been vomiting.
mah-tah vah-mah-nah-yah yah-nah-vaah — මට වමනය යනවා.

I can't sleep.
mah-tah nin-dhah
yahn-neh na-ha

මට නින්ද යන්නේ
නැහැ.

It hurts here.
me-thah-nah ri-dhe-nah-vaah

මෙතන රිදෙනව.

I have (a/an) ...	mah-tah ...	මට ...
	thi-ye-nah-vaah	තියෙනවා.
I've had (a/an) ...	mah-tah ... thi-bu-naah	මට ... තිබුණා.
allergy	a-lah-ji e-kahk	ඇලජි එකක්
anaemia	leh ah-du kah-mahk	ලේ අ කමක්
blister	bi-bi-lah	බිබිළ
bronchitis	u-gu-reh ah-maah-ru-wah	උගුරේ අමාරුව
burn	dha-vil-lah	දැවිල්ල
cancer	pi-li-kaah-wah	පිළිකාව
chicken pox	pa-po-lah	පැපොල
cold	hem-bi-ris-saah-wah	හෙම්බිරිස්සාව
constipation	bah-dhah veh-lee-mah	බඩ වේලීම
cough	kas-sah	කැස්ස
cramp	ken-dah pe-rah-lee-mah	කෙණ්ඩ පෙරළීම
diarrhoea	bah-dah bu-rul vee-mah	බඩ බුරුල් වීම
fever	u-nah	උණ
gastroenteritis	bah-dah-val i-dhi-mu-mah	බඩවැල් ඉදිමුම
glandular fever	grahn-thee-yah u-nah	ග්‍රන්ථිය උණ
hayfever	pee-nahs roh-gah-yah	පීනස් රෝගය
headache	hi-sah rah-dhah-yah	හිස රදය
heart	pa-pu-weh	පපුවේ
condition	ah-maah-ru-wah	අමාරුව
hepatitis	he-pah-tai-tis	හෙපටයිටිස්
indigestion	ah-jeer-nah-yah	අජීර්ණය
infection	bo-we-nah yah-mahk	බෝවෙන යමක්
inflammation	dha-vil-lah sah-hi-thah	දැවිල්ල සහිත ඉදිමුම
	i-dhi-mu-mah	
influenza	sem-prah-thish-yaah	සෙම්ප්‍රතිශ්‍යා
	u-nah	උණ
lice	u-ku-nahn	උකුණන්

lump	gu-li-yahk	ගුලියක්
migraine	mai-grehn	මයිග්‍රෙන්
	hi-sah-rah-dhah-yah	හිසරදය
pain	kahk-ku-mah	කැක්කුම
rash	raahsh e-kah; dhah-dhah	රෑෂ් එක; දද
sore throat	u-gu-rah ba-rahn-di-yah	උගුර බැරන්ඩිය
sprain	u-luk-ku-wah	උළුක්කුව
stomachache	bah-deh kak-ku-mah	බඩේ කැක්කුම
sunburn	av-vah-tah	අව්වට
	pich-chee-mah	පිච්චීම
travel sickness	gah-mahn	ගමන්
	ki-ree-meh-dee	කිරීමේදි
	a-thi-wah-nah	ඇතිවන
	vah-mah-nah-yah	වමනය
urinary infection	mu-thraah roh-gah	මුත්‍රා රෝග
venereal disease	mai-thoo-nah roh-gah	මයිතුන රෝග
worms	pah-nu ah-maah-ru-wah	පණු අමාරුව

I feel ...   mah-tah ...   මට ...
   dizzy   ka-rah-kil-lai   කැරකිල්ලයි
   shivery   vev-lah-nah-vaah   වෙව්ලනවා
   nauseous   ok-kaah-rah-yah vah-geh   ඔක්කාරය
වගේ
   weak   dhur-vah-lai vah-geh   දුර්වලයි වගේ

I feel better/worse.
   dhan mah-tah hon-dhai/   දැන් මට හොඳයි/
   an-thai vah-geh   අන්තයි වගේ.

This is my usual medicine.
   meh mah-geh saah-maahn-yah   මේ මගේ සාමාන්‍ය
   be-he-thah   බෙහෙත.

I don't want a blood transfusion.
   mah-tah leh dhen-nah   මට ලේ දෙන්න
   oh-neh na-ha   ඕනෙ නැහැ.

Can I have a receipt for my insurance?
   mah-geh rahk-shah-nah-yah-tah   මගේ රක්ෂණයට
   ri-seet e-kahk gahn-nah   රිසිට් එකක් ගන්න

HEALTH

HEALTH

THEY MAY SAY ...

mo-kah-dhah vu-neh?	මොකද වුනේ?
What's the matter?	
o-bah-tah kak-ku-mah dha-ne-nah-vaah-dhah?	ඔබට කැක්කුම දැනෙනවාද?
Do you feel any pain?	
ko-heh-dhah ri-dhen-neh?	කොහේද රිදෙන්නේ?
Where does it hurt?	
o-bah-tah u-nah thi-yeh-dhah?	ඔබට උණ තියේද?
Do you have a temperature?	
me-heh-mah ve-laah dhan koch-chah-rah kahl-dhah?	මෙහෙම වෙලා දැන් කොච්චර කල්ද?
How long have you been like this?	
mee-tah kah-lin meh-kah ha-di-lah thi-yeh-dhah?	මීට කලින් මේක හැදිල තියේද?
Have you had this before?	
o-bah dhan be-heth bo-nah-vaah-dhah?	ඔබ දැන් බෙහෙත් බොනවාද?
Are you on medication?	
o-bah dhum bo-nah-vaah-dhah?	ඔබ දුම් බොනවාද?
Do you smoke?	
o-bah mahth-pan paah-vich-chi kah-rah-nah-vaah-dhah?	ඔබ මත්පැන් පාවිච්චි කරනවාද?
Do you drink?	
o-bah mahth drahv-yah paah-vich-chi kah-rah-nah-vaah-dhah?	ඔබ මත් දුවය පාවිච්චි කරනවාද?
Do you take drugs?	
o-bah mo-nah-vaah-tah hah-ri a-lah-jik-dhah?	ඔබ මොනවට හරි ඇලජික්ද?
Are you allergic to anything?	

WOMEN'S HEALTH

කාන්තා සෞඛ්‍යය

Could I see a female doctor?
mah-tah ga-hu-nu dhos-thah-rah
ke-nek bah-lahn-nah
pu-lu-vahn-dhah?

මට ගැහැණු
දොස්තර කෙනෙක්
බලන්න පුළුවන්ද?

I'm pregnant.
mah-mah ga-bi-niy

මම ගැබිණියි.

I think I'm pregnant.
mah-mah hi-thahn-neh
mah-mah ga-bi-niy ki-yaah

මම හිතන්නේ මම
ගැබිණියි කියා.

I'm on the pill.
mah-mah pe-thi paah-vich-chi
kah-rah-nah-vaah

මම පෙති පාච්චිචි
කරනවා.

I haven't had my period for ... weeks.
sah-thi ...-tah mah-tah o-sahp
vee-mah thi-bu-neh na-ha

සති ...ට මට ඔසප්
වීම තිබුණේ නැහැ.

I'd like to use contraception.
pi-li-si-dhee-mah va-lak-vee-meh
krah-mah paah-vich-chi
kah-rahn-nah mah-mah
ka-mah-thiy

පිළිසිදම
වැළැක්විමේ කුම
පාච්චිචි කරන්න මම
කැමතියි.

I'd like to have a pregnancy test.
gab ga-nee-meh
pah-reek-shah-nah-yahk
mah-tah kah-rah-gahn-nah
oh-neh

ගැබ් ගැනීමේ
පරීක්ෂණයක් මට
කරගන්න ඕනේ.

G'DAY!

If you come face to face with a pregnant woman,
you're supposed to have a good day.

abortion	gahb-saah-vah	ගබ්සාව
cystitis	oh-jahs sah-hi-thah	ඕජස් සහිත
	ge-di ni-saah	ගෙඩි නිසා
	mu-thraah-shah-yeh	මුත්‍රාශයේ
	i-dhi-mu-mah	ඉදිමුම
diaphragm	mah-haah	මහා ප්‍රාවිරය
	praah-chee-rah-yah	
IUD	ai-yoo-dee e-kah	අයි.යූ.ඩී. එක
mammogram	ma-moh-graam e-kah	මැමෝග්‍රම් එක
menstruation	o-sahp vee-mah	ඔසප් වීම
miscarriage	gahb-saah vee-mah	ගබ්සා වීම
pap smear	pap-smi-yah e-kah	පැප්ස්මිය එක
period pain	o-sahp ru-dhaah	ඔසප් රුදා
the Pill	peth-thah	පෙත්ත
premenstrual	o-sahp poor-vah	ඔසප් පූර්ව
tension	kah-lah-hah gah-thi-yah	කලහ ගතිය
thrush	ak-kaah-rah-mah	අක්කාරම
ultrasound	ah-thi dhvah-nee-yah	අති ද්වනිය
	shahb-dhah thah-rahn-gah	ශබ්ද තරංග

THEY MAY SAY ...

o-bah-tah dhan o-sahp vee-mah ath-dhah?	ඔබට දැන් ඔසප් විම ඇත්ද?
Are you menstruating?	
o-bah gahr-bah-nee-dhah?	ඔබ ගර්භනීද?
Are you pregnant?	
o-bah pi-li-si-dhee-mah va-lak-vee-mah-tah pe-thi gahn-nah-vaah-dhah?	ඔබ පිළිසිදීම වැළැක්වීමට පෙති ගන්නවාද?
Are you on the Pill?	

HEALTH

SPECIAL HEALTH NEEDS

විශේෂ සෞඛ්‍ය අවශ්‍යතා

I'm ...	mah-mah ... ath-thek	මම ... ඇත්තෙක්
anaemic	leh ah-du-paah-du	ලේ අපා
asthmatic	a-dhu-mah	ඇදුම
diabetic	dhi-yah-va-di-yaah-vah	දියවැඩියාව

I'm allergic to ...	mah-tah ... ah-pahth-thyai	මට ... අපත්‍යයි.
antibiotics	an-ti-bah-yah-tik	ඇන්ටිබයටික්
aspirin	as-prin	ඇස්ප්‍රින්
bees	mee mas-soh	මී මැස්සෝ
codeine	koh-deen	කෝඩීන්
dairy products	ki-ri aah-haah-rah	කිරි ආහාර
penicillin	pe-ni-si-lin	පෙනිසිලින්
pollen	mahl reh-nu	මල් රේණු

I have a skin allergy.
mah-geh hah-meh
ah-saahth-mi-kah gah-thi-yahk
thi-ye-nah-vaah

මගේ හමේ
අසාත්මික
ගතියක් තියෙනව.

I have high/low blood pressure.
mah-tah thi-yen-neh
ah-dhi-kah/ah-du ru-dhee-rah
pee-dah-nah-yah

මට තියෙන්නේ
අධික/අඩු රුධිර
පීඩනය.

I have a weak heart.
mah-geh hahr-dhah-yah
vahs-thu-wah hah-ri
dhur-vah-lai

මගේ හෘදය වස්තුව
හරි දුර්වලයි.

I've had my vaccinations.
mah-geh ahth en-nahth
kah-rah-lai thi-ye-neh

මගේ අත් එන්නත්
කරලයි තියෙන්නේ.

Is that a new syringe you're using?
o-bah meh paah-vich-chi
kah-rahn-neh ah-luth
si-rin-jah-rah-yahk-dhah?

ඔබ මේ පාච්චිච්
කරන්නේ අලුත්
සිරින්ජරයක්ද?

HEALTH

I have my own syringe.
mah-tah mah-geh
si-rin-jah-rah-yah
thi-ye-nah-vaah

මට මගේ සිරින්ජරය
තියෙනවා.

I'm on medication for ...
mah-mah ...-tah be-heth
bo-nah-vaah

මම ...ට බෙහෙත්
බොනවා.

I'm on a special diet.
mah-mah kahn-neh
vi-sheh-shah kaa-mah

මම කන්නේ විශේෂ
කෑම.

I need a new pair of glasses.
mah-tah ah-luth kahn-naah-di
kut-tah-mahk oh-neh

මට අළුත් කන්නාඩි
කුට්ටමක් ඕනේ.

addiction	ab-ba-hi vee-mah	ඇබ්බැහි වීම
bite	sah-paah kaa-mah	සපා කෑම
blood test	leh pah-reek-sha-nah-yah	ලේ පරීක්ෂණය
inhaler	u-rah-nah-yah	උරණය
injection	in-jek-shahn e-kah	ඉන්ජෙක්ෂන් එක
injury	ah-nah-thu-rah	අනතුර
pacemaker	pehs-meh-kah-rah-yah	පේස්මේකරය
wound	thu-waah-lah-yah	තුවාලය

HEALTH

PARTS OF THE BODY   ශාරීරික අවයව

My ... hurts.
mah-geh ... ri-dhe-nah-vaah

මගේ ... රිදෙනවා.

I have a pain in my ...
mah-geh ... kak-ku-mahk
thi-ye-nah-vaah

මගේ ... කැක්කුමක්
තියෙනවා.

I can't move my ...
mah-geh ... so-lah-vahn-nah
ba-ha

මගේ ... සොලවන්න
බැහැ.

English	Pronunciation	Sinhala
ankle	vah-lah-lu-kah-rah-yah	වළලුකරය
appendix	un-du-kah	උණ්ඩුක
	puch-chah-yah	පුච්ඡය
arm	baah-hu-wah	බාහුව
back	kon-dhah	කොන්ද
bladder	muth-thraah-shah-yah	මූතාශය
blood	leh	ලේ
bone	kah-tu	කටු
chest	pa-pu-wah	පපුව
ears	kahn	කන්
eye	a-ha	ඇහැ
finger	an-gil-lah	ඇඟිල්ල
foot	paah-dhah-yah	පාදය
hand	ah-thah	අත
head	o-lu-wah	ඔළුව
heart	hah-dhah-wah-thah	හදවත
jaw	hahk-kah	හක්ක
kidney	vah-ku-gah-du	වකුගඩු
knee	dhah-nah-hi-sah	දණහිස
leg	kah-ku-lah	කකුල
liver	ak-maah-wah	අක්මාව
lungs	pe-nah-hah-lu	පෙනහළු
mouth	kah-tah	කට
muscle	maahn-shah peh-sheen	මාංශ පේශින්
nose	nah-hah-yah/	නහය/
	naah-sah-yah	නාසය
ribs	i-lah a-tah	ඉළ ඇට
shoulders	u-rah-his	උරහිස්
skin	hah-mah	හම
spine	kon-dhah	කොන්ද
stomach	bah-dah	බඩ
teeth	dhahth	දත්
throat	u-gu-rah	උගුර
vein	nah-hah-rah	නහර

HEALTH

ALTERNATIVE TREATMENTS

විකල්ප වෙදකම්

Alternative treatments, including homeopathy and Ayurveda, are available at specialist medical clinics.

acupuncture	kah-tu chi-kith-saah-wah	කටු විකිත්සාව
aromatherapy	su-gahn-dhi-kah	සුගන්ධික
	he-dhah-kah-mah	හෙදකම
chiropractor	thu-nah-ti-yeh	තුනටියේ
	ve-dhah-kahm	වෙදකම්
	kah-rahn-naah	කරන්නා
faith healer	aah-gahm bhahk-thi-kah	ආගම් භක්තික
	he-dhah-kah-mah	හෙදකම
herbalist	au-shah-<u>dha</u>-veh-dhee	ඖෂධවේද
homeopathy	hoh-mi-yoh-pah-thy	හෝමියෝපති
	ve-dhah-kah-mah	වෙදකම
massage	mah-saahj e-kah	මසාජ් එක
meditation	bhaah-vah-naah ki-ree-mah	භාවනා කිරීම
naturopathy	swaah-baah-vi-kah	ස්වාභාවික
	krah-mah ve-dhah-kah-mah	කුම වෙදකම
reflexology	prah-thyaah-vahr-thi-thah	පුත්යාවර්තිත
	vi-dhyaah-vah	විද්යාව
yoga	yoh-gee vi-dhyaah-vah	යෝගී විද්යාව

AT THE CHEMIST

ඉංගීුසි බෙහෙත් සාප්පුවේදි

Is there an all-night chemist nearby?
raah-three be-heth
saahp-pu-wahk lahn-gah
thi-yeh-dhah?

රාතී බෙහෙත්
සාප්පුවක් ළඟ
තියේද?

I need something for ...
mah-tah ...-tah mo-nah-vaah
hah-ri oh-neh

මට ...ට මොනවා
හරි ඕනේ.

Do I need a prescription for ...?
...-tah be-heth thun-du-vahk
oh-ne-dhah?

...ට බෙහෙත්
තුන්වක් ඕනෙද?

HEALTH

I have a prescription.
 mah-tah be-heth thun-du-vahk   මට බෙහෙත්
 thi-yah-nah-vaah   තුන්වක් තියෙනවා .

How many times a day?
 dhah-vah-sah-tah kee   දවසට කී
 sa-rah-yahk-dhah?   සැරයක්ද ?

Twice a day (with food).
 dhah-vah-sah-tah dhe-sa-rah-yahk   දවසට දෙසරයක්
 (kaa-mah ek-kah)   (කෑම එක්ක) .

Can I drive on this medication?
 meh be-heth a-rah-ge-nah   මේ බෙහෙත්
 mah-tah e-lah-vahn-nah   අරගෙන මට
 pu-lu-vahn dhah?   එළවන්න පුළුවන්ද ?

Will it make me drowsy?
 meh be-he-thah-tah mah-tah   මේ බෙහෙතට මට
 ni-dhi-mah-thah ei-dhah?   නිදිමත එයිද ?

antibiotics	an-ti-bah-yah-tiks	ඇන්ටිබයටික්ස්
antiseptic	vi-shah naah-shah-kah	විෂ නාශක
aspirin	as-prin	ඇස්ප්‍රින්
bandage	ve-lum pah-ti	වෙළුම් පටි
Band-aids	ve-lum pah-ti thee-ru	වෙළුම් පටි තීරු
condoms	kon-dom pah-<u>thah</u>	කොන්ඩොම් පට
contraceptives	pi-li-si-dhee-mah	පිළිසිඳීම
	va-lak-vee-meh dheh-vahl	වැළැක්වීමේ දේවල්
cotton balls	pu-lun ka-bah-li boh-lah	පුළුන් කැබලි බෝල
cough	kas-sah-tah gahn-nah	කැස්සට
medicine	be-heth	ගන්න බෙහෙත්
gauze	gors kaa-li	ගෝස් කෑලි
laxatives	vi-reh-kah-yahn	විරේකයන්
painkillers	veh-dhah-naah	වේදනා
	naah-shah-kah-yahn	නාශකයන්
sleeping pills	ni-dhi pe-thi	නිදි පෙති
vitamins	vi-tah-min	විටමින්

See Shopping (page 120) for general toiletries.

HEALTH

AT THE DENTIST

දන්ත වෛද්‍ය
ශල්‍යාගාරයේදී

I have a toothache.
mah-tah dhah-theh kak-ku-mahk
thi-ye-nah-vaah

මට දතේ කැක්කුමක්
තියෙනව.

I have a cavity.
mah-geh dhah-theh
ku-hah-rah-yahk thi-ye-nah-vaah

මගේ දතේ කුහරයක්
තියෙනව.

I've lost a filling.
mah-geh dhah-theh
pi-rah-vee-mah ga-lah-vi-laah

මගේ දතේ
පිරවීම ගැලවිල.

I've broken my tooth.
mah-geh dhah-thah ga-lah-vi-laah

මගේ දත ගැලවිල.

My gums hurt.
mah-geh vi-dhu-ru-mahs
ri-dhe-nah-vaah

මගේ විදුරුමස්
රිදෙනව.

I don't want it extracted.
dhah-thah gah-lah-vahn-nah
mah-tah oh-neh na-ha

දත ගලවන්න
මට ඕනේ නැහැ.

Please give me an anaesthetic.
kah-ru-naah-kah-rah mah-tah
hi-ri waht-tan-nah be-he-thah
dhen-nah

කරුණාකර මට හිරි
වට්ටන බෙහෙත
දෙන්න.

Ouch!
aah-i!

ආයි!

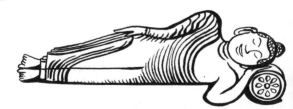

DISABLED TRAVELLERS
ආබාධිත සංචාරකයන්

I'm disabled.
  mah-mah aah-baah-<u>dhi</u>-thah-yek   මම ආබාධිතයෙක්.

I need assistance.
  mah-tah u-dhahv
  u-pah-kaah-rah oh-neh   මට උදව්
  උපකාර ඕනේ.

What services do you have
for disabled people?
  aah-baah-<u>dhi</u>-thah-yahn-tah   ආබාධිතයන්ට
  mo-nah seh-vaah-vahn-dhah   මොන සේවාද
  ath-theh?   ඇත්තේ?

Is there wheelchair access?
  roh-dhah pu-tu sah-dhah-haah   රෝද පුටු සඳහා
  pah-hah-su-kahm thi-yeh-dhah?   පහසුකම් තියෙද?

I'm deaf.
  mah-mah bi-hi-riy   මම බිහිරියි.

I have a hearing aid.
  kahn a-see-mah-tah mah-mah   කන් ඇසීමට මම
  u-pah-kah-rah-nah-yahk   උපකරණයක් පාච්චි
  paah-vich-chi kah-rah-nah-vaah   කරනවා.

Speak more loudly, please.
  kah-ru-naah-kah-rah hai-yen   කරුණාකර හයියෙන්
  kah-<u>thaah</u> kah-rahn-nah   කථා කරන්න.

Are guide dogs permitted?
  mah-gah pen-vah-nah bahl-lahn   මහ පෙන්වන
  sah-dhah-haah ah-vah-sah-rah   බල්ලන් සඳහා
  ath-dhah?   අවසර ඇත්ද?

braille library	brehl pus-thah-kaah-lah-yah	බ්‍රේල් පුස්තකාලය
guide dog	mah-gah pen-vah-nah bahl-lahn	මහ පෙන්වන බල්ලන්
wheelchair	roh-dhah pu-tu-wah	රෝද පුටුව

TRAVELLING WITH THE FAMILY

සිය පවුලත් සමහ ගමන් යෑම

Are there facilities for babies?
lah-dhah-ru-wahn sah-dah-haah
pah-hah-su-kahm ath-dhah?

ළදරුවන් සඳහා
පහසුකම් ඇත්ද?

Do you have a child-minding service?
lah-mun bah-laah ga-nee-meh
seh-vaah-vahk thi-yeh-dhah?

ළමුන් බලා ගැනීමේ
සේවාවක් තියේද?

Where can I find a (English-speaking) babysitter?
(in-gree-si kah-thaah kah-rah-nah)
lah-mun bah-laah gahn-naah
ke-nek mah-mah so-yaah gahn-neh
ko-hen-dhah?

(ඉංගුීසි කථා කරන)
ළමුන් බලා ගන්නා
කෙනෙක් මම සොයා
ගන්නේ කොහෙන්ද?

Can you put an (extra) bed/ cot in the room?
(va-di-pu-rah) an-dahk/
tho-til-lahk kaah-mah-rah-yeh
dhah-mahn-nah pu-lu-vahn-dhah?

(වැඩිපුර) ඇඳක්/
තොට්ටිල්ලක් කාමරයෙ
දමන්න පුළුවන්ද?

Is there a family discount?
pah-vu-lah-kah-tah
mi-lah ah-du-dhah?

පවුලකට මිළ අඩ?

Are children allowed?
lah-mah-yin-tah yahn-nah
pu-lu-vahn-dhah?

ළමයින්ට යන්න
පුළුවන්ද?

Do you have a children's menu?
lah-mah-yin-tah ve-nah-mah
aah-haah-rah thi-yeh-dhah?

ළමයින්ට වෙනම
ආහාර තියේද?

Are there any activities for children?
lah-mah-yin-tah ve-nah-mah
kri-yaah-kaah-rah-kahm
thi-yeh-dhah?

ළමයින්ට වෙනම
කියාකාරකම්
තියේද?

Is there a playground nearby?
sel-lahm pi-ti-yahk
lahn-gah thi-yeh-dhah?

සෙල්ලම් පිටියක්
ළඟ තියේද?

PILGRIMAGE & RELIGION

වන්දනා සහ ආගම

What's your religion?	o-bah mo-nah aah-gah-meh-dhah?	ඔබ මොන ආගමේද?
I'm ...	mah-mah ...	මම ...
Buddhist	budh-<u>dh</u>aah-gah-meh	බුද්ධාගමේ
Christian	kris-thi-yaah-ni aah-gah-meh	ක්‍රිස්තියානි ආගමේ
Hindu	hin-du aah-gah-meh	හින්දු ආගමේ
Jewish	yu-dhev aah-gah-meh	යූදෙව් ආගමේ
Muslim	mus-lim aah-gah-meh	මුස්ලිම් ආගමේ

I (don't) believe in God.
mah-mah dhe-vi-yahn
vish-vaah-sah (no) kah-rah-mi

මම දෙවියන් විශ්වාස (නො) කරමි.

I (don't) believe in rebirth.
mah-mah
pu-nah-ruth-pahth-thi-yah
vish-vaah-sah (no) kah-rah-mi

මම පුනරුත්පත්තිය විශ්වාස (නො) කරමි.

I am religious.
mah-mah aah-gah-mah-tah
la-dhiy

මම ආගමට ලැදියි.

I am not religious.
mah-mah aah-gah-mah-tah
la-dhi na-ha

මම ආගමට ලැදි නැහැ.

DREAMS OF THE EAST

When sleeping, people generally lie with their heads to the east (the direction Buddha is believed to have come from). The dead, however, are placed with their heads to the west as it's thought they shouldn't lie in the same direction as the living.

SPECIFIC NEEDS

Can I attend this service/mass?
    meh dheh-vah me-he-yah/
    poo-jaah-vah-tah mah-tah
    sah-hah-baah-gi vi-yah
    ha-ki-dhah?

මේ දේව මෙහෙයට/
පූජාවට මට
සහභාගි විය
හැකිද?

Can I pray here?
    mah-tah me-thah-nah
    yaahk-gnaah kah-rahn-nah
    pu-lu-vahn-dhah?

මට මෙතන යාච්ඤා
කරන්න පුළුවන්ද?

Where can I pray/worship?
    mah-tah yaahk-gnaah/
    van-dhah-naah
    kah-rahn-nah pu-lu-vahn
    ko-heh-dhah?

මට යාච්ඤා/
වන්දනා කරන්න
පුළුවන් කොහේද?

STONY FACED

A gift of a religious statue is said to end a friendship.

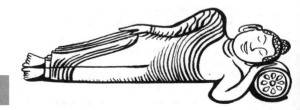

TELLING THE TIME   වේලාව කියවීම

You'll notice that telling the time in Sinhala is just as simple as saying it in English – you follow the same pattern. Numerically speaking, you'll need to know the Sinhalese version of your figures up to sixty (see pages 173 and 174).

What time is it?
    veh-laah-vah kee-yah-dhah?   **වේලාව කියද?**
It's (one) o'clock.
    dhan veh-laah-vah (e-kai)   **දැන් වේලාව (එකයි).**
    (lit: now time one)
Half past one.
    e-kah-hah-maah-rai   **එකහමාරයි.**
    (lit: one-half)
Quarter past one.
    e-kai kah-lai   **එකයි කාලයි.**
    (lit: one quarter)
Quarter to one.
    e-kah-tah kaah-lai   **එකට කාලයි.**
    (lit: to-one quarter)
Twenty to one.
    e-kah-tah vis-sai   **එකට විස්සයි.**
    (lit: to-one twenty)

DAYS OF THE WEEK   සතියේ දින

Monday	sahn-dhu-dhaah	සඳුදා
Tuesday	ahn-gah-hah-ru-vaah-dhaah	අඟහරුවාදා
Wednesday	bah-dhaah-dhaah	බදාදා
Thursday	brah-has-pah-thin-dhaah	බුහස්පතින්දා
Friday	si-ku-raah-dhaah	සිකුරාදා
Saturday	se-nah-su-raah-dhaah	සෙනසුරාදා
Sunday	i-ri-dhaah	ඉරිදා

TIME, DATES
& FESTIVALS

MONTHS   මාසයන්

January	jah-nah-vaah-ri	ජනවාරි
February	pe-bah-rah-vaah-ri	පෙබරවාරි
March	maahr-thu	මාර්තු
April	ahp-rehl	අප්‍රේල්
May	ma-yi	මැයි
June	joo-ni	ජුනි
July	joo-li	ජුලි
August	ah-gohs-thu	අගෝස්තු
September	sep-tham-bahr	සෙප්තැම්බර්
October	ok-thoh-bahr	ඔක්තෝබර්
November	no-vam-bahr	නොවැම්බර්
December	dhe-sahm-bahr	දෙසැම්බර්

SEASONS   සෘතු/කාල

summer	greesh-mah kaah-lah-yah	ග්‍රීෂ්ම කාලය
autumn	sah-rahth kaah-lah-yah	සරත් කාලය
winter	shee-thah kaah-lah-yah	ශීත කාලය
spring	wah-sahn-thah kaah-lah-yah	වසන්ත කාලය

For more on weather, see In the Country, page 142.

DATES   දින

What date it is today?
    ah-dhah dhi-nah-yah   අද දිනය මොකක්ද?
    mo-kahk-dhah?
It's 18 October.
    ah-dhah ok-thoh-bahr 18   අද ඔක්තෝබර් 18 වෙනිදා.
    ve-ni-dhaah

TIME, DATES & FESTIVALS

PRESENT — වර්තමානය

today	ah-dhah	අද
this morning	ah-dhah u-dheh	අද උදේ
this afternoon	ah-dhah dhah-vahl	අද දවල්
tonight	ah-dhah raa	අද රෑ
this week	meh sah-thi-yeh	මේ සතියේ
this month	meh maah-sah-yeh	මේ මාසයේ
this year	meh ah-vu-rud-dheh	මේ අවුරුද්දේ
now	dhan	දැන්
right now	dhan-mah	දැන්ම

PAST — අතීතය

yesterday	ee-yeh	ඊයේ
day before yesterday	pe-reh-dhaah	පෙරේදා
yesterday ...	ee-yeh ...	ඊයේ
morning	u-dheh	උදේ
afternoon	dhah-vahl	දවල්
evening	han-daa-veh	හැන්දෑවේ
last night	ee-yeh raa	ඊයේ රෑ
last week	gi-yah sah-thi-yeh	ගිය සතියේ
last month	gi-yah maah-sah-yeh	ගිය මාසයේ
last year	gi-yah ah-vu-rudh-dheh	ගිය අවුරුද්දේ
(half an hour) ago	(pa-yah bhaah-gah-yah) kah-tah is-sah-rah	(පැය භාගය) කට ඉස්සර
(three) days ago	dhah-vahs (thu-nah)-kah-tah kah-lin	දවස් (තුන)කට කලින්
(five) years ago	ah-vu-rudh-dhu (pah-hah)-kah-tah is-sah-rah	අවුරුදු (පහ) කට ඉස්සර
a while ago	kah-lah-kah-tah pe-rah	කලකට පෙර
since (May)	(ma-yi) maah-seh si-tah	(මැයි) මාසේ සිට

TIME, DATES
& FESTIVALS

FUTURE අනාගතය

tomorrow	he-tah	හෙට
day after tomorrow	ah-nidh-dhaah	අනිද්දා
tomorrow ...	he-tah ...	හෙට ...
morning	u-dheh	උදේ
afternoon	dhah-vahl	දවල්
evening	han-dhaa-weh	හෙ හැන්දෑවේ
next week	ee-lahn-gah sah-thi-yeh	ඊළඟ සතියේ
next month	ee-lahn-gah maah-sah-yeh	ඊළඟ මාසයේ
next year	ee-lahn-gah ah-vu-rudh-dheh	ඊළඟ අවුරුද්දේ
in (five) minutes	vi-naah-di (pah-hah)-kin	විනාඩි (පහ)කින්
in (six) days	dhi-nah (hah-yah)-kin	දින (හය)කින්
until (June)	(joo-ni) maah-sah-yah thek	(ජූනි) මාසය තෙක්

DURING THE DAY දවස තුළ

It's early.	veh-laah-sah-nai	වේලාසනයි.
It's late.	pah-rahk-kuy	පරක්කුයි.
afternoon	dhah-vahl	දවල්
dawn	paahn-dhah-ra	පාන්දර
day	dhah-vah-sah	දවස
early	veh-laah-sah-nah	වේලාසන
evening	han-dhaa-wah	හැන්දෑව
lunchtime	dah-vahl kaa-mah veh-laah-vah	දවල් කෑම වේලාව
midday	dhah-hah-vah-lah	දහවල
midnight	ma-dhi-yahm ra-yah	මැදියම් රැය
morning	u-dheh	උදේ
night	raa	රෑ
noon	dhah-vahl	දවල්
sunrise	hi-ru u-dhaah-vah	හිරු උදාව
sunset	hi-ru ba-see-mah	හිරු බැසීම

FESTIVALS & NATIONAL HOLIDAYS
උත්සව සහ ජාතික නිවා

With a diversity of cultural and religious festivals, Sri Lankans have developed a flair for pageantry and ceremony – almost every month brings with it a celebration. Certain festival dates may vary as they are governed by the lunar calendar. Some of the major festivals are:

Dhuruthu Perahera   දුරුතු පෙරහැර
a religious pageant in January at the Kelaniya Temple, commemorating the first visit of Lord Buddha to Sri Lanka 2540 years ago

Thai Pongal   තායි පොන්ගල්
a Hindu festival celebrating the harvest, and offering thanks giving to the Sun God, held on 14 or 15 January

Independence Day   නිදහස් සමරු උළෙල
celebrated on 4 February, commemorating the end of 450 years of colonial rule in 1948

Ramzan Festival   රාමිසාන් උත්සවය
also known as Id-Ul-Fitr, this Islamic celebration, usually celebrated in March, marks the end of Ramadan fasting

Sinhalese &   සිංහල සහ
Hindu New Year   හින්දු අවුත් අවුරුද්ද
celebrated on 13 and 14 April, marking the end of harvest and the start of the south-west monsoon

Vesak Full   වෙසක් පුර
Moon Day   පසළොස්වක දින
a two-day celebration in May, commemorating the birth, enlightenment and death of Buddha

Poson Full   පොසොන් පුර
Moon Day   පසළොස්වක දින
held in June, commemorating the arrival of Buddhism to
Sri Lanka in the 3rd century BC

The Kandy Perahera   නුවර පෙරහැර
a spectacular pageant and festival honouring the Sacred Tooth
Relic of Buddha, held over 12 days in July/August

Kataragama Festival   කතරගම උත්සවය
an August festival honouring a shrine dedicated to the god
Kataragama, located in the south-east of the island

The Dondra Festival   දෙවුන්දර උත්සවය
another August festival, held in Dondra, south of Colombo,
around a shrine dedicated to the Hindu god, Vishnu

Sri Pada   ශ්‍රී පාද වන්දනාව
a multi-denominational pilgrimage in December, venerating
a footprint, believed to be Buddha's, located at the summit of
Sri Pada, also known as Adam's Peak

CELEBRATIONS   උත්සව

When's your birthday?
  o-beh u-pahn dhi-nah-yah
  kah-vah-dhaah-dah?

ඔබේ උපන් දිනය
කවදාද?

My birthday is on (25 January).
  mah-geh u-pahn dhi-nah-yah
  (jah-nah-vaah-ri 25)

මගේ උපන් දිනය
(ජනවාරි 25).

Happy birthday!
  su-bhah u-pahn dhi-nah-yahk!

සුභ උපන් දිනයක්!

PLANETARY PLANNING

Horoscopes carry a lot of weight in Sri Lanka – even cutting a child's hair for the first time or introducing them to solids is done in consultation with their horoscope.

Christmas Day	nath-thahl dhah-va-sah	නතතල් දවස
Christmas Eve	nath-thahl dhi-nah-tah pe-rah dhi-nah	නතතල් දිනට පෙර දින
Happy Christmas!	su-bhah nath-thah-lak!	සුභ නත්තලක්!
New Year's Eve	ah-luth ahv-rudh-dhah-tah pe-rah dhi-nah	අළුත් අවුරුද්දට පෙර දින
New Year's Day	ah-luth ahv-ru-dhu dhaah	අළුත් අවුරුදු දා
Happy New Year!	su-bhah ah-luth ahv-rudh-dhahk!	සුභ අළුත් අවුරුද්දක්!
Easter	paahs-ku	පාස්කු
Happy Easter!	su-bhah paahs-ku dhi-nah-yahk!	සුභ පාස්කු දිනයක්!

TIME, DATES
& FESTIVALS

TOASTS & CONDOLENCES

සුබදිය පිරවීම හා අනුශෝචනය

Bon voyage!	su-bhah gah-mahn!	සුභ ගමන්!
Cheers!	waah-sah-naah-vahn!	වාසනාවන්!
Congratulations!	su-bhah ah-shin-sah-nah!	සුභ ආශිංසන!
Get well soon.	ik-mah-nin su-wah veh-vah	ඉක්මනින් සුව වේවා.
Good luck!	waah-sah-naah veh-waah!	වාසනා වේවා!
I'm very sorry.	mah-tah bo-hoh-mah kah-nah-gaah-tuy	මට බොහෝම කණගාටුයි.
My deepest sympathy.	mah-geh dha-di show-kah-yah	මගේ දැඩි ශෝකය.
My thoughts are with you.	mah-tah o-bah ni-thah-rah si-hi ve-nah-vaah	මට ඔබ නිතර සිහි වෙනවා

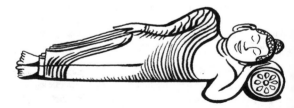

If you follow the pattern of Sinhalese numbers, you'll notice that one to 12 differ from one another, but from 20 onwards there is a set pattern, with only a change in each series of tens up to one hundred.

CARDINAL NUMBERS ශුඛාංක

1	e-kah	එක
2	dhe-kah	දෙක
3	thu-nah	තුන
4	hah-thah-rah	හතර
5	pah-hah	පහ
6	hah-yah	හය
7	hah-thah	හත
8	ah-tah	අට
9	nah-vah-yah	නවය
10	dhah-hah-yah	දහය
11	e-ko-lah-hah	එකොළහ
12	dho-lah-hah	දොළහ
13	dhah-hah-thu-nah	දහතුන
14	dhah-hah-hah-thah-rah	දහහතර
15	pah-hah-lah-vah	පහළොව
16	dhah-hah-sah-yah	දහසය
17	dhah-hah-hah-thah	දහහත
18	dhah-hah-ah-tah	දහඅට
19	dhah-hah-nah-vah-yah	දහනවය

FIGURING IT OUT

In Sinhala, figures are only written in script when they're spelled out – the figures themselves are written as in English.

NUMBERS & AMOUNTS

20	vis-sah	විස්ස
Numbers 21-29 start with vis-si-:		විස්
21	vis-si-e-kah	විස්එක
22	vi-si-dhe-kah	විස්දෙක
30	thi-hah	තිහ
Numbers 31-39 start with this-:		තිස්
33	this-thu-nah	තිස්තුන
37	this-hah-thah	තිස්හත
40	hah-thah-li-hah	හතළිහ
Numbers 41-49 start with ha-thah-lis:		හතළිස්
43	hah-thah-lis thu-nah	හතළිස් තුන
46	hah-thah-lis hah-yah	හතළිස් පහ
50	pah-nah-hah	පනහ
Numbers 51-59 start with pah-nahs:		පනස්
52	pah-nahs dhe-kah	පනස් දෙක
55	pah-nahs pah-hah	පනස් පහ
60	ha-tah	හැට
Numbers 61-69 start with ha-tah:		හැට
61	ha-tah e-kah	හැට එක
66	ha-tah hah-yah	හැට හය
70	hath-thaa-wah	හැත්තෑව
Numbers 71-79 start with hath-thaah:		හැත්තෑ
73	hath-thaah thu-nah	හැත්තෑ තුන
75	hath-thaah pah-hah	හැත්තෑ පහ
80	ah-soo-wah	අසූව
Numbers 81-89 start with ah-soo:		අසූ
84	ah-soo hah-thah-rah	අසූ හතර
88	ah-soo ah-tah	අසූ අට
90	ah-noo-wah	අනූව
Numbers 81-89 start with ah-noo:		අනූ
96	ah-noo hah-yah	අනූ හය
99	ah-noo nah-vah-yah	අනූ නවය

All numbers in the hundreds end with see-yah:

100	e-kah see-yah	එකසිය
200	dhe-see-yah	දෙසිය
300	thun-see-yah	තුන්සිය
400	haah-rah-see-yah	හාරසිය
500	pahn-see-yah	පන්සිය
600	hah-yah-see-yah	හයසිය
700	hath-see-yah	හත්සිය
800	ah-tah-see-yah	අටසිය
900	nah-vah-see-yah	නවසිය
1000	e-kah-daah-hah	එකදාහ
one lakh (100,000)	ek lahk-shah-yah	එක ලක්ෂය
one million	mi-li-yah-nah-yah	මිලියනය

ORDINAL NUMBERS   කුම්ාංක

1st	pah-lah-mu-ve-ni	පළමුවෙනි
2nd	dhe-vah-ni	දෙවනි
3rd	thun-ve-ni	තුන්වෙනි
4th	hah-thah-rah-ve-ni	හතරවෙනි
5th	pahs-ve-ni	පස්වෙනි

FRACTIONS   භාග

a quarter	kaah-lah	කාල
a half	bhaah-gah-yah	භාගය
a third	thu-nen pahn-gu-wah	තුනෙන් පංගුව
three-quarters	hah-thah-ren thu-nah	හතරෙන් තුන

USEFUL AMOUNTS   ප්‍රයෝජනවත් ප්‍රමාණ

How much?	koch-chah-rah-dhah?	කොච්චරද?
How many?	kee-yahk-dhah?	කියක්ද?
Could you	kah-ru-naah-kah-rah	කරුණාකර
please give me ...?	mah-tah ... dhen-nah?	මට ... දෙන්න?
I need ...	mah-tah ... oh-neh	මට ... ඕනේ

all	sahm-poor-nah-yah	සම්පූර්ණය
double	dhe-kah dhe-kah	දෙක දෙක
a dozen	dhu-si-mahk	දුසිමක්
half a dozen	dhu-sim baah-gah-yahk	දුසිම් භාගයක්
(a) few	ti-kahk	ටිකක්
less	ah-du	අ
a little	bo-hoh-mah ti-kahk	බොහෝම ටිකක්
a lot	hun-gahk	හුඟාක්
(too) many	bo-hoh (va-di)	බොහෝ (වැඩි)
more	thah-vah	තව
(too) much	go-daahk (va-di)	ගොඩක් (වැඩි)
none	ki-si-wahk na-thi	කිසිවක් නැති
a pair	joh-du-wahk/dhe-kahk	ජෝඩුවක්/දෙකක්
some	sah-mah-hah-rehk	සමහරෙක්

a bottle/jar	boh-thah-lah-yahk	බෝතලයක්
a packet	pa-kaht-tu-wahk	පැකට්ටුවක්
a slice	peth-thahk	පෙත්තක්
a tin	tin e-kahk	ටින් එකක්

| once | ek vah-rahk | එක් වරක් |
| twice | dhe-sa-rah-yahk | දෙසැරයක් |

EMERGENCIES

GENERAL   පොදු

Help!	kau-ruth nadh-dhah?	කවුරුත් නැද්ද?
	(lit: anyone isn't here?)	
Stop!	nah-vah-thin-nah!	නවතින්න!
Go away!	yahn-nah!	යන්න!
Thief!	ho-rek!	හොරෙක්!
Fire!	gin-nahk!	ගින්නක්!
Watch out!	bah-laah-ge-nai!	බලාගෙනයි!
It's an	meh-kah	මේක
emergency!	hah-dhis-si-yahk!	හදිස්සියක්!

Could you help us please?
    kah-ru-naah-kah-rah-lah   කරුණාකරල අපට
    ah-pah-tah u-dhahv kah-rahn-nah   උදව් කරන්න
    pu-lu-vahn-dhah?   පුළුවන්ද?

Could I please use the telephone?
    kah-ru-naah-kah-rah-lah   කරුණාකරල මට
    mah-tah te-li-fohn e-kah   ටෙලිෆෝන් එක
    paah-vich-chi kah-rahn-nah   පාවිච්චි කරන්න
    pu-lu-vahn-dhah?   පුළුවන්ද?

I'm lost.
    mah-mah na-thi-ve-laah   මම නැතිවෙලා.

Where are the toilets?
    toi-laht/va-si-ki-li-yah   ටොයිලට්/වැසිකිළිය
    ko-heh-dhah thi-yen-neh?   කොහේද තියෙන්නේ?

EMERGENCIES

177

POLICE   පොලිසිය

Call the police!
po-lee-si-yah-tah kah-<u>thaah</u>
kah-rahn-nah!

පොලිසියට කථා
කරන්න!

Where's the police station?
po-lee-si-yah ko-heh-dhah
thi-yen-neh?

පොලිසිය කොහේද
තියෙන්නේ?

We want to report an offence.
va-rah-dhi va-dhahk ga-nah
ah-pah-tah pa-mi-ni-li
kah-rahn-nah oh-neh

වැරදි වැඩක් ගැන
අපට පැමිණිලි
කරන්න ඕනේ.

I've been raped/assaulted.
maah-vah dhoo-shah-nah-yah
kah-laah; mah-tah ga-hu-vaah

මාව දූෂණය
කළා; මට ගැහුවා.

I've been robbed.
mah-gen so-raah gahth-thaah

මගෙන් සොරා ගත්තා.

My ... was/were stolen.	mah-geh ... so-rah-kahm ke-ru-waah	මගේ ... සොරකම් කෙරුවා.
backpack	bak-pak e-kah	බැක්පැක් එක
bags	baag/mahl-lah	බෑග්/මල්ල
handbag	ahth baag e-kah	අත් බෑග් එක
money	sahl-li	සල්ලි
papers	ko-lah	කොළ
travellers cheques	tra-vah-lah chek-pahth	ට්‍රැවල වෙක්පත්
passport	paahs-poht e-kah	පාස්පෝට් එක
wallet	pers e-kah	පර්ස් එක

My possessions are insured.
mah-geh bah-du
rahk-shah-nah-yah
kah-rah-lai thi-yen-neh

මගේ බඩ රකෂණය
කරලයි තියෙන්නේ.

EMERGENCIES

I'm sorry; I apologise.
   kah-nah-gaah-tuy; mah-tah
   sah-maah ven-nah

කණගාටුයි; මට සමා
වෙන්න.

I didn't realise I was doing
anything wrong.
   mah-mah vah-rah-dhahk
   kah-rah-nah bah-vah mah-tah
   va-tah-hu-neh na-ha

මම වරදක් කරන
බව මට වැටහුණේ
නැහැ.

I didn't do it.
   mah-mah ke-ru-veh na-ha

මම කෙරුවේ නැහැ.

We're innocent.
   ah-pi nir-dhoh-shai

අපි නිර්දෝෂයි.

We're foreigners.
   ah-pi vi-dheh-shi-kah-yoh

අපි විදේශිකයෝ.

I want to contact my
embassy/consulate.
   mah-geh thaah-naah-pah-thi/
   kon-sahl kahn-thoh-ru-wah-tah
   mah-tah kah-<u>t</u>haah kah-rahn-nah
   oh-neh

මගේ තානාපති/
කොන්සල්
කන්තෝරුවට මට
කථා කරන්න ඕනේ.

Can I call someone?
   kaah-tah hah-ri kah-<u>t</u>haah
   kah-rahn-nah mah-tah
   pu-lu-vahn-dhah?

කාට හරි කථා
කරන්න මට
පුළුවන්ද?

Can I have a lawyer who speaks English?
   in-gree-si kah-<u>t</u>haah kah-rah-nah
   nee-theeg-gnah vah-rah-yek
   mah-tah gahn-nah
   pu-lu-vahn-dhah?

ඉංග්‍රීසි කථා කරන
නීතිඥ වරයෙක් මට
ගන්න පුළුවන්ද?

Is there a fine we can pay to clear this?
   dhah-dhah mu-dhah-lahk
   ge-vah-lah ah-pah-tah meh-ken
   ni-dhah-hahs ven-nah
   pu-lu-vahn-dhah?

දඩ මුදලක්
ගෙවල අපට
මේකෙන් නිදහස්
වෙන්න පුළුවන්ද?

I (don't) understand.
  mah-tah theh-ren-neh
  (na-ha)

මට තේරෙන්නේ
(නැහැ).

I know my rights.
  mah-geh hi-mi-kahm ga-nah
  mah-mah dahn-nah-vaah

මගේ හිමිකම් ගැන
මම දන්නවා.

What am I accused of?
  mo-nah vah-rah-dhah-
  kah-tah-dhah mah-tah
  choh-dhah-naah kah-rahn-neh?

මොන වරදකටද
මට චෝදනා
කරන්නේ?

arrested	ahth ah-dan-gu-wah-tah gahth	අත් අඩංගුවට-ගත්
cell	si-rah koo-du-wah	සිර කුව
consulate	kon-sahl kahn-thoh-ru-wah	කොන්සල් කන්තෝරුව
embassy	thaah-nah-pah-thi kahn-thoh-ru-wah	තානාපති කන්තෝරුව
fine (payment)	dhah-dah-yah	දඩය
guilty	vah-rah-dhah-kaah-rai	වරදකාරයි
lawyer	nee-theeg-gnah-vah-rah-yaah	නීතිඥවරයා
not guilty	nir-dhoh-shai	නිර්දෝෂයි
police officer	po-lis ni-lah-<u>dh</u>aah-ree	පොලිස් නිළධාරී
police station	po-lis sthaah-nah-yah	පොලිස් ස්ථානය
prison	si-rah ge-dhe-rah	සිර ගෙදර
trial	nah-dhu vi-bhaah-gah-yah	න විභාගය

You'll/He'll/She'll	... ga-nah o-bah/	... ගැන
be charged with ...	o-hu/a-yah	ඔබ /ඔහු /ඇය
	choh-dhah-naah	චෝදනා ලබන
	lah-bah-nu a-thah	ඇත .
anti-	rah-jah-yah-tah-	රජයට-
government	vi-rudh-dhah-vah	විරුද්ධව
activity	kri-yaah ki-ree-mah	ක්‍රියා කිරීම
assault	pah-hah-rah dhee-mah	පහර දීම
disturbing	saah-mah-yah	සාමය කඩ
the peace	kah-dhah ki-ree-mah	කිරීම
possession	(nee-thi vi-roh-dhee	(නීති විරෝධි
(of illegal	dheh) lahn-gah	දේ) ළඟ තබා
substances)	thah-baah ga-nee-mah	ගැනීම
illegal entry	nee-thyaah-nu-koo-lah	නීත්‍යානුකූල
	no-voo pa-mi-nee-mah	නොවූ පැමිණීම
laundering	ho-rah mu-dhal noht-tu	හොර මුදල්
	gah-nu-dhe-nu-wah	නෝට්ටු ගනුදෙනුව
murder	mi-nee-ma-ru-mah	මිනීමැරුම
not having	vee-saah e-kahk	විසා එකක්
a visa	no-thi-bee-mah	නොතිබීම
overstaying	o-bah-geh/o-hu-geh/	ඔබගේ /ඔහුගේ /
your/his/	a-yah-geh vee-saah	ඇයගේ විසා
her visa	e-kah ik-mah-vaah	එක ඉක්මවා
	si-tee-mah	සිටීම
paedophilia	baah-lah pahk-shaah-	බාල
	dhoo-shah-nah-yah	පක්ෂාදූෂණය
rape	dhoo-shah-nah-yah	දූෂණය
robbery/theft	so-rah-kah-mah	සොරකම
shoplifting	saahp-pu bah-du	සාප්පු බඩු
	ho-ren ga-nee-mah	හොරෙන් ගැනීම
traffic	prah-vaah-hah-nah	ප්‍රවාහණ
violation	nee-thi kah-dah	නීති කඩ
	ki-ree-mah	කිරීම
working without	ah-vah-sah-rah-yahk	අවසරයක්
a permit	na-thi-wah va-dah	නැතිව වැඩ
	ki-ree-mah	කිරීම

HEALTH

සෞඛ්‍යය

Call a doctor!
dhos-thah-rah ke-nek-tah
kah-<u>thaah</u> kah-rahn-nah!

දොස්තර කෙනෙක්ට
කථා කරන්න!

Call an ambulance!
am-byu-lahns e-kah-kah-tah
kah-<u>thaah</u> kah-rahn-nah!

එම්බියුලන්ස් එකකට
කථා කරන්න!

I'm ill.
mah-tah sah-nee-pah na-ha

මට සනීප නැහැ.

My friend is ill.
mah-geh yah-hah-lu-waah-tah
sah-nee-pah na-ha

මගේ යහළුවාට
සනීප නැහැ.

I have medical insurance.
mah-tah wai-dyah rahk-shah-nah
thi-ye-nah-waah

මට වෛද්‍ය රක්ෂණ
තියෙනවා.

EMERGENCIES

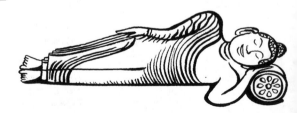

- Where there's more than one Sinhalese entry for an English word, the alternatives are separated by a bullet:

  difficult   ah-maah-ru • ah-pah-hah-su

- Where two words are interchangeable, they're separated by a slash:

  double bed   lo-ku/dah-bahl an-dhah
  (meaning either   lo-ku an-dhah or dah-bahl an-dhah)

- Masculine and feminine forms of the same word are also separated by a slash:

  artist   chith-rah shil-pi-yek/
              shil-pi-ni-yahk (m/f)

- All verbs are listed in the present/future tense, which is the dictionary form in Sinhala, and are followed by '(v)'. Nouns are not indicated.

A

be able (can, v)	ha-ki ve-nah-vaah	හැකි වෙනවා
abortion	gab-saah-vah	ගබ්සාව
above	u-dah	උඩ
abroad	pi-tah-rah-tah	පිටරට
accept (v)	pi-li-gahn-nah-vaah	පිළිගන්නවා
accident	ah-nah-thu-rah	අනතුර
accommodation	i-dhum hi-tum	ඉදුම් හිටුම්
across	hah-rah-haah	හරහා
activist	kri-yaath-mah-kah-yaah	ක්‍රියාත්මකයා
adaptor	a-dahp-tah-rah-yah	ඇඩප්ටරය
addiction	ab-ba-hi-vee-mah	ඇබ්බැහිවීම
address	li-pi-nah-yah	ලිපිනය
admission	a-thul-vee-mah	ඇතුල්වීම
adult	va-di-hi-ti	වැඩිහිටි
advantage	va-dah-dhaah-yee	වැඩදායි
advice	ah-vah-vaah-dhah	අවවාද
aeroplane	ah-hahs yaah-nah-yah	අහස් යානය
be afraid of (v)	bah-yah ve-nah-vaah	භය වෙනවා
after	pah-su-wah	පසුව
afternoon	dhah-vahl	දවල්
in the afternoon	dhah-vaah-leh	දවාලේ
(spoken language)		
again	na-vah-thah	නැවත
against	vi-rudh-dhah-vah	විරුද්ධව
age	vah-yah-sah	වයස

aggressive	kah-lah-hah-kaah-ree	කලහකාරී
(a while) ago	(kah-lah-kah-tah)	(කලකට)
	u-dah-dhee	උඩදි
agree (v)	e-kahn-gah ve-nah-vaah	එකඟ වෙනවා

> I don't agree.
> mah-mah e-kahn-gah   මම එකඟ
> ven-neh na-ha   වෙන්නේ නැහැ.

> Agreed!
> e-kahn-gai!   එකඟයි!

agriculture	kru-shi-kar-mah	කෘෂිකර්ම
ahead	kah-lin •	කලින් • ඉස්සර
	is-sah-rah ve-laah	වෙලා
aid (help)	aah-dhaah-rah	ආධාර
AIDS	ehds roh-gah-yah	ඒඩ්ස් රෝගය
air	vaah-thah-yah	වාතය
air-conditioning	vaah-yu	වායු
	sah-mee-kah-rah-nah-yah	සමීකරණය
	kah-rah-nah lah-dhah	කරන ලද
air mail	gu-wahn tha-pal	ගුවන් තැපැල්
airport	gu-wahn tho-tu-pah-lah	ගුවන් තොටුපළ
alarm clock	ah-vah-dhi kah-rah-vah-nah	අවදි කරවන
	o-rah-loh-su-wah	ඔරලෝසුව
all	si-yahl-lah • ok-ko-mah	සියල්ල • ඔක්කොම
allergy	ah-pah-thyah •	අපත්‍ය •
	ah-saahth-mi-kah	අසාත්මික
allow (v)	i-dah dhee-mah •	ඉඩ දීම •
	ah-vah-sah-rah dhee-mah	අවසර දීම

> It's not allowed.
> ah-vah-sah-rah (na-ha)   අවසර (නැහැ).

almost	on-nah-men-nah	ඔන්න-මෙන්න
alone	thah-ni-vah	තනිව
already	dha-nah-tah-mahth	දැනටමත්
also	thah-vah-dhah	තවද
altitude	u-sah prah-maah-nah-yah	උස පුමාණය
always	sa-mah-vi-tah-mah	සැමවිටම
among	ah-thah-rah	අතර
ancient	aah-dhi-kaah-lee-nah/	ආදිකාලීන/පුරාණ
	pu-raah-nah	
and	sah-hah	සහ
angry	thah-rah-hah • kehn-thi	තරහ • කේන්ති
animals	sah-thun	සතුන්
answer	pi-li-thu-rah	පිළිතුර
antibiotics	an-ti-bah-yah-tik	ඇන්ටිබයටික්
antique	i-pa-rah-ni	ඉපැරණි
antiseptic	vi-shah naah-shah-kah	විෂ නාශක

any	oh-naa-mah	ඕනෑම
appointment	dhi-nah yo-dhaah-gahth	දින යොදාගත්
archaeological	pu-raah-vahs-thu-kah	පුරාවස්තුක
architecture	nir-maah-nah shil-pah-yah	නිර්මාණ ශිල්පය
argue (v)	vaah-dhah kah-rah-nah-vaah	වාද කරනවා
arm	baah-hu-wah	බාහුව
arrivals	pa-mi-neem	පැමිණීම්
arrive (v)	pa-mi-ne-nah-vaah	පැමිණෙනවා
art	kah-laah-wah	කලාව
art gallery	kah-laah bhah-vah-nah-yah	කලා භවනය
artist	chith-rah shil-pi-yek/	චිත්‍ර ශිල්පියෙක්/
	shil-pi-ni-yahk (m/f)	ශිල්පිනියක්
ask (for something, v)	il-lah-nah-vah	ඉල්ලනවා
ask (a question, v)	ah-hah-nah-vah	අහනවා
aspirin	as-prin	ඇස්ප්‍රින්
atmosphere	vaah-thaah-vah-rah-nah-yah	වාතාවරණය
aunt	nan-dhaah •	නැන්දා •
	(father's sister)	
	lo-ku ahm-maah •	ලොකු අම්මා •
	(mother's older sister)	
	pun-chi ahm-maah •	පුංචි අම්මා •
	(mother's younger sister)	
automatic teller (ATM)	eh-tee-em e-kah	ඒ.ටී.එම්. එක
autumn	sah-rahth ir-thu-wah	සරත් සෘතුව
awful	ahn-thi-mai	අන්තිමයි

B

baby	lah-dhah-ru-waah	ළදරුවා
baby food	lah-dhah-ru aah-haah-rah	ළදරු ආහාර
baby powder	lah-dhah-ru pu-yah-rah	ළදරු පියර
babysitter	lah-mun bah-laah	ළමුන් බලා
	gahn-naah ah-yah	ගන්නා අය
back (body)	pi-tah	පිට
at the back (behind)	pi-tu-pah-sah	පිටුපස
backpack	bak-pak e-kah	බැක්පැක් එක
bad	nah-rah-kah	නරක
bag	baag e-kah	බෑග් එක
baggage	bah-du mah-lu	බඩු මළු
baggage claim	bah-du mah-lu bhaah-rah	බඩු මළු භාර
	ga-nee-mah	ගැනීම
bakery	beh-kah-ri-yah	බේකරිය
balcony	sah-dhah-lu-thah-lah-yah	සඳළුතලය
ball (game)	boh-lah-yah	බෝලය
ball (dance)	baahl na-tu-mah	බෝල් නැටුම
ballet	nruth-thyah • rahn-gah-nah	නෘත්‍ය • රංගන
band (music)	vaah-dhah-kah	වාදක
	mahn-dah-lah-yah •	මණ්ඩලය •
	baand e-kah	බෑන්ඩ් එක

bandage	ve-lum pah-ti	වෙළුම් පටි
bank	ban-ku-wah	බැංකුව
baptism	bau-thees-mah	බෞතීස්ම
basket	koo-dah-yah	කූඩය
bath	naa-mah	නෑම
bathroom	naah-nah kaah-mah-rah-yah	නාන කාමරය
battery	ba-tah-ri-yah	බැටරිය
beach	mu-hu-dhu ve-rah-lah	මුහුදු වෙරළ
beautiful	lahs-sah-nah	ලස්සන
because	ni-saah	නිසා
bed	an-dhah	ඇඳ
bedroom	ni-dhah-nah kaah-mah-rah-yah	නිදන කාමරය
before	kah-lin	කලින්
beggar	si-gahn-naah	සිඟන්නා
begin	pah-tahn gahn-nah	පටන් ගන්න
behind	pah-su-pah-sah	පසුපස
below	yah-tah	යට
beside	ai-neh	අයිනේ
best	i-thaah-mahth hon-dhah	ඉතාමත් හොඳ
bet	ot-tu-wah	ඔට්ටුව
better	i-thaah hon-dah	ඉතා හොඳ
between	ah-thah-rah-thu-rah	අතරතුර
bicycle	bai-si-kah-lah-yah	බයිසිකලය
big	lo-ku	ලොකු
bill (account)	bi-lah	බිල
binoculars	dhoo-rah-dhahr-shah kahn-naah-di-yah	දුරදර්ශ කන්නාඩිය
biodegradable	jee-vah naah-shah-kah	ජීව නාශක
bird	ku-rul-laah	කුරුල්ලා
birthday	u-pahn dhi-nah-yah	උපන් දිනය
bite (dog)	sah-paah kaa-mah	සපා කෑම
bite (insect)	vi-dhee-mah (kroo-mi)	විදීම (කෘමි)
black	kah-lu	කළු
B&W (camera film)	kah-lu su-dhu film rohl e-kah	කළු සුදු ෆිල්ම් රෝල් එක
blanket	blan-kaht-tu-vah	බ්ලැන්කට්ටුව
bless (v)	aah-sheer-vaah-dhah kah-rah-nah-vaah	ආශීර්වාද කරනවා

Bless you! (when sneezing)
dhe-vi pi-hi-tai! දෙවි පිහිටයි!

blind	ahn-dhah	අන්ධ
blood	leh	ලේ
blood group	leh kaahn-dah-yah	ලේ කාණ්ඩය
blood pressure	ru-dhi-rah pee-dah-nah-yah	රුධිර පීඩනය
blood test	leh pah-reek-shah-nah-yah	ලේ පරීක්ෂණය

blue	nil	නිල්
board (ship, etc, v)	na-gee-mah	නැගීම
boarding pass	boh-din paahs e-kah	බෝඩිං පාස් එක
boat	boht-tu-wah	බෝට්ටුව
body	an-gah	ඇඟ

Bon voyage!
su-bhah gah-mahn! — සුහ ගමන්!

bone	kah-tu-wah	කටුව
book (n)	po-thah	පොත
book (v)	kah-lin ven kah-rah-vaah	කලින් වෙන්
	gahn-nah-vaah	කරවා ගන්නවා
bookshop	poth saahp-pu-wah	පොත් සාප්පුව
boots	boot sah-path-thu	බූට් සපත්තු
bored	kaahn-si-yah	කාන්සිය
boring	kaahn-si-mahth	කාන්සිමත
borrow (v)	nah-yah-tah gahn-nah-vaah	ණයට ගන්නවා
both (inanimate)	dhe-kah-mah	දෙකම
both (animate)	dhen-nah-mah	දෙන්නම
bottle	boh-thah-lah-yah	බෝතලය
bottle opener	boh-thahl ari-nah-yah	බෝතල් අරිනය
(at the) bottom	yah-tah	යට
box	pet-ti-yah	පෙට්ටිය
boy	pi-ri-mi lah-mah-yaah	පිරිමි ළමයා
boyfriend	pem-wah-thaah	පෙම්වතා
brave	nir-bhee-thah	නිර්භීත
bread	paahn	පාන්
break (v)	kah-dah-nah-vaah	කඩනවා
breakfast	u-dheh kaa-mah	උදේ කෑම
breathe (v)	hus-mah gahn-nah-vaah	හුස්ම ගන්නවා
bribe	ahl-lah-sah	අල්ලස
bridge	paah-lah-mah	පාලම
brilliant	is-thah-rahm	ඉස්තරම්
bring (v)	ge-ne-nah-vaah	ගෙනෙනවා
broken	ka-du-nu	කැඩුනු
brother	ai-yaah (older)	අයියා
	mahl-lee (younger)	මල්ලී
	so-ho-yu-raah (refers to either)	සොහොයුරා
brown	dhum-bu-ru paah-tah	දුඹුරු පාට
bruise	see-ree-mah	සීරීම
bucket	pah-nit-tu-wah	පනිට්ටුව
building	go-dah-na-gil-lah	ගොඩනැඟිල්ල
bus (city)	bahs e-kah	බස් එක
bus (intercity)	nah-gah-rah ahn-thah-rah	නගර අන්තර
	bahs e-kah	බස් එක
bus stop	bahs staand e-kah •	බස් ස්ටෑන්ඩ් එක •
	bahs na-vah-thum po-la	බස් නැවතුම් පොළ
business	vyaah-paah-rah-yah	ව්‍යාපාරය

businessperson	paah-ri-kah-yek/vyaah-paah-ri-kaah-vak (m/f)	ව්‍යාපාරිකයෙක්/ ව්‍යාපාරිකාවක්
busy	va-dah ah-di-kah	වැඩ අධික
but	nah-muth	නමුත්
butterfly	sah-mah-nah-lah-yaah	සමනළයා
button	both-thah-mah	බොත්තම
buy (v)	gahn-nah-vaah	ගන්නවා

> I'd like to buy ...
> mah-tah ... gahn-nah ka-mah-thiy
> මට ... ගන්න කැමතියි.
>
> Where can I buy a ticket?
> mah-mah ti-kaht e-kahk gahn-neh ko-hen-dah?
> මම ටිකට් එකක් ගන්නේ කොහෙන්ද?

C

cafe	theh pan	තේ පැන්
	hoh-tah-lah-yah	හෝටලය
calendar	ka-lahn-da-rah-yah	කැලැන්ඩරය
camera	ka-mah-raah-vah	කැමරාව
camera shop	ka-mah-raah saahp-pu-wah	කැමරා සාප්පුව
can (be able, v)	ha-ki ve-nah-vaah	හැකි වෙනවා
can (aluminium)	tin	ටින්
can opener	tin ah-ri-nah e-kah	ටින් අරින එක
cancel (v)	ah-vah-lahn-gu kah-rah-nah-vaah	අවලංගු කරනවා
candle	i-ti-pahn-dhah-mah	ඉටිපන්දම
car	kaahr e-kah	කාර් එක
cards	kaahd	කාඩ්
care (about, v)	sa-lah-ki-li-mahth ve-nah-vaah	සැලකිලිමත් වෙනවා
care (for someone, v)	bah-laah gahn-nah-vaah	බලා ගන්නවා

> Careful!
> prah-veh-sah-min!
> ප්‍රවේසමින්!

carry (v)	o-sah-vah-nah-vaah	ඔසවනවා
cashier	ah-yah-ka-mi-yaah	අයකැමියා
cassette	ka-saht pah-ti-yah	කැසට් පටිය
cat	bah-lah-laah	බළලා
cathedral	dhev ma-dhu-rah	දෙව් මැදුර
cave	gu-haah-wah	ගුහාව
CD	see-dee •	සී.ඩී. •
	sahn-yuk-thah tha-ti	සංයුක්ත තැටි
celebrate (v)	uth-sah-vah pah-vahth vah-nah-vaah	උත්සව පවත්වනවා
centimetre	sen-ti-mee-tah-rah-yah	සෙන්ටිමීටරය
chair	pu-tu-wah	පුටුව

championships	shoo-rah-taah	ශූරතා
chance	vaah-rah-yah	වාරය
change (v)	ve-nahs kah-rah-nah-vaah	වෙනස් කරනවා
change (coins)	maah-ru sahl-li	මාරු සල්ලි
chat up (v)	kah-thaah-rah-tah	කථාවට මුල
	mu-lah pu-rah-nah-vaah	පුරනවා
cheap	laah-bah	ලාභ

| Cheat! | | |
| vahn-chaah-kaah-rah-yaah! | | වංචාකාරයා! |

check-in (desk)	vaahr-thaah ki-ree-mah	වාර්තා කිරීම
cheese	chees	චීස්
chemist	au-shah-dah-veh-dhee	ඖෂධවේදි
chess	ches kree-daah-vah	චෙස් ක්‍රීඩාව
chest	pa-pu-wah	පපුව
chewing gum	chu-wing gahm	චුවිං ගම්
chicken (meat)	ku-kul mahs	කුකුළු මස්
child	lah-mah-yaah	ළමයා
childminding	lah-mun bah-laah	ළමුන් බලා
	ga-nee-mah	ගැනීම
children	lah-mah-yin	ළමයින්
chocolate	cho-co-laht	චොක්ලට්
choose (v)	thoh-rah-nah-vaah	තෝරනවා
Christmas Day	nahth-thahl dhi-nah	නත්තල් දින
Christmas Eve	nahth-thahl dhi-nah-tah	නත්තල් දිනට
	pe-rah di-nah	පෙර දින
church	pahl-li-yah	පල්ලිය
cigarette papers	si-gah-raht ko-lah	සිගරට් කොළ
cigarettes	si-gah-raht	සිගරට්
cinema	si-ni-maah-wah	සිනමාව
citizenship	pu-rah-va-si	පුරවැසි
	bhaah-vah-yah	භාවය
city/city centre	nah-gah-rah-yah	නගරය
clean	pi-ri-si-dhu	පිරිසිදු
cleaning	pi-ri-si-dhu ki-ree-mah	පිරිසිදු කිරීම
client	ah-nu-graah-hah-kah	අනුග්‍රාහකයා
cliff	kahn-dhu	කඳු ප්‍රපාතය
	prah-paah-thah-yah	
climb (v)	nah-gi-nah-vaah	නගිනවා
cloakroom	kah-baah	කබා කාමරය
	kaah-mah-rah-yah	
clock	o-rah-loh-su-wah	ඔරලෝසුව
close (v)	va-hah-nah-vaah	වහනවා
closed	vah-saah a-thah	වසා ඇත
clothing	an-dum	ඇඳුම්
clothing store	an-dum saahp-pu-wah	ඇඳුම් සාප්පුව
cloudy	vah-laah-ku-lu sah-hi-thai	වලාකුළු සහිතයි

C

coast	mu-hu-dhu-bah-bah-dah	මුහුදුබඩ
coat	kah-baah-yah	කබාය
coins	kaah-si	කාසි
cold	hem-bi-ris-saah-wah	හෙම්බිරිස්සාව
cold (adj)	see-tha-la	සිතල

It's cold.
see-tha-lai · සිතලයි .

cold water	al wha-thu-rah	ඇල් වතුර
colleague	sah-gah-yaah	සගයා
college	paah-<u>t</u>ah-shaah-laah-wah	පාඨශාලාව
colour	paah-tah	පාට
comb	pah-naah-wah	පනාව
come (v)	e-nah-vaah	එනවා
comedy	vi-kah-tah	විකට
comfortable	su-wah-dhaah-yah-kai	සුවදායකයි
communion	sam-bahn-dhah-kah-mah •	සම්බන්ධකම •
	sath-pra-saah-dhah	සත්ප්‍රසාද
communist	ko-mu-nis vaah-dhi-yaah	කොමියුනිස් වාදියා
companion	sah-gah-yaah •	සගයා •
	sah-hah-chah-rah-yaah	සහචරයා
company	sah-maah-gah-mah	සමාගම
compass	maah-li-maah	මාලිම
	yahn-thrah-yah	යන්ත්‍රය
computer	pah-ri-ghah-nah-kah-yah	පරිගණකය
concert	ran-gah dhak-mahk	රඟ දැක්මක්
confession (religious)	paah-poch-chaah-rah-nah-yah	පාපෝච්චාරණය
confirm (v) (a booking)	thah-hah-vu-ru kah-rah-nah-vaah	තහවුරු කරනවා

Congratulations!
su-bhah aah-shin-sah-nah! · සුභ ආශිංසන !

conservative	gah-thaah-nu-gah-thi-kah	ගතානුගතික
be constipated (v)	bah-dah veh-lah-nah-vaah	බඩ වේලනවා
consulate	kon-sahl vah-rah-yaah	කොන්සල් වරයා
contact lenses	spahr-shah len-sah-yah	ස්පර්ශ ලෙන්සය
contraceptives	pi-li-si-dheeh-mah	පිළිසිඳීම වැළැක්වීමේ
	va-lak-vee-meh dheh-vahl •	දේවල් •
	gab ga-nee-mah	ගැබ් ගැනීම
	va-lak-vee-meh	වැළැක්වීමේ
	u-pahk-krah-mah	උපක්‍රම
convent	kahn-yaah-raah-mah-yah	කන්‍යාරාමය
cook (v)	u-yah-nah-vaah	උයනවා
cool (colloquial)	shohk	ෂෝක්
corner	ko-nah	කොණ
corrupt	dhoo-shi-thah	දූෂිත

| cost (v) | va-yah ve-nah-vaah | වැය වෙනවා |

How much does it cost to go to ...?
...-tah yahn-nah   ...ට යන්න
kee-yahk vei-dhah? කියක් ගන්නවාද?

cotton	kah-pu	කපු
country	rah-tah	රට
countryside	gahm-bah-dhah	ගම්බද
cough (n)	kas-sah	කැස්ස
count (v)	gah-nahn kah-rah-nah-vaah	ගණන් කරනවා
cow	e-lah-dhe-nah	එළදෙන
crazy	un-mahth-thah	උන්මත්ත
credit card	kre-dit kaahd e-kah	ක්‍රෙඩිට් කාඩ් එක

Can I pay by credit card?
kre-dit kaahd e-kehn ge-vahn-nah   ක්‍රෙඩිට් කාඩ් එකෙන්
pu-lu-vahn-dhah?   ගෙවන්න පුළුවන්ද?

cricket	kri-kaht	ක්‍රිකට්
cross (religious)	ku-ru-sah-yah	කුරුසය
cup	kohp-pah-yah	කෝප්පය
cupboard	kah-bahd e-kah •	කබඩ් එක •
	al-maah-ri-yah	අල්මාරිය
customs (traditions)	chaah-rith-rah	චාරිත්‍ර
customs (airport)	reh-gu-wah	රේගුව
cut (v)	kah-pah-nah-vaah	කපනවා
cycle (v)	bai-si-kahl pa-dhee-mah	බයිසිකල් පැදීම
cyclist	bai-si-kahl kah-ru	බයිසිකල් කරු

D

dad	thaahth-thaah • pi-yaah	තාත්තා • පියා
daily	saa-mah-dhaah-mah	සෑමදාම
dairy products	ki-ri aah-haah-rah	කිරි ආහාර
dance (v)	nah-tah-nah-vaah	නටනවා
dangerous	ahn-thah-raah-dhaah-yee	අන්තරාදායි
dark	kah-lu-wah-rah	කළුවර
date	dhah-vah-sah •	දවස • දිනය
	dhi-nah-yah	
date (someone, v)	aah-dhah-rah hah-mu-wah	ආදර හමුව
date of birth	u-pahn dhi-nah-yah	උපන් දිනය
daughter	dhu-wah	දූ
dawn	ah-lu-yah-mah	අලුයම
day	dhah-vah-sah	දවස
day after tomorrow	ah-nidh-dhaah	අනිද්දා
day before yesterday	pe-reh-dhaah	පෙරේදා
dead	ma-ri-lah • mi-yah gos	මැරිල • මිය ගොස්
deaf	bi-hi-ri	බිහිරි
death	mah-rah-nah-yah	මරණය

decide (v)	thee-rah-nah-yah kah-rah-nah-vaah	තීරණය කරනවා
deep	gam-bu-ru	ගැඹුරු
deer	mu-waah	මුවා
deforestation	ka-laa vahn-dhah ki-ree-mah	කැලෑ වද කිරීම
delay	prah-maah-dhah-yah	පුමාදය
delicatessen	see-thah kah-lah mahs	සිත කල මස්
	mahn-shah ah-le-vi hah-lah	මාංශ අලෙවි හළ
democracy	prah-jaah-thahn-thrah-vaah-dhah-yah	පුජාතන්තුවාදය
demonstration (protest)	pe-lah-paah-li-yah	පෙළපාළිය
dentist	dhahn-thah	දන්ත
	vai-dhyah-vah-rah-yaah • dhahth dhos-thah-rah	වෛද්‍යවරයා • දත් දොස්තර
deny (something, v)	pi-li no-gahn-nah-vaah	පිළි නොගන්නවා
deodorant	dhu-gahn-dha nahs-nah-yah	දුගඳ නස්නය
depart (leave, v)	yah-nah-vaah	යනවා
departure	ba-ha-rah-wah yaa-mah	බැහැරව යෑම
desert	tha-ni-kah-rah yaa-mah	තනිකර යෑම
destination	gah-mah-naahn-thah-yah	ගමනාන්තය
destroy (v)	vi-naah-shah kah-rah-nah-vaah	විනාශ කරනවා
diabetic	dhi-yah-va-di-yaah roh-gee	දියවැඩියා රෝගි
dial tone	dah-yahl tohn e-kah	ඩයල් ටෝන් එක
diaper (nappy)	na-pi-yah	නැපිය
diarrhoea	paah-chah-nah-yah	පාචනය
diary	dhi-nah po-thah	දින පොත
dictionary	shahb-dhah-koh-shah-yah	ශබ්දකෝෂය
die (v)	ma-re-nah-vah	මැරෙනවා
different	ve-nahs	වෙනස්
difficult	ah-maah-ru • ah-pah-hah-su	අමාරු • අපහසු
dining car	aah-pah-nah rah-thah-yah	ආපන රථය
dinner	raa kaa-mah	රෑ කෑම
direct	ke-lin	කෙළින්
dirty	ki-li-ti	කිලිටි
disabled	aah-baah-dhi-thah	ආබාධිත
disadvantage	ah-vaah-si	අවාසි
discount	vaht-tah-mah	වට්ටම
discover (v)	so-yaah gahn-nah-vaah	සොයා ගන්නවා
discrimination	ve-nahs-kahm ki-ree-mah	වෙනස්කම් කිරීම
disease	roh-gah-yah	රෝගය
diving	ki-mi-dhee-mah	කිමිදීම
dizzy	ka-rah-kil-lah	කැරකිල්ල
do (v)	kah-rah-nah-vaah	කරනවා

What are you doing?		
o-bah mo-kah-dhah kah-rahn-neh?		ඔබ මොකද කරන්නේ?

I didn't do it.		
mah-mah eh-kah ke-ru-weh na-ha		මම ඒක කෙරුවේ නැහැ.

doctor	dhos-thah-rah •	දොස්තර •
	vai-dhyah-vah-rah-yek/	වෛද්‍යවරයෙක්/
	vai-dhyah-vah-ri-yahk (m/f)	වෛද්‍යවරියක්
documentary	tho-rah-thu-ru	තොරතුරු
	vaahr-thaah	වාර්තා
dog	bahl-laah	බල්ලා
doll	boh-nik-kaah	බෝනික්කා
door	dho-rah	දොර
dope (drugs)	mahth dhrahv-yah	මත් ද්‍රව්‍ය
double	dhe-kah dhe-kah	දෙක දෙක
double bed	lo-ku/dah-bahl an-dhah	ලොකු/ඩබල් ඇඳ
double room	lo-ku kaah-mah-rah-yah	ලොකු කාමරය
dozen	dhu-si-mah	දුසිම
drama	naaht-tya-yah	නාට්‍යය
dramatic	naaht-tya-yah-kaah-rah	නාට්‍යකාර
dream (v)	si-hi-nah bah-lah-nah-vaah	සිහින බලනවා
dress	an-dhu-mah	ඇඳුම
drink	bee-mahk	බීමක්
drink (v)	bo-nah-vaah	බොනවා
drive (v)	pah-dhah-vah-nah-vaah	පදවනවා
drivers licence	ri-yah-dhu-ru	රියදුරු
	bah-lah-pahth-rah-yah •	බලපත්‍රය •
	lai-sahn e-kah	ලයිසන් එක
drugs	mahth-dhrah-vyah	මත්ද්‍රව්‍ය
drums (instrument)	be-rah	බෙර
dummy (baby's)	soop-pu-wah	සූප්පුව

E

each	e-kah-e-kah	එක-එක
ear	kah-nah	කණ
early	veh-laah-sah-nin	වේලාසනින්
earn (v)	u-pah-yah-nah-vaah •	උපයනවා •
	hahm-bah	හම්බ
	kah-rah-nah-vaah	කරනවා
earrings	kah-raah-bu	කරාබු
Earth	loh-kah-yah	ලෝකය
earthquake	bhoo-mi kahm-paah-wah	භූමි කම්පාව
east	na-ge-nah-hi-rah	නැගෙනහිර
Easter	paahs-ku	පාස්කු

easy	leh-si • pah-hah-su	ලේසි • පහසු
eat (v)	kah-nah-vaah	කනවා
economy	aahr-thi-kah-yah	ආර්ථිකය
education	ahdh-yah-pah-nah-yah	අධ්‍යාපනය
elections	ma-thi-vah-rah-nah	මැතිවරණ
electricity	vi-dhu-li-bah-lah-yah	විදුලිබලය
elephant	ah-li-yaah	අලියා
elevator	uth-thoh-lah-kah-yah	උත්තෝලකය
embarrassed	vik-ship-thah vee-mah • lahj-jaah vee-mah	විකිම්පිත වීම • ලජ්ජා වීම
embassy	thaah-naah-pah-thi kaar-yaah-lah-yah	තානාපති කාර්යාලය
emergency	hah-dis-si-yahk • hah-di-si ah-vahs-thaah-vah	හදිස්සියක් • හදිසි අවස්ථාව
employee	seh-vah-kah-yaah	සේවකයා
employer	seh-vaah yoh-jah-kah-yaah	සේවා යෝජකයා
empty	his	හිස්
end	ahn-thi-mah • ah-vah-saah-nah-yah	අන්තිම • අවසානය
engagement	raah-jah-kaahr-yaah-yahk • vi-vaah-hah gi-vi-sah ga-nee-mah	රාජකාරියයක් • විවාහ ගිවිස ගැනීම
engine	en-ji-mah	එන්ජිම
engineering	in-ji-neh-ru shi-pah-yah	ඉන්ජිනේරු ශිල්පය
English	in-gree-si	ඉංගිසි
enjoy (oneself, v)	pree-thi ve-nah-vaah	පීති වෙනවා
enough	a-thi	ඇති
enter (v)	a-thul ve-nah-vaah	ඇතුල්වෙනවා
entertaining	aah-gahn-thu-kah sahth-kaah-rah-yah	ආගන්තුක සත්කාරය
envelope	li-yum kah-vah-rah-yah	ලියුම් කවරය
environment	pah-ri-sah-rah-yah	පරිසරය
equality	sah-maah-nahth-mah-thaah-vah-yah	සමානාත්මතාවය
euthanasia	ah-naah-yaah-sah mah-rah-nah-yah	අනායාස මරණය
evening	han-dhaa-vah	හැන්දෑව
every day	sa-mah-dhaah-mah	සෑමදාම
example	u-dhaah-hah-rah-nah-yah	උදාහරණය
excellent	bo-hoh-mah hon-dhai • vi-shish-tai	බොහොම හොඳයි • විශිෂ්ටයි
exchange (v)	hu-wah-maah-ru kah-rah-nah-vaah	හුවමාරු කරනවා
exchange rate	vi-dheh-shah vi-ni-mah-yah gaahs-thu	විදේශ විනිමය ගාස්තු
excluded	i-vahth ko-tah	ඉවත් කොට

Excuse me.		
mah-tah sah-maah-vahn-nah		මට සමාවන්න .

exhibition	prah-dhar-shah-nah-yah	පුදර්ශනය
exit	pi-tah-vee-mah	පිටවීම
expensive	va-di mi-lah	වැඩි මිළ
exploitation	soo-rah kaa-mah	සූරා කෑම
express	see-grah-gaah-mi	සීඝුගාමී
eye	a-ha	ඇහැ

F

face	mu-hu-nah	මුහුණ
factory	kahm-hah-lah	කම්හල
family	pah-vu-lah	පවුල
famous	keer-thi-mahth	කීර්තිමත්
fan (hand-held)	ah-vaah-nah	අවාන
fan (machine)	pah-vahn-kaah-wah	පවන්කාව
fan (of a team)	kree-daah loh-lah-yah	කුීඩා ලෝලයා
far	dhu-rah	දුර
farm	go-vi-pah-lah	ගොවිපළ
farmer	go-vi-yek/	ගොවියෙක්/
	go-vi kaahn-thaah-vahk (m/f)	ගොවි කාන්තාවක්
fast	ik-mah-nin	ඉක්මනින්
fat	mah-hah-thah	මහත
father	thaath-thaah	තාත්තා
father-in-law	maah-maah	මාමා
fault (someone's)	vah-rah-dhah	වරද
fear	bhah-yah • bhi-yah	භය • භිය
feel (v)	dha-ne-nah-vaah	දැනෙනවා
feelings	han-geem	හැඟීම්
fence	va-tah	වැට
festival	uth-sah-vah-yah	උත්සවය
fever	u-nah	උණ
few	sah-mah-hah-rehk	සමහරෙක්
fiance	pem-wah-thaah	පෙම්වතා
fiancee	pem-wah-thi-yah	පෙම්වතිය
fiction	mith-yah kah-thaah-vah	මිථ්‍යා කථාව
field (rice paddy)	kum-bu-rah	කුඹුර
fight (v)	rahn-du • kah-lah-hah	රණ්ඩු •
	kah-rah-nah-vaah	කලහ කරනවා
fill (v)	pu-rah-vah-nah-vaah	පුරවනවා
film (cinema)	chith-rah-pah-ti-yah	චිතුපටිය
film (for camera)	film rohl e-kah	ෆිල්ම් රෝල් එක
film speed	dhaah-vi-thaah-vah-yah	ධාවිතාවය
find (v)	so-yaah gahn-nah-vaah	සොයා ගන්නවා
fine (penalty)	dhah-dah-yah	දඩය
finger	an-gil-lah	ඇඟිල්ල

fire	gin-dhah-rah	ගින්දර
first	pah-lah-mu-wah-nah	පළමුව
first-aid kit	prah-thah-maah-dhaah-rah	පුථමාධාර
	kaht-tah-lah-yah	කට්ටලය
fish	maah-lu	මාලු
flag	ko-di-yah	කොඩිය
flat (land, etc)	sah-mah-thah-laah	සමතලා
flea	mak-kaah	මැක්කා
flashlight (torch)	flash lait e-kah	ෆ්ලැෂ් ලයිට් එක
flight	flait e-kah • gu-wahn	ෆ්ලයිට් එක •
	gah-mah-nah	ගුවන් ගමන
floor (ground)	po-lo-wah	පොළව
floor (storey)	mah-hah-lah	මහල
flour	pi-ti	පිටි
flower	mah-lah	මල
fly	mas-saah	මැස්සා

It's foggy.
mee dhum sah-hi-thai   මී දුම් සහිතයි .

follow (v)	anu-gah-mah-nah-yah	අනුගමනය කරනවා
	kah-rah-nah-vaah	
food	kaa-mah • aah-haah-rah	කෑම • ආහාර
foot	kah-ku-lah	කකුල
football (soccer)	paah-pahn-dhu	පාපන්දු
footpath	ah-di-paah-rah	අඩිපාර
foreign	vi-dheh-shee-yah	විදේශීය
forest	ka-lah-yah	කැලය
forever	sah-dhaah-kaah-li-kah-vah	සදාකාලිකව
forget (v)	ah-mah-thah-kah	අමතක කරනවා
	kah-rah-nah-vah	

I forget.
mah-tah ah-mah-thah-kah   මට අමතක වෙනවා .
ve-nah-vaah

Forget about it! (don't worry)
eh-kah ah-mah-thah-kah kah-rah-nah!   ඒක අමතක කරන්න !

forgive (v)	sah-maah-vah dhe-nah-vaah	සමාව දෙනවා
fortnight	dhe-sah-thi-yah-kah-tah	දෙසතියකට
	vah-rahk • sah-thi	වරක් • සති
	dhe-kah-tah vah-rahk	දෙකකට වරක්
free (not bound)	ni-dhah-hahs	නිදහස්
free (of charge)	no-mi-lah-yeh	නොමිළයේ
fresh	ah-luth	අළුත්
Friday	si-ku-raah-dhaah	සිකුරාදා

G

friend	yah-hah-lu-waah • mi-thu-raah	යහළුවා • මිතුරා
frozen foods	shee-thah kah-lah aah-haah-rah	ශීත කළ ආහාර
fruit picking	pah-lah-thu-ru ka-dee-mah	පළතුරු කැඩීම
full	pi-ri-lah	පිරිලා
fun	vi-noh-dhah-yah	විනෝදය
have fun (v)	vi-noh-dhah ve-nah-vaah	විනෝද වෙනවා
funeral	mah-rah-nah-yah	මරණය
future	ah-naah-gah-thah-yah	අනාගතය

G

game	sel-lahm	සෙල්ලම්
game (sport)	kree-daa-vah	ක්‍රීඩාව
garage	gah-raah-jah-yah	ගරාජය
garbage	kah-sah-lah	කසළ
gardening	vah-thu va-dah	වතු වැඩ
garden	(mahl-)vahth-thaah	(මල්)වත්ත
gas cartridge	gaas un-dah-yah	ගෑස් උණ්ඩය
gate	geht-tu-wah	ගේට්ටුව
gay	mai-thoo-nah	මයිතුන
general	saah-maahn-yah	සාමාන්‍ය

| **Get lost!** | |
| pah-lah-yahn yahn-nah! | **පලයන් යන්න !** |

gift	thaag-gah	තෑග්ග
girl	ga-ha-nu lah-mah-yaah	ගැහැණු ළමයා
girlfriend	yah-hah-lu ga-ha-nu lah-mah-yaah • pem-wah-thi-yah	යහළු ගැහැණු ළමයා • පෙම්වතිය
give (v)	dhe-nah-vah	දෙනවා

| **Could you give me ...?** | |
| mah-tah ... dhen-nah pu-lu-vahn-dhah? | **මට ... දෙන්න පුළුවන්ද?** |

| glass | vee-dhu-ru-vah | විදුරුව |
| go (v) | yah-nah-vah | යනවා |

| **Let's go.** | |
| yah-mu | **යමු .** |

goal	dhi-num sthaah-nah-yah • gohl e-kah	දිනුම් ස්ථානය • ගෝල් එක
goat	e-lu-waah	එළුවා
God	dhe-vi-yahn	දෙවියන්
gold	rath-rahn	රත්රන්

H

Good afternoon.	su-bhah dhah-hah-vah-lahk	සුභ දහවලක්.
Good evening/night.	su-bhah san-dhaa-vahk/ raahth-ri-yahk	සුභ සැන්දෑවක්/ රාතියක්.
Good luck!	vaah-sah-naah-vahn!	වාසනාවන්!
Good morning.	su-bhah u-dhaa-sah-nahk	සුභ උදෑසනක්.
Goodbye.	aah-yu-boh-vahn	ආයුබෝවන්.

government	rah-jah-yah	රජය
gram (weight)	graam e-kah	ගුෑම් එක
gram (pulse)	kah-dah-lah	කඩල
grandchild	mu-nu-pu-raah (m) • mi-ni-pi-ri-yah (f)	මුනුපුරා • මිනිපිරිය
grandfather	see-yaah	සීයා
grandmother	aahch-chee	ආච්චි
grapes	mi-di	මිදි තණ කොළ
grass	thah-nah ko-lah	තණ කොළ
grave	so-ho-nah	සොහොන
great	lo-ku • mah-haah	ලොකු • මහ
greengrocer	sil-lah-rah ve-len-dhaah	සිල්ලර වෙළෙන්දා
grey	ah-lu paah-tah	අළු පාට
guess (v)	hi-thah-lah ki-yah-nah-vaah	හිතල කියනවා
guide (person)	gaid ke-nek	ගයිඩ් කෙනෙක්
guidebook	maahr-goh-pah-dheh-shah po-thah	මාර්ගෝපදේශ පොත
guitar	gi-taah-rah-yah	ගිටාරය
gym (weights)	vyaah-yaahm shaah-laah-wah	වෘායාම් ශාලාව
gymnastics	sah-rahm-bah kree-daah	සරඹ කීඩා

H

hair	kon-dah-yah	කොණ්ඩය
hairbrush	kon-daah bu-ru-su-wah	කොණ්ඩා බුරුසුව
half	bhaah-gah-yah	භාගය
ham	ham	හැම්
hammer	mi-ti-yah	මිටිය
hammock	el-le-nah tho-til-lah	එල්ලෙන තොට්ල්ල
hand	ah-thah	අත
handbag	ahth baa-gah-yah	අත් බෑගය
handicrafts	ath-kahm	අත්කම්

198

handmade	ah-thin ni-mah-voo	අතින් නිමවූ
handsome	pi-yah-kah-ru •	පියකරු •
	lahs-sah-nah	ලස්සන
happy	pree-thi-mahth •	පුීතිමත් •
	sahn-thoh-shah-vahth	සන්තෝෂවත්

Happy birthday!
su-bah u-pahn dhi-nah-yahk!   සුභ උපන් දිනයක්!

harbour	vah-raah-yah	වරාය
hard (solid)	thah-dhah	තද
hard (difficult)	ah-maah-ru	අමාරු
harrassment	hi-ri-ha-rah-kahm	හිරිහැරකම්
have (v)	thi-yah-nah-vaah	තියනවා

Do you have ...?
o-bah-tah ...   ඔබට ...
thi-yah-nah-vaah-dhah?   තියනවාද?

hayfever	pee-nahs roh-gah-yah	පීනස් රෝගය
he	o-hu	ඔහු
head	o-lu-wah	ඔළුව
headache	hi-sah-rah-dhah-yah	හිසරදය
health	sau-khyah	සෞඛ්‍යය
hear (v)	a-he-nah-vaah	ඇහෙනවා
heart	hah-dhah-vah-thah	හදවත
heat	ush-nah-yah	උෂ්ණය
heavy	bah-rah	බර

Hello.
aah-yu-boh-wahn   ආයුබෝවන්.

| helmet | hel-maht e-kah | හෙල්මට් එක |
| help (v) | u-dhav kah-rah-nah-vaah | උදව් කරනවා |

Help!
kau-ruth nadh-dhah?   කවුරුත් නැද්ද?
(lit: anyone isn't-there?)

herbs	au-shah-dhah pa-lah	ඖෂධ පැල වර්ග
	vahr-gah	
herbalist	au-shah-dhah veh-dhee	ඖෂධ වේදි
here	me-thah-nah	මෙතන
hill	kahn-dhah	කන්ද
hire (v)	ku-li-yah-tah	කූලියට ගන්නවා
	gahn-nah-vaah	
HIV positive	ech-ai-vee	එච්.අයි.වි.
	sah-hi-thah-voo	සහිතවූ
holiday(s)	ni-vaah-du(-vah)	නිවාඩු(ව)
homeless	ah-naah-thah-voo	අනාථවූ

homeopathy	hoh-mi-yoh-pah-thi ve-dhah-kah-ma	හෝමියෝපති වෙදකම
homosexual	sah-mah lin-gi-kah	සම ලිංගික
honey	mee pa-ni	මී පැණි
honeymoon	mah-dhu sah-mah-yah	මධු සමය
horrible	ahn-thi-mai	අන්තිමයි
horse	ahsh-wah-yaah	අශ්වයා
horse riding	ahsh-wah-yaahn pa-dhee-mah	අශ්වයන් පැදීම
hospital	roh-hah-lah • is-pi-ri-thaah-lah-yah	රෝහල • ඉස්පිරිතාලය
hot	ush-nah	උෂ්ණ

It's hot.
rahs-nei   රස්නෙයි.

hot water	u-nu wah-thu-rah	උණු වතුර
house	ge-yah • ge-dhah-rah	ගෙය • ගෙදර
how	ko-ho-mah-dhah	කොහොමද

How do I get to ...?
...-tah mah-mah yahn-neh ko-ho-mah-dhah?   ...ට මම යන්නේ කොහොමද?

How do you say ...?
... ki-yahn-neh ko-ho-mah-dhah?   ... කියන්නේ කොහොමද?

hug	bah-dhaah ga-nee-mah	බදා ගැනීම
human rights	maah-nah-vah hi-mi-kahm	මානව හිමිකම්
hundred	see-yahk	සියක්
hungry	bah-dah-gi-ni	බඩගිනි
husband	sa-mi-yaah	සැමියා

I

I	mah-mah	මම
ice	ais • hi-mah	අයිස් • හිම
ice cream	ais-kreem	අයිස්ක්‍රීම්
identification	han-dhu-naah ga-nee-mah	හඳුනා ගැනීම
identification card	han-dhu-num pah-thah	හැඳුනුම් පත
idiot	moh dah-yaah	මෝඩයා
ill	ah-sah-nee-pah • le-dah	අසනීප • ලෙඩ
immediately	dhan-mah	දැන්ම
immigration	aah-gah-mah-nah	ආගමන
important	va-dhah-gahth	වැදගත්

It's (not) important.
eh-kah va-dhah-gahth (na-ha)   ඒක වැදගත් (නැහැ).

included	a-thu-lahth	ඇතුළත්
indigestion	ah-jee-rah-nah-yah	අජීරණය
inequality	ah-sah-maah-nahth-vah-yah	අසමානත්වය
injection	be-heth vi-dhee-mah	බෙහෙත් විදීම
injury	thu-vaah-lah-yah	තුවාලය
inside	a-thu-lah • a-thu-lah-thah	ඇතුළ • ඇතුළත
insurance	rahk-shah-nah-yah	රැකණය
interesting	sith a-lum kah-rai	සිත් ඇලුම් කරයි
international	jaah-thyaahn-thah-rah	ජාත්‍යාන්තර
interview	sahm-mu-khah	සම්මුඛ
	pah-reek-shah-nah-yah	පරීක්ෂණය
island	dhoo-pah-thah •	දූපත •
	dhi-vah-yi-nah	දිවයින
itch	ka-sil-lah	කැසිල්ල
itinerary	gah-mahn vis-thah-rah-yah	ගමන් විස්තරය

J

jail	si-rah-ge-yah	සිරගෙය
jar	joh-gu-wah	ජෝගුව
jealous	eer-shyaah-vah	ඊර්ෂ්‍යාව
jeans	kah-li-sah-mah	කලිසම
jeep	jeep e-kah	ජීප් එක
jewellery	aah-bhah-rah-nah	ආභරණ
job	rahk-shaah-wah	රැකියාව
jockey	ahsh-vah	අශ්ව රෝහකයා
	roh-hah-kah-yaah	
joke	vi-hi-lu-wah	විහිළුව
joke (v)	vi-hi-lu kah-rah-nah-vaah	විහිළු කරනවා
journalist	leh-khah-kah-yek/	ලේඛකයෙක්/
	leh-khah-kaah-vi-yahk (m/f)	ලේඛිකාවියක්
journey	gah-mah-nah	ගමන
judge	vi-ni-su-ru	විනිසුරු •
	vi-nish-chah-yah-kah-ru	විනිශ්චයකරු
juice	yu-shah • is-mah	යුෂ • ඉෂ්ම
jump (v)	pah-ni-nah-vaah	පනිනවා
jumper	jahm-pah-rah-yah	ජම්පරය
justice	yuk-thi-yah	යුක්තිය

K

key	yah-thu-rah	යතුර
kick	pah-yin gah-sah-nah-vaah	පයින් ගහනවා
kill (v)	mah-rah-nah-vaah	මරනවා
kilogram	ki-loh-graa-mah-yah	කිලෝග්‍රෑමය
kilometre	ki-loh-mee-tah-rah-yah	කිලෝමීටරය
kind	kaah-ru-naah-vahn-thah	කරුණාවන්ත
kindergarten	baah-laahn-shah-yah	බාලාංශය

king	rah-jah	රජ
kiss	choom-bah-nah-yah	චුම්බනය
kitchen	kus-si-yah •	කුස්සිය •
	mu-lu-than ge-yah	මුළුතැන් ගෙය
kitten	bah-lahl pa-ti-yaah	බළල් පැටියා
knapsack	pi-tah mahl-lah	පිට මල්ල
knee	dhah-nah-hi-sah	දණහිස
knife	pi-hi-yah	පිහිය
know (v)	dha-nah gahn-nah-vaah	දැන ගන්නවා

I (don't) know.
mah-mah dhahn-neh (na-ha)   මම දන්නේ (නැහැ).

lace	rehn-dhah-yah	රේන්දය
lake	wa-vah	වැව
land	i-dah-mah	ඉඩම
languages	bhaah-shaah-vahn	භාෂාවන්
large	vi-shaah-lah • lo-ku	විශාල • ලොකු
last	ahn-thi-mah	අන්තිම
last month	pah-su-gi-yah maah-sah-yah	පසුගිය මාසය
last night	ee-yeh raa	ඊයේ රෑ
last week	pah-su-gi-yah sah-thi-yah	පසුගිය සතිය
last year	pah-su-gi-yah	පසුගිය
	ah-vu-rudh-dhah	අවුරුද්ද
late	pah-rahk-kuy	පරක්කුයි
laugh (n)	si-nah-hah-wah	සිනහව
launderette	lon-dah-ri-yah	ලොන්ඩරිය
law	nee-thi-yah	නීතිය
lawyer	nee-thee-gnah vah-rah-yek/	නීතිඥ වරයෙක්/
	vah-ri-yak (m/f)	වරියක්
laxatives	vi-reh-kah-yahn	විරේකයන්
lazy	kahm-ma-li	කම්මැලි
leaded (petrol)	ee-yahm sah-hi-thah	ඊයම් සහිත
learn (v)	i-ge-nah gahn-nah-vaah	ඉගෙන ගන්නවා
leather	hahm	හම්
be left	ahth-ha-rah yah-nah-vaah •	අත්හැර යනවා •
(behind/over, v)	i-thu-ru ve-nah-vaah	ඉතුරු වෙනවා
left (not right)	vah-mah	වම
left luggage	thah-baah gi-yah bah-du	තබා ගිය බඩු
left-wing	vaah-maahn-shah-yah	වාමාංශය
leg	kah-ku-lah	කකුළ
legalisation	nee-thi-gah-thah	නීතිගත කිරීම
	ki-ree-mah	
legislation	vyaah-vahs-thaah-vahn	ව්‍යවස්ථාවන්

lens	kahn-naah-di	කන්නාඩි
(camera/glasses)	vee-dhu-ru-wah	විදුරුව
lesbian	ga-ha-nu mai-thoo-nah	ගැහැණු මයිථුන
less	ah-du	අ
letter	li-pi-yah • li-yu-mah	ලිපිය • ලියුම
liar	bo-ru-kaah-rah-yaah	බොරුකාරයා
library	pus-thah-kaah-lah-yah	පුස්තකාලය
lice	u-ku-nahn • thah-di	උකුණන් • තඩි
lie (v)	bo-ru ki-yah-nah-vaah	බොරු කියනවා
life	jee-vi-thah-yah	ජීවිතය
lift (elevator)	uth-thoh-lah-kah-yah •	උත්තෝලකය •
	lift e-kah	ලිෆ්ට් එක
light (lamp)	lait e-kah	ලයිට් එක
light (not heavy)	sa-hal-lu	සැහැල්ලු
light (daylight)	e-li-yah	එළිය
lightbulb	vi-dhu-li bu-bu-lu-wah	විදුලි බුබුලුව
lighter	lai-tah-rah-yah	ලයිටරය
lighthouse	prah-dee-paah-gaah-rah-yah •	ප්‍රදීපාගාරය •
	lait hous e-kah	ලයිට් හවුස් එක
like (v)	ka-mah-thi ve-nah-vaah	කැමති වෙනවා
line	i-rah • reh-khaah-wah	ඉර • රේඛාව
lips	thol	තොල්
listen (v)	ah-saah si-ti-nah-vaah	අසා සිටිනවා
little (small)	po-di • ku-daah	පොඩි • කුඩා
a little (amount)	ti-kai	ටිකයි
live (v)	jee-vi-thah ve-nah-vaah	ජීවත් වෙනවා
local	pah-laah-theh	පළාතේ
lock	ah-gu-lah • lok e-kah	අගුල • ලොක් එක
lock (v)	yah-thu-ru/ah-gu-lu	යතුරු/අගුලු දමනවා
	dhah-mah-nah-vaah	
long	dhi-gah	දිග
long distance	dhu-rah prah-maah-nah-yah	දුර ප්‍රමාණය
look (v)	bah-lah-nah-vaah	බලනවා
look after (v)	bah-laah gahn-nah-vaah	බලා ගන්නවා
look for (v)	so-yah-nah-vaah	සොයනවා
lose (v)	na-thi kah-rah-nah-vaah	නැති කරනවා
a lot	go-dahk	ගොඩක්
loud	han-dah na-gee-mah	හඬ නැගීම
love (v)	aah-dhah-rah-yah	ආදරය කිරීම
	ki-ree-mah	
low	pah-hahth • ah-du	පහත් • අ
lucky	waah-sah-naah-wahn-thah	වාසනාවත්
luggage	bah-du mah-lu	බඩු මළු
luggage lockers	bah-du sehp-pu	බඩු සේප්පු
lunch	dhah-vahl kaa-mah	දවල් කෑම
luxury	su-koh-pah-boh-gee	සුබෝපභෝගී

M

machine	yahn-thrah-yah • me-shin e-kah	යන්තුය • මෙෂින් එක
mad	pis-su • ol-maah-dhah	පිස්සු • ඔල්මාද
magazine	sahn-gah-raah-wah	සඟරාව
mail	tha-pal	තැපැල්
mailbox	li-yum pet-ti-yah	ලියුම් පෙට්ටිය
main road	mah-hah-paah-rah	මහපාර
majority	va-di sahn-kyaah-wah	වැඩි සංඛ්‍යාව
make (v)	saah-dhah-nah-vaah	සාදනවා
make-up	sa-dhum lah-nah • o-pah gan-vee-mah	සැදුම් ලන • ඔප ගැන්වීම
man	mi-ni-saah	මිනිසා
manager	kah-lah-mah-naah-kaah-rah • ma-neh-jahr	කළමනාකාර • මැනේජර්
many	hun-gahk • bo-hoh-mah-yahk	හුඟාක් • බොහොමයක්
map	si-thi-yah-mah	සිතියම
marijuana	mah-ru-vaah-naah mahth dhrahv-yah	මරුවානා මත් දුවෳ
market	ve-lahn-dhah-po-lah • maah-kaht e-kah	වෙළඳපොළ • මාකට් එක
marriage	vi-vaah-hah-yah • kah-saah-dhah-yah	විවාහය • කසාදය
marry (v)	vi-vaah-hah ve-nah-vaah • kah-saah-dhah bahn-di-nah-vaah	විවාහ වෙනවා • කසාද බඳිනවා
marvellous	aash-chair-yah-mahth	ආශ්චර්යමත්
mass (Catholic)	poo-jaah-wah	පූජාව
massage	sahm-bhaah-yah-nah-yah	සම්භාහනය
match (sport)	mach e-kah • thah-rahn-gah-yah	මැච් එක • තරඟය
matches	gi-ni-koo-ru	ගිනිකූරු

It doesn't matter.
kah-mahk na-ha | කමක් නැහැ.

What's the matter?
mo-kah-dhah ve-laah thi-yehn-neh? | මොකද වෙලා තියෙන්නේ?

mattress	met-tah-yah	මෙට්ටය
maybe	ven-nah pu-lu-vahn	වෙන්න පුළුවන්
mechanic	yaahr-three-kah • kaahr-mi-kah shil-pi-yek/ shil-pi-ni-yahk (m/f)	යාන්තික • කාර්මික ශිල්පියෙක්/ශිල්පිනියක්
medicine	be-heth	බෙහෙත්
meet (v)	hah-mu ve-nah-vaah	හමු වෙනවා
member	saah-maah-ji-kah-yaah	සාමාජිකයා

M

menstruation	o-sahp vee-mah	ඔසප් වීම
menu	kaa-mah waht-toh-ru-wah	කෑම වට්ටෝරුව
message	pah-ni-vu-dah-yah	පණිවුඩය
metal	loh-hah	ලෝහ
metre	mee-tah-rah-yah	මීටරය
midnight	mah-dhyah-mah ra-yah	මධ්‍යම රැය
migraine	i-ru-waah rah-dhah-yah	ඉරුවා රදය
military service	hah-mu-dhaah seh-vah-yah	හමුදා සේවය
milk	ki-ri	කිරි
millimetre	mi-li-mee-tah-rah-yah	මිලිමීටරය
million	mi-li-yuh-nah-yah •	මිලියනය •
	dhah-shah lahk-shah-yah	දශ ලක්ෂය
mineral water	bim jah-lah-yah	බිම් ජලය
minute (time)	vi-naah-di-yahk	විනාඩියක්

Just a minute.
vi-naah-di-yahk in-nah   විනාඩියක් ඉන්න .

mirror	kahn-naah-di-yah	කන්නාඩිය
miscarriage	gahb-saah-vah	ගබ්සාව
miss (feel absence, v)	paah-lu-wah dha-ne-nah-vaah	පාළුව දැනෙනවා
mistake	ba-ri-vee-mah •	බැරිවීම •
	va-rah-dhee-mah	වැරදීම
mix (v)	mish-rah kah-rah-nah-vaah	මිශ්‍ර කරනවා
mobile phone	moh-bail fohn e-kah	මොබයිල් ෆෝන් එක
modem	moh-dahm e-kah	මොඩම් එක
moisturising cream	aah-leh-pah-yah • kreem	ආලේපය • ක්‍රිම්
monastery	thaah-pah-saah-raah-mah-yah	තාපසාරාමය
money	sahl-li • mu-dhahl	සල්ලි • මුදල්
monk	bhik-shu-wah	භික්ෂුව
month	maah-sah-yah	මාසය
monument	smaah-rah-kah-yah	ස්මාරකය
more	thah-vahth	තවත්
morning	u-dheh vah-ru-wah	උදේ වරුව
mosque	mus-lim pahl-li-yah	මුස්ලිම් පල්ලිය
mosquito coil	mah-dhu-ru dahn-gah-rah	මදුරු දඟර
mosquito net	mah-dhu-ru da-la	මදුරු දැල
mother	ahm-maah	අම්මා
mother-in-law	nan-dhahm-maah	නැන්දම්මා
motorboat	moh-toh both-tu-wah	මෝටෝ බෝට්ටුව
motorcycle	moh-toh bai-si-kah-lah-yah	මෝටෝ බයිසිකලය
mountain	kahn-dhah	කන්ද
mountain path	kahn-dhu maah-wah-thah	කදු මාවත
mouse	mee-yaah	මීයා
mouth	kah-tah	කට

D I C T I O N A R Y

movie	chith-rah-pah-ti-yah	චිත්‍රපටිය
mud	mah-dah	මඩ
Mum	ahm-maah	අම්මා
muscle	maahn-shah peh-sheen	මාංශ පේශින්
museum	kau-thu-kaah-gaah-rah-yah • kah-tu-ge-yah	කෞතුකාගාරය • කටුගෙය
music	sahn-gee-thah-yah	සංගීතය

N

name	nah-mah	නම
nappy	na-pi-yah	නැපිය
national park	jaah-thi-kah u-dhyaah-nah-yah	ජාතික උද්‍යානය
nationality	jaah-thi-kahth-vah-yah	ජාතිකත්වය
nature	so-baah-dhah-hah-mah	සොබාදහම
naturopath	swaah-bhaa-vi-kah vai-dhyah	ස්වාභාවික වෛද්‍ය
nausea	vah-mah-nah-yah gah-thi-yah	වමනය ගතිය
near	lahn-gah • kit-tu-wah	ළඟ • කිට්ටුව
necessary	ah-vah-shyah	අවශ්‍ය
necklace	maah-lah-yah	මාලය
need (v)	ah-vah-shyah ve-nah-vaah	අවශ්‍ය වෙනවා
needle (sewing)	in-dhi-kah-tu-wah	ඉඳිකටුව
needle (syringe)	si-rin-jahr kah-tu-wah	සිරින්ජර් කටුව
neither	hoh	හෝ
net	net e-kah	නෙට් එක
never	kah-vah-dhaah-vahth na-ha	කවදාවත් නැහැ
new	ah-luth	අලුත්
news	prah-vruth-thi • pu-wahth	ප්‍රවෘත්ති • පුවත්
newspaper	pu-wahth-pah-thah	පුවත්පත
New Year's Day	ah-luth ahv-ru-dhu dhi-nah	අලුත් අවුරුදු දින
New Year's Eve	ah-luth ahv-ru-dhu dhi-nah-tah pe-rah dhi-nah	අලුත් අවුරුදු දිනට පෙර දින
next	ee-lahn-gah	ඊළඟ
next month	ee-lahn-gah maah-sah-yah	ඊළඟ මාසය
next week	ee-lahn-gah sah-thi-yah	ඊළඟ සතිය
nice	lahs-sah-nai • hon-dhai	ලස්සණයි • හොඳයි
night	raa • raahth-ri-yah	රෑ • රාත්‍රිය

| No. | | |
| na-ha | | නැහැ . |

noisy	shahb-dhah-vahth	ශබ්දවත්
none	ki-si-ve-ku no-veh	කිසිවෙකු නොවේ
noon	dhah-hah-vah-lah	දහවල

O

north	u-thu-rah	උතුර
nose	nah-hah-yah • naah-sah-yah	නහය • නාසය
notebook	noht po-thah	නෝට් පොත
nothing	ki-si-vahk na-ha	කිසිවක් නැහැ
now	dhan	දැන්
nun	me-he-ni-yah • bhik-shu-ni-yah	මෙහෙණිය • භික්ෂුණිය
nurse	he-dhi-yah • saahth-thu seh-vah-kah-yek seh-vi-kaah-vahk (m/f)	හෙදිය • සාත්තු සේවකයෙක්/ සේවිකාවක්

O

obvious	prah-thyahk-shah	පුතාක්ෂ
ocean	mu-hu-dhah	මුහුද
offence	vah-rah-dhah	වරද
office	kahn-thoh-ru-wah	කන්තෝරුව
often	ni-thah-rah	නිතර
oil (cooking)	thel	තෙල්
oil (crude)	ah-mu thel	අමු තෙල්

| OK. | | |
| hon-dhai | | හොඳයි. |

old	pah-rah-nah	පරණ
olive oil	o-liv thel	ඔලිව් තෙල්
olives	ve-rah-lu	වෙරළු
Olympic Games	o-lim-pik kree-daah	ඔලිම්පික් කිුඩා
on	u-dah • mah-thah	උඩ • මත
on time	ve-laah-vah-tah	වේලාවට
once	e-kah vah-thaah-vahk	එක වතාවක්
one-way (ticket)	ek dhi-saah-vah-kah-tah	එක දිසාවකට
only	pah-mah-nai • vi-thah-rai	පමණයි • විතරයි
open	vi-vur-thah • a-rah-lah	විවෘත • ඇරල
open (v)	ah-ri-nah-vaah	අරිනවා
opera	sahn-gee-thah naaht-yah	සංගීත නාට්‍ය
opera house	sahn-gee-thah naaht-yah shaah-laah-wah	සංගීත නාට්‍ය ශාලාව
operation	shahl-yah-kahr-mah-yah	ශල්‍යකර්මය
opinion	mah-thah-yah	මතය
opposite (facing)	i-dhi-ri-pi-tah • is-sah-rah-hah	ඉදිරිපිට • ඉස්සරහ
opposite (unlike)	vi-rudh-dhah (unlike)	විරුද්ද
or	hoh • nath-nahm	හෝ • නැත්නම්
orchestra	thoor-yah vaah-dhah-kah mahn-dah-lah-yah	තූර්ය වාදක මණ්ඩලය
order	pi-li-ve-lah	පිළිවෙළ
order (v)	il-lum kah-rah-nah-vaah	ඉල්ලුම් කරනවා

ordinary	saah-maahn-yah	සාමාන්‍ය
organise	sahn-vi-dhaah-nah-yah	සංවිධානය
original	mul	මුල්
other	ve-nahth	වෙනත්
outside	pi-tah-thah	පිට
over	hah-maah-rai • i-vah-rai	හමාරයි • ඉවරයි
overdose	be-heth prah-maah-nah-yah ik-mah-vee-mah	බෙහෙත් ප්‍රමාණය ඉක්මවීම
owe (v)	nah-yah ga-thi ve-nah vaah	ණය ගැති වෙනවා
owner	ai-thi-kah-ru	අයිතිකරු
oxygen	ok-si-jahn	ඔක්සිජන්
ozone layer	oh-sohn thah-lah-yah	ඕසෝන් තලය

P

pacifier (dummy)	soop-pu-wah	සූප්පුව
package	bah-du mi-ti-yah	බඩු මිටිය
packet	pa-kaht-tu-wah	පැකට්ටුව
padlock	ib-baah	ඉබ්බා
pain	ru-dhah-wah • kak-ku-mah	රුදාව • කැක්කුම
painful	kak-kum-mai	කැක්කුමයි
painkillers	ru-dhaah naah-shah-kah	රුදා නාශක
paint (v)	theen-thah gaah-nah-vaah	තීන්ත ගානවා
painting (the art)	chith-rah-kahr-mah-yah	චිත්‍රකර්මය
pair (a couple)	joh-du-wah	ජෝඩුව
palace	maah-li-gah-wah	මාලිගාව
pan	thaahch-chu-wah	තාච්චුව
pap smear	pap smi-yah pi-li-kaah pah-reek-shah-nah-yah	පැප් ස්මිය පිළිකා පරීක්ෂණය
paper	ko-lah	කොළ
paraplegic	kon-dhu-a-tah pahk-shaah-ghaah-thah-voo	කොන්දඇට පක්ෂාඝාතවූ
parcel	paahr-sah-lah-yah	පාර්සලය
parents	dhe-mahv-pi-yahn	දෙමව්පියන්
park	u-dhyaah-nah-yah	උද්‍යානය
park (v)	nah-thah-rah kah-rah thah-bah-nah-vaah	නතර කර තබනවා
parliament	paahr-li-mehn-thu-wah	පාර්ලිමේන්තුව
party (fiesta)	saah-dhah-yah	සාදය
party (politics)	pahk-shah-yah	පක්ෂය
pass	sah-maahr-thah-yah • pah-su ki-ree-mah	සමාර්ථය • පහසු කිරීම
passenger	mah-gi-yaah	මගියා
passport	gah-mahn bah-lah-pahth-rah-yah • paahs-poht e-kah	ගමන් බලපත්‍රය • පාස්පෝට් එක
passport number	paahs-poht an-kah-yah	පාස්පෝට් අංකය

P

past	ah-thee-thah-yah	අතීතය
path	ah-di-pah-rah • mah-gah	අඩිපාර • මග
patient (adj)	roh-gi-yaah	රෝගියා
pay (v)	ge-vah-nah-vaah	ගෙවනවා
peace	saah-mah-yah	සාමය
peak	mu-dhu-nah	මුදුන
pedestrian	mah-gi-yaah	මගියා
pen (ballpoint)	paa-nah	පෑන
pencil	pan-sah-lah	පැන්සල
penis	pu-ru-shah lin-gah-yah	පුරුෂ ලිංගය
penknife	ku-daah pi-hi-yah	කුඩා පිහිය
pensioner	vi-shraah-mi-kah-yaah	විශ්‍රාමිකයා
people	mah-hah-jah-nah-yaah •	මහජනයා •
	mi-nis-su	මිනිස්සු
pepper	gahm-mi-ris	ගම්මිරිස්
percent	prah-thi-shah-thah-yah	ප්‍රතිශතය
performance	rahn-gah dhak-mah	රඟ දැක්ම
period pain	o-sahp ru-dhaah	ඔසප් රුදා
permanent	sthee-rah	ස්ථිර
permission	ah-vah-sah-rah-yah	අවසරය
permit	bah-lah-pahth-rah-yah •	බලපත්‍රය •
	ah-vah-sah-rah	අවසරය
person	pudh-gah-lah-yaah	පුද්ගලයා
petrol	pet-rohl	පෙට්‍රෝල්
pharmacy	in-gree-si be-heth	ඉංග්‍රීසි බෙහෙත්
	shaa-laa-wah	ශාලාව
phone book	te-li-fohn ahn-kah	ටෙලිෆෝන් අංක
	po-thah	පොත
phone box	po-du	පොදු
	dhu-rah-kah-thah-nah-yahk	දුරකථනයක
phonecard	te-li-fohn kaahd e-kah	ටෙලිෆෝන්
		කාඩ් එක
photo	chaah-yaah-roo-pah-yah	ඡායාරූපය

> May I take a photo?
> mah-mah pin-thoo-rah-yahk
> gahn-nah-dhah?
>
> මම පින්තූරයක්
> ගන්නද?

pie	pai e-kah	පයි එක
piece	kaal-lah	කෑල්ල
pig	oo-raah	ඌරා
pill	be-heth peth-thah	බෙහෙත් පෙත්ත
the Pill	pi-li-si-dhee-mah	පිළිසිඳීම
	va-lak-vee-meh be-he-thah	වැළැක්වීමේ
		බෙහෙත
pillow	kot-tah-yah	කොට්ටය
pillowcase	kot-tah u-rah-yah	කොට්ට උරය
pine	pah-yin gah-sah	පයින් ගස

**D
I
C
T
I
O
N
A
R
Y**

pink	roh-sah paah-tah	රෝස පාට
pipe	paip-pah-yah	පයිප්පය
place	sthaah-nah-yah	ස්ථානය
plain (not mixed)	nu-mu-hun	නුමුහුන්
plain (field)	tha-ni-thah-laah-wah	තැනිතලාව
plane	ah-hahs yaah-nah-yah	අහස් යානය
plant	pa-lah-yah	පැලය
plastic	plaahs-tik	ප්ලාස්ටික්
plate	pi-gaah-nah	පිඟාන
plateau	tha-ni-thah-laah-wah	තැනිතලාව
platform	veh-dhi-kaah-wah	වේදිකාව
play (theatre)	naah-dhah-gahm	නාඩගම්
play (a game, v)	sel-lahm kah-rah-nah-vaah	සෙල්ලම් කරනවා
play (music, v)	vaah-dhah-nah-yah kah-rah-nah-vaah	වාදනය කරනවා
player (sport)	kree-dah-kah-yaah	ක්‍රීඩකයා
plug (bath)	a-bah-yah	ඇබය
plug (electricity)	plahg e-kah	ප්ලග් එක
pocket	saahk-ku-wah	සාක්කුව
poetry	kah-vi	කවි
point (v)	an-gil-len pen-vah-nah-vaah	ඇඟිල්ලෙන් පෙන්වනවා
police	po-lee-si-yah	පොලීසිය
politics	dheh-shah-paah-lah-nah-yah	දේශපාලනය
pollen	mahl-reh-nu	මල්රේණු
pollution	dhoo-shah-nah-yah	දූෂණය
poor	dup-path	දුප්පත්
popular	jah-nah-pri-yah	ජනප්‍රිය
port	vah-raah-yah	වරාය
possible	ha-ki	හැකි

It's (not) possible.
(no) ha-ki   (නො) හැකි .

postcard	tha-pal pah-thah	තැපැල් පත
post code	tha-pal sahn-keh-thah	තැපැල් සංකේත
post office	tha-pal kahn-thoh-ru-wah	තැපැල් කන්තෝරුව
pottery	ma-ti kahr-mahn-thah-yah	මැටි කර්මාන්තය
poverty	dhi-lin-dhu bah-vah	දිළිඳු බව
power	bah-lah-yah	බලය
prayer	yaag-gnaah-wah	යාඥාව
prefer (v)	vah-daahth ka-mah-thi ve-nah-vaah	වඩාත් කැමති වෙනවා
pregnant	gab-bah-rah	ගැබ්බර

ENGLISH – SINHALA

pre-menstrual tension	o-sahp vee-mah-tah pe-rah a-thi-vah-nah ah-sah-hah-nah thaah-vah-yah	ඔසප් වීමට පෙර ඇතිවන අසහන තාවය
prepare (v)	soo-dhaah-nahm ve-nah-vaah	සූදානම් වෙනවා
present (gift)	thaag-gah	තෑග්ග
president	sah-baah-pah-thi	සභාපති
pressure	pee-dah-nah-yah	පීඩනය
pretty	pi-yah-kah-ru	පියකරු
prevent	va-lak-vee-mah	වැළැක්වීම
price	mi-lah	මිල
pride	ah-hahn-kaah-rah-yah	අහංකාරය
priest	poo-jah-kah-vah-rah-yaah	පූජකවරයා
prime minister	ah-gah-ma-thi	අගමැති
prison	si-rah ge-yah • bahn-dhah-naah-gaah-rah-yah	සිර ගෙය • බන්ධනාගාරය
private	pudh-gah-li-kah	පුද්ගලික
profession	vruth-thee-yah	වෘත්තිය
profit	laah-bah	ලාභ
program	va-dah-sah-tah-hah-nah	වැඩසටහන
promise	po-ron-dhu-wah	පොරොන්දුව
protect (v)	aah-rahk-shaah kah-rah-nah-vaah	ආරක්ෂා කරනවා
protest	vi-roh-dhah-yah	විරෝධය
public toilet	po-dhu va-si-ki-li	පොදු වැසිකිළි
pull (v)	ah-dhi-nah-waah	අදිනවා
pump	pom-pah-yah	පොම්පය
puncture	hi-lahk	හිලක්
punish (v)	dhah-du-vahm ki-ree-mah	දඬුවම් කිරීම
pure	pi-ri-si-dhu	පිරිසිදු
purple	dhahm paah-tah	දම් පාට
push (v)	thahl-lu kah-rah-nah-vaah	තල්ලු කරනවා

Q

qualifications	su-dhu-su-kahm	සුදුසුකම්
quality	thahth-vah-yah	තත්වය
quarantine	ni-roh-dhaah-yah-nah-yah	නිරෝධායනය
quarter	kaah-lah	කාල
question	prahsh-nah-yah	ප්‍රශ්නය
queue	poh-li-mah	පෝලිම
quick	ik-mah-nin	ඉක්මනින්
quiet	ni-hahn-dah • nish-shahb-dhah	නිහඬ • නිශ්ශබ්ද
quit (v)	i-vahth ve-nah-vaah	ඉවත් වෙනවා

D
I
C
T
I
O
N
A
R
Y

R

rabbit	haah-waah	හාවා
race (breed)	jaah-thi-yah	ජාතිය
race (sport)	thah-rahn-gah dhi-vee-mah	තරහ දිවීම
racism	jaah-thi vi-roh-dhah-yah	ජාති විරෝධය
racquet	dhal pith-thah • ra-kaht e-kah	දැල් පිත්ත • රැකට් එක
railway station	dhum-ri-yah staah-nah-yah	දුම්රිය ස්ථානය
rain	vas-sah	වැස්ස

It's raining.

va-hi vah-hi-nah-vaah	වැහි වහිනවා .

rape	dhoo-shah-nah-yah	දූෂණය
rare	dhur-lah-bah	දුර්ලභ
rash	kush-tah-yah	කුෂ්ඨය
raw	ah-mu	අමු
razor	dha-li pi-hi-yah	දැලි පිහිය
razor blades	blehd thah-lah	බ්ලේඩ් තල
read (v)	ki-yah-vah-nah-vaah	කියවනවා
ready	soo-dhaah-nahm • laas-thi	සූදානම් • ලැස්ති
realise (v)	va-tah-he-nah-vaah	වැටහෙනවා
reason	heh-thu-vah	හේතුව
receipt	ku-vi-thaahn-si-yah	කුවිතාන්සිය
receive (v)	la-be-nah-vaah	ලැබෙනවා
recent(ly)	maa-thah(-kah-dee)	මෑත(කදී)
recognise (v)	hahn-dhu-naah gahn-nah-vaah	හඳුනා ගන්නවා
recommend (v)	nir-dheh-shah kah-rah-nah-vaah	නිර්දේශ කරනවා
recycling	prah-thi-chah-kree-yah- kah-rah-nah-yah	පුතිවකුියකරණය
referee	mah-dhyahs-thah-kah-ru	මධ්‍යස්ථකරු
refrigerator	shee-thah-kah-rah-nah-yah	ශීතකරණය
refugee	sah-rah-naah-gah-thah-yaah	සරණාගතයා
refund	aah-pah-su ge-vee-mah	ආපසු ගෙවීම
refuse (v)	prah-thik-sheh-pah kah-rah-nah-vaah	පුතිෂෙප කරනවා
registered mail	li-yaah pah-dhin-chi tha-pal	ලියා පදිංචි තැපැල්
relationship	sahm-bahn-dhah- thaah-vah-yah	සම්බන්ධතාවය
relax (v)	vi-veh-kah gahn-nah-vaah	විවෙක ගන්නවා
religion	aah-gah-mah	ආගම
remember (v)	si-hi-pahth/mah-thahk kah-rah-nah-vaah	සිහිපත්/මතක කරනවා

R

rent (v)	ku-li-yah-tah	කුලියට දෙනවා
	dhe-nah-vaah	
repair (v)	ah-luth-va-dhi-yaah	අලුත්වැඩියා
	kah-rah-nah-vaah	කරනවා
reservation	ven-kah-rah-nah lah-dhah	වෙන්කරන ලද
reserve (v)	kah-lin	කලින්
	ven kah-rah-nah-vaah	වෙන් කරනවා
rest (relaxation)	vi-veh-kah-yah	විවේකය
rest (what's left)	i-thi-ri-yah	ඉතිරිය
rest (v)	vi-veh-kah gahn-nah-vaah	විවේක ගන්නවා
restaurant	aah-pah-nah	ආපන ශාලාව
	shaah-laah-wah	
resume (cv)	vis-tha-rah	විස්තර
	sahn-ksheh-pah-yah	සංකේෂපය
retired	vi-shraah-mi-kah	විශ්‍රාමික
return (ticket)	yaah-mah-tah eh-mah-tah	යාමට ඒමට
return (v)	aah-pah-su	ආපසු පැමිණෙනවා
	pa-mi-ne-nah-vaah	
rice	bahth	බත්
rich (wealthy)	po-ho-sath	පොහොසත්
right (correct)	ni-va-rah-dhi • hah-ri	නිවැරදි • හරි

You're right.
o-bah hah-ri   ඔබ හරි.

right (not left)	dhah-ku-nah	දකුණ
right-wing	dhah-ku-nu	දකුණු පාර්ශවය
	paahr-shah-vah-yah	
ring (on finger)	mudh-dhah	මුද්ද
ring (of phone)	naah-dhah-ya	නාදය
rip-off	gah-saah ka-mah	ගසා කෑම
risk	u-vah-dhu-rah	උවදුර
river	gahn-gah	ගංගා
road (main)	(mah-hah) paah-rah	(මහ) පාර
road map	maahr-gah si-thi-yah-mah	මාර්ග සිතියම
rock	pahr-vah-thah-yah	පර්වතය
room	kaah-mah-rah-yah	කාමරය
rope	kahm-bah-yah	කඹය
round	rah-vum	රවුම්
(at the) roundabout	vah-tah-rah-vu-mah(dee)	වට රවුම(දී)
rowing	o-ru pa-dhee-mah	ඔරු පැදීම
rubbish	ku-nu	කුණු
rug	pah-lah-sah	පලස
ruins	nah-tah-bun	නටබුන්
rules	nee-thi	නීති
run (v)	dhu-wah-nah-vaah	දුවනවා

S

English	Pronunciation	Sinhala
sad	dhu-kah	දුක
safe (n)	sehp-pu-wah	සේප්පුව
safe (adj)	aah-rahk-shaah-vai	ආරක්ෂාවයි
safe sex	aah-rahk-shi-thah lin-gi-kah sahn-sahr-gah-yah	ආරක්ෂිත ලිංගික සංසර්ගය
saint	saahn-thu-vah-rah-yaah	සාන්තුවරයා
salary	va-tu-pah	වැටුප
(on) sale	vi-ki-nee-mah-tah	විකිණීමට
salt	lu-nu	ලුණු
same	eh-kah-mah	එකම
sand	va-li	වැලි
sanitary napkins	o-sahp paad e-kah	ඔසප් පැඩ් එක
save (v)	i-thi-ri kah-rah-nah-vaah	ඉතිරි කරනවා
say (v)	ki-yah-nah-vaah	කියනවා
scarf	skaahf e-kah	ස්කාර්ෆ් එක
school	paah-sa-lah • is-koh-leh	පාසැල • ඉස්කෝලේ
science	vidh-yaah-vah	විද්‍යාව
scissors	kah-thu-rah	කතුර
score (v)	lah-ku-nu lah-baah gahn-nah-vaah	ලකුණු ලබා ගන්නවා
sculpture	prah-thi-maah nir-maah-nah-yah	ප්‍රතිමා නිර්මාණය
sea	mu-hu-dhah	මුහුද
seasick	mu-hu-dhu yaa-meh-dee a-thi-vah-nah vah-mah-nah-yah	මුහුදු යෑමේදී ඇතිවන වමනය
seat	ah-su-nah • seet e-kah	අසුන • සීට් එක
seatbelt	aah-sah-nah pah-ti	ආසන පටි
second (time)	thaht-pah-rah-yah	තත්පරය
second (not first)	dhe-vah-ni	දෙවනි
see (v)	bah-lah-nah-vaah	බලනවා

We'll see.
bah-lah-mu
බලමු.

I see. (understand)
mah-tah theh-re-nah-vaah
මට තේරෙනවා.

See you later.
pahs-seh hah-mu-ve-mu
පස්සේ හමුවෙමු.

English	Pronunciation	Sinhala
self-employed	swah-yahn ra-ki-yaah-veh ni-yu-thu	ස්වයං රැකියාවේ නියුතු
selfish	aahth-maar-thah-kaah-mee	ආත්මාර්ථකාමී
self-service	swah-yahn seh-vaah	ස්වයං සේවා
sell (v)	vi-ku-nah-nah-vaah	විකුණනවා

send (v)	e-vah-nah-vaah	එවනවා
sensible	budh-dhi-mahth	බුද්ධිමත්
sentence (words)	vaahk-yah-yah	වාකාය
sentence (prison)	si-rah dhahn-du-wah-mah	සිර දඩුවම
separate (v)	ven kah-rah-nah-vaah	වෙන් කරනවා
series	kaahn-dah-yah	කාණ්ඩය
serious	bah-lah-vahth • dhah-ru-nu	බලවත් • දරුණු
several	no-yek • vi-vi-dah	නොයෙක් • විවිධ
sex	lin-gah-yah • lin-gi-kah	ලිංගය •
	sahn-sahr-gah-yah	ලිංගික සංසර්ගය
sexism	lin-gi-kahth-vah-yah	ලිංගිකත්වය
shade	se-vah-nah	සෙවන
shampoo	sham-poo	ෂැම්පු
share (with, v)	be-dhaah gahn-nah-vaah	බෙදා ගන්නවා
shave (v)	ra-vu-lah baah-nah-vaah	රැවුල බානවා
she	a-yah	ඇය
sheep	ba-tah-lu-waah	බැටළුවා
sheet (bed)	a-thi-ril-lah •	ඇතිරිල්ල •
	sheet e-kah	සීට් එක
sheet (of paper)	ko-lah-yah	කොළය
shell	sip-pi kah-tu	සිප්පි කටු
shelves	thaht-tu	තට්ටු
ship	na-vah	නැව
shirt	kah-mi-sah-yah	කමිසය
shoes	sah-pahth-thu	සපත්තු
shop	saahp-pu-wah	සාප්පුව
go shopping (v)	saahp-pu yah-nah-vaah	සාප්පු යනවා
short (length)	ke-ti	කෙටි
short (height)	ko-tah	කොට
shorts	ko-tah kah-li-sahn	කොට කලිසම්
shoulders	u-rah-his	උරහිස්
shout (v)	kaa gah-sah-nah-vaah	කෑ ගසනවා
show	rahn-gah dhak-mah	රඟ දැක්ම
show (v)	pen-vah-nah-vaah	පෙන්වනවා

Can you show me on the map?
mah-tah si-thi-yah-meh
pen-vahn-nah pu-lu-vahn-dhah?
මට සිතියමේ
පෙන්වන්න පුළුවන්ද?

shower	wah-thu-rah mah-lah •	වතුර මල •
	shah-vahr e-kah	ෂවර් එක
shrine	poo-jaah sthaah-nah-yah	පූජා ස්ථානය
shut (v)	vah-hah-nah-vaah	වහනවා
sick	ah-sah-nee-pai	අසනීප
sign	sah-lah-ku-nah	සලකුණ
signature	ahth-sah-nah	අත්සන
silk	silk	සිල්ක්
silver	ri-dhee	රිදී

S

similar	sah-maah-nah	සමාන
since (May)	si-tah/i-dahn (ma-yi)	සිට/ඉදන් (මැයි)
sing (v)	sin-dhu ki-yah-nah-vaah	සින්දු කියනවා
singer	gaah-yah-kah-yaah	ගායකයා
single (person)	thah-ni	තනි
single (unique)	ah-sah-haah-yah	අසහාය
single room	thah-ni kaah-mah-rah-yah	තනි කාමරය
sister	ahk-kaah (older)	අක්කා
	nahn-gee (younger)	නංගී
	so-hoh-yu-ri-yah (refers to either)	සොහොයුරිය
sit (v)	in-dhah gahn-nah-vaah	ඉඳ ගන්නවා
size (of anything)	prah-maah-nah-yah • thah-rah-mah	පුමාණය • තරම
size (clothes • shoes)	sais e-kah	සයිස් එක
skin	hah-mah	හම
sky	ah-hah-sah	අහස
sleep (v)	ni-dhah-nah-vaah	නිදනවා
sleeping bag	slee-pin baag e-kah	ස්ලිපිං බෑග් එක
sleeping car	ni-dhah-nah ma-di-ri-yah	නිදන මැදිරිය
sleeping pills	ni-dhi pe-thi	නිදි පෙති
slide (film)	dhah-lah seh-yaah pah-ti-yah	දළ සේයා පටිය
slow	he-min	හෙමින්
slowly	he-min	හෙමින්
small	pun-chi • po-di	පුංචි • පොඩි
smell	su-wahn-dhah	සුවඳ
smile (v)	si-naah se-nah-vaah	සිනාසෙනවා
smoke (v)	dhum =bo-nah-vaah	දුම් බොනවා
soap	sah-bahn	සබන්
soccer	paah-pahn-dhu	පාපන්දු
social security	sah-maah-jah aah-rahk-shaah-vah	සමාජ ආරක්ෂාව
social welfare	sah-maah-jah ah-bhi-vrudh-dhi-yah	සමාජ අභිවෘද්ධිය
socialist	sah-maah-jah-vaah-dhee	සමාජවාදී
solid	ghah-nah	ඝන
some	a-tham	ඇතැම්
someone	kahv-ru hoh	කව්රු හෝ
something	yah-mahk	යමක්
sometimes	a-tham vi-tah	ඇතැම් විට
son	pu-thaah	පුතා
song	gee-thah-yah	ගීතය
soon	ik-mah-nin	ඉක්මනින්

I'm sorry.
mah-tah kah-nah-gaah-tuy මට කණගාටුයි .

| south | dhah-ku-nah | දකුණ |

216

S

souvenir	sa-mah-ru bhaahn-dah-yah • smaah-rah-kah-yah	සැමරු භාණ්ඩය • ස්මාරකය
speak (v)	kah-thaah kah-rah-nah-vaah	කථා කරනවා

Do you speak English?
o-bah in-gree-si kah-<u>thaah</u>
kau-rah-nah-vaah-dhah?

ඔබ ඉංග්‍රීසි කථා
කරනවාද?

special	vi-sheh-shah	විශේෂ
speed	veh-gah-yah	වේගය
speed limit	veh-gah see-maah-wah	වේග සීමාව
spicy (hot)	ku-lu-bah-du ye-doo	කුළුබඳු යෙදූ
sport	kree-daah	ක්‍රීඩා
sprain	u-luk-ku-wah	උළුක්කුව
spring (season)	wah-sahn-thah kaah-lah-yah	වසන්ත කාලය
square (in town)	chah-thu-rahsh-rah-yah	චතුරශ්‍රය
stadium	kree-daahn-gah-nah-yah	ක්‍රීඩාංගනය
stage	kah-rah-li-yah • veh-dhi-kaah-wah	කරලිය • වේදිකාව
stairway	pah-dhi pe-lah	පඩි පෙළ
stale	pah-rah-nai/nah-rahk ve-laah	පරණයි/නරක් වෙලා
stamp	mudh-dhah-rah-yah	මුද්දරය
standard (usual)	saah-maahn-nyah-yah	සාමාන්‍ය
start (v)	pah-tahn gahn-nah-vaah	පටන් ගන්නවා
station	pola • sthaah-nah-yah	පොළ • ස්ථානය
stationers	li-pi drahv-yah saahp-pu-wah	ලිපි දුවා සාප්පුව
statue	pra-thi-maah-wah	ප්‍රතිමාව
stay (remain, v)	in-nah-vaah	ඉන්නවා
stay (somewhere, v)	nah-vah-thi-nah-vaah	නවතිනවා
steal (v)	so-rah-kahm ki-ree-mah	සොරකම් කිරීම
steep	ah-di-kah baa-vum sah-hi-thah	අධික බෑවුම් සහිත
step	pah-di-yah	පඩිය
stomach	bah-dah	බඩ
stomachache	bah-deh kak-ku-mah	බඩේ කැක්කුම
stone	gah-lah	ගල
stop (v)	nah-vah-thin-nah-vaah	නවතිනවා

Stop!
nah-vah-thin-nu!

නවතිනු!

storm	ku-naah-tu-wah	කුණාටුව
story	kah-thaahn-thah-rah-yah	කථාන්තරය
straight	ke-lin	කෙළින්
strange	pu-dhu-mah sah-hah-gah-thah	පුදුම සහගත
stranger	naahn-dhu-nah-nah ke-nek	නාඳුනන කෙනෙක්
stream	a-lah	ඇල

D
I
C
T
I
O
N
A
R
Y

street	vee-thi-yah	වීථිය
strike	va-dah	වැඩ
	vahr-jah-nah-yah	වර්ජනය
string	lah-nu-wah	ලනුව
strong	shahk-thi-mahth	ශක්තිමත්
student	shish-yah-yek/	ශිෂ්‍යයෙක්/
	shish-yaah-wahk (m/f)	ශිෂ්‍යාවක්
stupid	mot-tah • ah-mah-nah	මෝට්ට • අමන
subtitles	u-pah sheer-shah	උප ශීර්ෂය
suburb	pah-laah-thah	පළාත
success	sah-maahr-thah-yah	සමාර්ථය
suffer (v)	dhuk vin-dhi-nah-waah	දුක් විඳිනවා
sugar	see-ni	සීනි
suitcase	soot-kehs e-kah	සූට්කේස් එක
summer	ush-nah kaah-lah-yah	උෂ්ණ කාලය
sun	i-rah • hi-ru	ඉර • හිරු
sunburn	ahv rahsh-nah-yah-tah	අව් රෂ්ණයට
	pich-chee-mah	පිච්චීම
sunglasses	ahv-kahn-naah-di	අව්කන්නාඩි
sunny	ahv-vai	අව්වයි
sunrise	hi-ru u-dhaah-vah	හිරු උදාව
sunset	hi-ru bas-mah	හිරු බැස්ම
surface mail	saah-maahn-yah tha-pal	සාමාන්‍ය තැපැල්
surname	vaah-sah-gah-mah	වාසගම
surprise	bah-laah-po-roth-thu	බලාපොරොත්තු
	no-voo • pu-dhu-mah-yah	නොවූ • පුදුමය
survive (v)	no-ma-ree jee-vahth	නොමැරී ජීවත්
	ve-nah-waah	වෙනවා
sweet	pa-ni rah-sah	පැණි රස
swim (v)	pi-hi-nah-nah-waah	පිහිනනවා
swimming pool	pool e-kah • pi-hi-num	පූල් එක • පිහිනුම්
	thah-taah-kah-yah	තටාකය
swimsuit	pi-hi-num an-dhum	පිහිනුම් ඇඳුම්
	kaht-tah-lah-yah	කට්ටලය
sympathetic	saah-nu-kahm-pi-thah	සානුකම්පිත
synagogue	yu-dhev	යුදෙව්
	poo-jahs-sthaah-nah-yah	පූජාස්ථානය
synthetic	kru-thri-mah	කෘත්‍රිම
syringe	si-rin-jah-rah-yah	සිරින්ජරය

T

table	meh-sah-yah	මේසය
table tennis	teh-bahl te-nis	ටේබල් ටෙනිස්
	kree-daah-vah	ක්‍රීඩාව
tail	vah-li-gah-yah	වලිගය
take (away, v)	pah-se-kah-tah	පැසෙකට ගන්නවා
	gahn-nah-vaah	

T

take (food, v)	gahn-nah-vaah	ගන්නවා
take (train, v)	yah-nah-vaah	යනවා
take photographs (v)	pin-thoo-rah gahn-nah-vaah	පින්තූර ගන්නවා
talk (v)	kah-thaah kah-rah-nah-vaah	කථා කරනවා
tall	u-sah	උස
tampons	o-sahp ahn-dhah-nah-yahn	ඔසප් අඳනයන්
tasty	rah-sah	රස
tax	bah-dhu	බදු
taxi stand	ku-lee rah-thah gaah-lah	කුලී රථ ගාල
team	kahn-daah-rah-mah	කණ්ඩායම
tear (crying)	kahn-dhu-lah	කඳුළු
teeth	dhahth	දත්
telegram	vi-dhu-li pah-ni-vu-dhah-yah	විදුලි පණිවුඩය
telephone	dhu-rah-kah-thah-nah-yah	දුරකථනය
telephone (v)	te-li-fohn kah-rah-nah-vaah	ටෙලිෆෝන් කරනවා
telephone office	dhu-rah-kah-thah-nah kahn-thoh-ru	දුරකථන කන්තෝරුව
television	roo-pah-vah-hi-ni-yah	රූපවාහිනිය
tell (v)	ki-yah-nah-vaah	කියනවා
temperature (fever)	u-nah	උණ
temperature (weather)	ush-nahth-vah-yah	උෂ්ණත්වය
temple	pahn-sah-lah	පන්සල
tennis	te-nis kree-daah-wah	ටෙනිස් ක්‍රීඩාව
tent	koo-dhaah-rah-mah	කූඩාරම
tent pegs	koo-daah-rahm a-bah	කූඩාරම් ඇබ
terrible	bhah-yaah-nah-kai	භයානකයි
test	pah-reek-shah-nah-yah	පරීක්ෂණය
thank (v)	sthoo-thi kah-rah-nah-vaah	ස්තුති කරනවා

| Thank you. | | ස්තූතියි . |
| sthoo-thiy | | |

theatre	nru-thyah shaah-laah-wah	නෘත්‍ය ශාලාව
they	o-vun	ඔවුන්
thick	ghah-nah	ඝන
thief	ho-raah	හොරා
thin	thu-nee	තුනී
think (v)	hi-thah-nah-vaah	හිතනවා
third	thun-ve-ni	තුන්වෙනි
thirsty	pi-paah-sah-yah • thi-bah-hah	පිපාසය • තිබහ
this (one)	meh-kah	මේක
thought	si-thu-vi-li	සිතුවිලි
throat	u-gu-rah	උගුර
ticket	ti-kaht e-kah	ටිකට් එක
ticket collector	ti-kaht e-kah-thu kah-rahn-naah	ටිකට් එකතු කරන්නා

D
I
C
T
I
O
N
A
R
Y

ticket machine	ti-kaht ma-shi-nah	ටිකට් මැෂිම
ticket office	ti-kaht kahn-thoh-ru-wah	ටිකට් කන්තෝරුව
time	veh-laah-vah	වේලාව
timetable	kaah-lah-sah-tah-hah-nah	කාලසටහන
tin (can)	tin e-kah	ටින් එක
tin opener	tin ah-ri-nah e-kah	ටින් අරින එක
tip (gratuity)	tip e-kahk	ටිප් එකක්
tired	mah-hahn-siy	මහන්සියි
tissues	pah-tah-lah	පටල
tobacco	dhum-ko-lah	දුම්කොළ
tobacco kiosk	dhum-ko-lah kah-deh	දුම්කොළ කඩේ
today	ah-dhah	අද
together	e-kah-tah ek-vah	එකට එක්ව
toilet paper	toi-laht peh-pahr	ටොයිලට් පේපර්
toilets	va-si-ki-li	වැසිකිළි
tomorrow	he-tah	හෙට
tonight	ah-dhah raa	අද රෑ
too (as well)	…-th	…ත්
too expensive	mi-lah va-diy	මිල වැඩි
too much/many	va-di • hun-gaahk	වැඩි • හුඟාක්
tooth	dhah-thah	දත
toothbrush	dhahth bu-ru-su-wah	දත් බුරුසුව
toothpaste	dhahth be-heth	දත් බෙහෙත්
toothpick	dhahth kah-tu-wah	දත් කටුව
torch (flashlight)	tohch e-kah	ටෝච් එක
touch (v)	ahl-lah-nah-vaah	අල්ලනවා
tour	sahn-chaah-rah-yah	සංචාරය
tourist	sahn-chaah-rah-kah-yaah	සංචාරකයා
tourist information	sahn-chaah-rah-kah	සංචාරක
office	tho-rah-thu-ru	තොරතුරු
	kaahr-yaah-lah-yah	කායර්ාලය
towards	ve-thah-tah	වෙතට
towel	thu-waah-yah	තුවාය
track (path)	ah-di-paah-rah	අඩිපාර
trade union	vruth-thee-yah	වෘත්තීය සංගමය
	sahn-gah-mah-yah	
traffic	rah-thah-vaah-hah-nah	රථවාහන
	gah-mah-naah-	ගමනාගමනය
	gah-mah-nah-yah	
traffic lights	tra-fik lait	ට්‍රැෆික් ලයිට්
trail (route)	paah-rah • maahr-gah-yah	පාර • මාර්ගය
train	dhum-ri-yah	දුම්රිය
train station	dhum-ri-yah sthaah-nah-yah	දුම්රිය ස්ථානය
translate (v)	pah-ri-vahr-thah-nah-yah	පරිවර්තනය
	kah-rah-nah-vaah	කරනවා

travel (v)	sahn-chaah-rah-yah kah-rah-nah-vaah	සංචාරය කරනවා
travel agency	sahn-chaah-rah-kah eh-jahn-si-yah	සංචාරක ඒජන්සිය
travel sickness	gah-mahn ki-ree-meh-dee a-thi-vah-nah vah-mah-nah-yay	ගමන කිරීමේදී ඇතිවන වමනය
travellers cheques	tra-vah-lah chek-pahth	ටුැවලර් චෙක්පත්
tree	gah-hah	ගහ
trek	dhu-rah gah-mah-nahk	දුර ගමනක්
trip	gah-mah-nahk	ගමනක්
trousers	kah-li-sah-mah	කලිසම

> It's true.
> eh-kah ath-thah — ඒක ඇත්ත .

trust (v)	vish-waah-sah kah-rah-nah-vaah	විශ්වාස කරනවා
truth	ath-thah	ඇත්ත
try (v)	uth-sah-hah kah-rah-nah-vaah	උත්සාහ කරනවා
T-shirt	tee-shaht e-kah	ටි-ෂර්ට් එක

> Turn left.
> vah-mah-tah ha-ren-nah — වමට හැරෙන්න .

> Turn right.
> dhah-ku-nah-tah ha-ren-nah — දකුණට හැරෙන්න .

twice	dhe-sah-rah-yahk	දෙසරයක්
twin beds	an-dhahn dhe-kah-dhe-kah	ඇඳන් දෙක-දෙක
typical	ni-yah-mai	නියමයි
tyres	tah-yahr	ටයර්

U

umbrella	ku-dah-yah	කුඩය
understand (v)	theh-rum gahn-nah-vaah	තේරුම් ගන්නවා

> I (don't) understand.
> mah-tah theh-ren-neh (na-ha) — මට තේරෙන්නේ (නැහැ) .

unemployed	ra-ki-yaah vi-rah-hi-thah	රැකියා විරහිත
unemployment	ra-ki-yaah vi-rah-hi-thah bhaa-vah-yah	රැකියා විරහිත භාවය
university	vish-vah vidh-yaah-lah-yah	විශ්ව විදාහලය
unleaded	ee-yahm rah-hi-thah	ඊයම් රහිත
unsafe	ah-naah-rahk-shi-thah	අනාරක්ෂිත
until (June)	thek (joo-ni)	තෙක් (ජූනි)
unusual	ah-saah-maahn-yah	අසාමාන්‍ය
up	u-dah	උඩ

uphill	kahn-dhahk nah-gi-nah-vaah	කන්දක් නගිනවා
urgent	hah-dhi-si	හදිසි
useful	prah-yoh-jah-nah-vahth	ප්‍රයෝජනවත්

V

vacant	his	හිස්
vacation	ni-vaah-du-wah	නිවාඩුව
vaccination	en-nah-thah	එන්නත
valley	mi-ti-yaah-wah-thah	මිටියාවත
valuable	wah-ti-naah	වටිනා
value (price)	ah-gah-yah	අගය
vegetable	e-lah-vah-lu	එළවළු
vegetarian	e-lah-vah-lu pah-mah-nahk kah-nah	එළවළු පමණක් කන්නා

I'm vegetarian.
| mah-mah e-lah-vah-lu pah-mah-nai kahn-neh | මම එළවළු පමණයි කන්නේ. |

vegetation	gahs ko-lahn	ගස් කොළ
venue	sthaah-nah-yah	ස්ථානය
very	bo-hoh	බොහෝ
videotape	vee-di-yoh pah-ti-yah	විඩියෝ පටිය
view	dhahr-shah-nah-yah	දර්ශනය
village	gah-mah	ගම
vineyard	mi-dhi wahth-thah	මිදි වත්ත
virus	vai-rah-sah-yah	වෛරසය
visa	vee-saah e-kah • aah-gah-mah-nah ah-vah-sah-rah-yah	විසා එක • ආගමන අවසරය
visit (v)	ba-ha dhah-ki-nah-vaah	බැහැ දකිනවා
vitamins	vi-tah-min	විටමින්
vote (v)	chahn-dhah-yah dhah-mah-nah-vaah	ජන්දය දැමීම

W

Wait!
| in-nah! | ඉන්න! |

waiter	weh-tahr • u-pah-tan vah-rah-yek/ vah-ri-yahk (m/f)	වේටර් • උපටැන් වරයෙක්/ වරියක්
waiting room	weh-tin room e-kah	වේටින් රූම් එක
walk (v)	a-vi-dhi-nah-vaah	ඇවිදිනවා
wall (inside)	a-thu-lah-thah bith-thi-yah	ඇතුළත බිත්තිය
wall (outside)	pi-tah-thah bith-thi-yah	පිටත බිත්තිය

want (v)	oh-neh ve-nah-vaah	ඕනේ වෙනවා
war	yudh-dhah-yah	යුද්ධය
wardrobe	ahl-maah-ri-yah	අල්මාරිය
warm	u-nu-sum	උණුසුම්
wash (v)	soh-dhah-nah-vaah	සෝදනවා
washing machine	re-dhi soh-dhah-nah	රෙදි සෝදන
	me-shin e-kah	මෙෂින් එක
watch	bah-lah-nah-vaah	බලනවා
watch (v)	bah-laah in-nah-vaah	බලා ඉන්නවා
water	wah-thu-rah	වතුර
mineral water	bim jah-lah-yah	බිම් ජලය
waterfall	dhi-yah al-lah	දිය ඇල්ල
wave (sea)	rah-lah	රළ
way	mah-gah	මග

Please tell me the way to ...
kah-ru-naah-kah-rah mah-tah   කරුණාකරල මට
... mah-gah pen-vahn-nah   ... මග පෙන්වන්න .

Which way?
koi path-then-dhah?   කොයි පැත්තෙන්ද ?

we	ah-pi	අපි
weak	dhur-wah-lah	දුර්වල
wealthy	po-ho-sahth	පොහොසත්
wear (v)	ahn-dhi-nah-vaah	අඳිනවා
weather	dheh-shah-gu-nah-yah	දේශගුණය
wedding	vi-vaah-hah	විවාහ මංගල්‍යය
	mahn-gahl-yah	
week	sah-thi-yah	සතිය
weekend	meh sah-thi ahn-thah-yah	මේ සති අන්තය
weigh (v)	ki-rah-nah-vaah	කිරනවා
welcome	saah-dhah-rah-yen	සාදරයෙන්
	pi-li-gah-ni-mu	පිළිගනිමු
well	sah-nee-pah-yah	සනීපය
west	bah-tah-hi-rah	බටහිර
wet	the-thah	තෙත
what	ku-mahk-dhah?/	කුමක්ද ?/
	mo-kahk-dhah	මොකක්ද

What happened?
ku-mahk-dhah vu-neh?   කුමක්ද වුණේ ?

| wheelchair | roh-dhah pu-tu-wah | රෝද පුටුව |
| when | kah-vah-dhaah-dhah | කවදාද |

When does it leave?
e-kah pi-tahth ven-neh   ඒක පිටත්
kah-vah-dhaah-dhah? •   වෙන්නේ කවදාද ? •
koi veh-laah-veh-dhah?   කොයි වේලාවේද ?

where	ko-heh-dhah	කොහේද

Where's the bank?
ban-ku-wah thi-yen-neh
ko-heh-dhah?
බැංකුව තියෙන්නේ
කොහේද?

which	koi e-kah-dhah	කොයි එකද
who	kau-dhah	කවුද

Who is it?
eh kau-dhah?
ඒ කවුද?

whole	sahm-poor-na	සම්පූර්ණ
why	a-yi	ඇයි
wide	pah-lahl	පළල්
wife	bi-rin-dhah	බිරිඳ
win (v)	dhi-nah-nah-vaah	දිනනවා
wind	su-lahn-gah	සුළඟ
window	jah-neh-lah-yah	ජනේලය
window-shopping (v)	saahp-pu-wah-lah bah-du bah-lah-min a-vi-di-nah-vaah	සාප්පුවල බඩ බලමින් ඇවිදිනවා
windscreen	vin skreen vee-du-ru-vah	වින් ස්ක්‍රීන් විදුරුව
wine	wain	වයින්
winner	jah-yah-grah-hah-kah-yaah	ජයග්‍රාහකයා
winter	see-thah kaah-lah-yah	සීත කාලය
wish (v)	pah-thah-nah-vah	පතනවා
with	sah-mah-gah	සමඟ
within	a-thu-lah-thah	ඇතුළත
within an hour	pa-yahk a-thu-lah-thah	පැයක් ඇතුළත
without	na-thi-vah	රහිතව

yet	thah-vah-mah	තවම
not yet	thah-vah-mah na-ha	තවම නැහැ
you	o-bah	ඔබ
young	thah-ru-nah	තරුණ
youth hostel	thah-ru-nah nah-vaah-tha-nah	තරුණ නවාතැන

zebra	see-braah	සීබ්‍රා
zodiac	grah-hah raah-shee chahk-rah-yah	ග්‍රහ රාශි චක්‍රය
zoo	sahth-vah ud-dhyaah-nah-yah	සත්ව උද්‍යානය

D I C T I O N A R Y

NOTES

SIGNS

CLOSED	වසා ඇත
DANGER!	අන්තරාදායකයි!
ENTRANCE	ඇතුල්වීම
EXIT	පිටවීම
INFORMATION	තොරතුරු
NO ENTRY	ඇතුල්වීම තහනම්
NO EXIT	පිටවීම තහනම්
NO SMOKING	දුම් බීම තහනම්
OPEN	විවෘතව ඇත
POLICE	පොලිසිය
PROHIBITED	අවසර නැත
RESERVED	වෙන් කර ඇත
STOP	නතර වෙන්න
TOILETS	වැසිකිළි